Hungry Translations

TRANSFORMATIONS: WOMANIST, FEMINIST, AND INDIGENOUS STUDIES

Edited by AnaLouise Keating

A list of books in the series appears at the end of this book.

Hungry Translations

Relearning the World through Radical Vulnerability

BY RICHA NAGAR
in journeys with
Sangtin Kisan Mazdoor Sangathan
and Parakh Theatre

UNIVERSITY OF ILLINOIS PRESS
Urbana, Chicago, and Springfield

The proceeds from the sales of this book will go
toward supporting the work and vision of Sangtin
Kisan Mazdoor Sangathan and Parakh Theatre

Library of Congress Control Number: 2019944466

The tide
the knife surging
          gently
rage that
rises
stubborn
cages of
bodies you guide
unlearning
fighting   we
breathe
Babuji

Contents

List of Photographs   ix

Series Editor's Foreword   xi

Note on Transliterations, Translations, and Poems   xiii

Aalaap   1

PART ONE
Staging Stories   5

PART TWO
Movement as Theater
Storylines, Scenes, Lessons, and Reflections

Walking Together   49

A Long War   66

The Journey Continues   86

PART THREE
Living in Character
"Kafan" as Hansa

Nourishment   107

Mumtaz and Budhiya   110

Hansa, Karo Puratan Baat!   123

Entangled Scripts and Bodies: Theater as Pedagogy   146

Hungry for *Hansa*   177

PART FOUR
Stories, Bodies, Movements
A Syllabus in Fifteen Acts

Prologue   199

One More Time   201

Synopsis and Backdrop   205

Initial Keywords, Props, Premises   211

Formal Outcomes, Expectations, Grades, and Assignments   215

The Fifteen Acts   218

Closing Notes: Retelling Dis/Appearing Tales
SIDDHARTH BHARATH, SARA MUSAIFER,
AND RICHA NAGAR   241

Backstage Pages   259

Glossary of Selected Words and Acronyms   265

Notes   269

Works Cited   277

Index   285

Photographs

Reena with Rani, the puppet   11

Tama's beats match Pita's notes while Kamlesh and Sarvesh
   look on   12

Sunita takes the dholak   13

Saathis watch Prakash during the making of *Inquilab Hamre
   Dum Se Aayi*   15

Tama engages his audience during a show of *Aag Lagi Hai
   Jangal Ma*   16

Kusuma and Prakash join their saathis to oppose corruption
   through theater   16

Rambeti demands justice   17

Saathis resist through melodies   17

Richa Nagar, Richa Singh, Rambeti, and Marvin Gomez Cerna
   after the CCAFS workshop in Cambodia   24

SKMS representatives outline our vision at the CCAFS workshop   25

Richa and Richa   50

Writing *Sangtin Yatra*   51

Shashibala reviewing a draft chapter   51

Sangtin Writers resolve to continue their journey   55

Job cards   71

Cooking rotis at the dharna site   76

Victory rally   83

May Day meeting of 2017   99

Mumtaz Sheikh and Gabbar Mukhiya during rehearsals of *Hansa*   120

Mumtaz as Budhiya   121

Bhagwan Das and Alok Panday as Ghisu and Madhav   164

Gaurav playing Madhav, with Mumtaz as Budhiya   173

The men dance to the tune of "Gagri Sambharo"   180

Mumtaz writes her reflections with Neeraj's help   183

Discussions become intense as the *Hansa* show draws near   183

The making of *Retelling Dis/Appearing Tales*   243

Transforming the classroom through *Retelling Dis/Appearing Tales*   247

Devleena playing Ana   247

Team members give feedback as class gets ready for the
   public performance   250

The group rehearses the last scene   250

Series Editor's Foreword

> The journeys shared in *Hungry Translations* travel in and across the interstitial spaces of being and becoming, of refusing and breaking, of rising and flowing from within the breaks, and of hungrily searching for relations and connections.
>
> —Siddharth Bharath, Sara Musaifer, and Richa Nagar

The hunger Richa Nagar explores with her co-travelers in *Hungry Translations: Relearning the World through Radical Vulnerability* resonates with my hunger for innovative, transformational scholarship, knowledge production, and community—a hunger that compelled me to initiate this book series. Grounded in the belief that radical progressive change—on individual, collective, national, transnational, and planetary levels—is urgently needed and in fact possible (although not easy to achieve), Transformations: Womanist, Feminist, and Indigenous Studies invites authors and readers to transgress the status quo (our conventional, unquestioned assumptions about consensus reality) by producing transdisciplinary scholarship informed by women-of-colors theories-praxes and post-oppositional perspectives. Based in a metaphysics of radical interconnectedness, post-oppositionality calls for and enacts relational approaches to knowledge production, social interactions, and identity formation that borrow from but do not become trapped within oppositional thought and action.

Post-oppositionality offers fresh alternatives to social justice work inside, outside, and straddling the academy. Post-oppositionality invites us to think differently, to step beyond our conventional rules, to liberate ourselves from the oppositionally based theories and practices we generally employ. Although post-oppositionality can take many forms, these forms share several characteristics, including the belief in people's interconnectedness with all that exists;

the acceptance of paradox and contradiction; the desire to be radically inclusive—to seek and create complex commonalities and broad-based alliances for social change; and intellectual humility—the recognition that our knowledge is always partial, incomplete, and thus open to revision.

Hungry Translations beautifully illustrates these characteristics, enacting bold post-oppositional interventions into western academic research methods and scholarship. I am especially struck by the role intellectual humility plays in this book. As the title phrase "Hungry Translations" might suggest, Nagar acknowledges the impossibility of perfect, complete translation, communication, or knowledge. Partiality is inevitable. We are partial; our work is partial; our insights are partial. But this recognition of partiality contains the promise of progressive change, the assurance that when we acknowledge and embrace partiality, we open ourselves to innovative possibilities and fresh perspectives.

But it is not easy to embrace partiality. Before we can do so, we must risk "radical vulnerability." We must step out of our self-enclosed boundaries and recognize our inevitable interconnectedness with others. Despite the fierce claims of radical individualism we encounter on a daily basis, we are not "autonomous or sovereign social beings"; rather, we are "intensely co-constituted and entangled with the other" (parts 1 and 4). As Nagar demonstrates, this interconnectivity (when acknowledged and explored) can transform our scholarship. When we recognize the community-based, relational nature of research and knowledge creation, we become co-learners, co-creators in our research projects. We reject the Enlightenment-based approach to research, which typically views marginalized research subjects as "raw materials or suppliers of stories," and redefine these subjects as radical collaborators. We become co-learners with them and, together, we co-produce liberatory knowledge. We learn to live with incommensurability while still struggling to co-understand more fully, to co-create points of connection that respectfully embrace differences.

AnaLouise Keating

Note on Transliterations, Translations, and Poems

Hindi, Urdu, and Awadhi words appear in the roman script throughout *Hungry Translations*. Rather than providing their literal translations, I convey their context-specific meanings in other ways that I feel do more justice to the spirit of what I intend to communicate through them. A glossary of selected words and acronyms appears at the end of the book, but it does not seek to provide a comprehensive list of all the Hindi, Urdu, and Awadhi words or acronyms I have used.

All the translations from Hindi, Urdu, and Awadhi into English have been done by Richa Nagar. These include the translation of the play *Hansa, Karo Puratan Baat!*, the writing done with members of Sangtin Kisan Mazdoor Sangathan, and the excerpts from journals of the participants in Parakh Theatre's workshop in Mumbai.

Unless otherwise indicated, all the poems in *Hungry Translations* have been written by Richa Nagar.

Aalaap

Theater
   dharati   dhaani
     dhamak dha nee
   translate
    no italics
surrender-blend
fuse-refuse
     tongues crushed by school benches
Mumtaz Sheikh
this aalaap this grunt
   this river rushing downhill
    to you i sing
manufactured skulls explode
      around us
   no edges

Rangmanch
   colors rub on soul-stage
   sun spreads on garbage heaps
      piercing plastic
    tickling unbearable

                    stench nourishing
              everything that walks
dogs
cats
pigs
rats
goats
humans
         cows   crows
                refuse   *refuse*

H a l a k-m a l a k   r i v e r s
         rise   kick   curse
         barren screaming acres
         wrinkled young bellies
         open up sorrowful
         ashes flowing livers
         aching finger joints
                serve meatless
                desires of eight kitchens a day
lids full of Ariel—detergent that whitens
         grime of countless laundry loads
         masters haunt for
         soil that feeds (in) rat race—
         burn skin   not soul

Dry hands
         fry fleshless   heavy woks
black hot iron sweat glistens
                unapologetically
         bones hold another pair
         sounds of marbles dropping
                anklets jingle
                               no silver
Dancing
trancing   together
              demanding
              lusting

submerging   surrendering
      intoxicating
           fires moving fates

Virodh vidroh vinash
      pyaas rooh jism
      rudan milan cheetkaar
for worldly has the shape of emptiness
        shor   angaar
    mold rift   d r i f t
                softly shrieking
      shaking   stretching
          shredding
six yards of handed down
        sari
        whirling monsoon winds
    rhythms roar
      scorch spirit
    revolting   revoluting
    sound of hell and heaven is vacuum

Bhookh
    ferocious loving
    spreading arms
        legs   heart
    finding in atma
        utterance denied
love sans knots and stitches
g h a d a r
rang aur jung ka manch
roz-dar-roz
   zindagi bina haare

        translation   transliteration

        tarjuma
          <u>no</u> italics

PART ONE

Staging Stories

Learning Moments

As my fingers begin to type these words, I am filled with a sense of deep humility. I recognize that for each one of us who is afforded the means or tools to step in with an authority to make knowledge claims, there are millions of others whose words and knowledges we stand on, but who have been systematically made invisible on the pages and spaces of formal learning—except as objects or subjects who must be researched, represented, discussed, and at times, 'uplifted' by the experts. In making a call to end the violence of such erasures, this book asks: Whom do we bring with ourselves onto the page or stage? Whose are the voices we rely on for weaving our stories, but whose tones and accents remain unheard and unacknowledged in our scripts? Who are the people who remain forgotten in our citational practices and for whom the conventional citations of the academy remain meaningless? Can we hope to achieve justice by radically reworking the ways in which these unheard tones, stolen voices, and erased knowledges are rendered through academic practices?

On the opening page of his *Politics in Emotion: The Song of Telangana*, Himadeep Muppidi reminds us of the art of storytelling, of proverbs and parables that can mend old tears and give birth to new solidarities, of words drunk with the "palm-oil" of stories and songs that can make bodies dance and sing and sway toward new horizons.[1] But he has a poignant reminder for us: even as the narrator whose own body migrates, learns, and writes in spaces along the banks of both the Mississippi in Minnesota and the Musi in Telangana, Muppidi realizes that his writing can only happen in the confines of "rooms secured with colonial and postcolonial pipelines." From these small rooms "where books flow ceaselessly out of diverse terminals," he can hear "a lot of agitation and energy out there." This agitation is made up of the voices and rhythms of the "villagers and villages near and far." He can feel their music and murmurs, their excitedly moving bodies. But the books on his walls, "English and Telugu alike," muffle the sounds from these places. Muppidi writes:

> Sometimes, if the winds and tubes and screens carry them right, the books are helpless against the music and the dancing and I feel a need to venture out of these small rooms . . . and wade into these new sources of epistemic energy. More often than not, however, I content myself with catching some notes and pulling together worldly pages on what those beats . . . those lyrics, do to me or mean to my body. Writing them down, recording them, in the confines of these rooms, is more compelling than joining the dances in the streets and towns and villages sprawling outside. . . . Could it be because, in this world of small rooms . . . politics should always be parlayed into newer and newer fabrications? Or, is it because my academic body, an assemblage of so many words, is incompetent at engaging politics otherwise?[2]

The idea of *hungry translations* is fired, in many ways, by the restlessness of those who believe in cracking the book-studded walls in the "world of small rooms" by bringing them into vibrant, even disturbing, epistemic conversations with the bodies "out there" that sing, perform, and protest. I engage the truths that often become muffled when words from one place are translated into more words of another language and robbed of their accents, melodies, and meanings; when the words are not accompanied by the embodied vocabularies and gestures that give them life after they are uttered. I am concerned about that which cannot be heard, seen, sensed, or felt through words alone, especially when those words are written down and caged in a regularized structure, in familiar fonts, in a predictable sequence of black and white pages. The translations I argue for emanate from long-term journeys with companions in multiple sites: journeys that produce yearnings for ways to refuse the seclusion of the small book-walled rooms and to build situated solidarities with those who protest and dance "out there," without romanticizing "their" voices and movements. These journeys hunger to continue to learn ways of being and doing that can make our collective knowledges abide by the terms of the struggles we stand with, even as they escape the limits imposed by the disciplined terms of the academy.

Learning from such journeys involves recognizing and sharing our most tender and fragile moments, our memories and mistakes, in moments of translation. This mode of being approaches translation as an act of love or radical openness that also unsettles and disrupts. To use Emily Apter's words, translation becomes a tool to reposition the subject "in the world and in history"—a way of denaturalizing citizenship by "rendering self-knowledge foreign to itself."[3] By embracing these challenges through an anti-definitional stance that uproots and reroots, I offer hungry translations as an agitation. This agitation narrates people, stories, events, and dreams through collectively owned journeys not in a hope to reach perfection, but in a hope to disorder the dominant languages and paradigms through which we often encounter knowledges and knowledge makers.

To begin performing these hungry translations, I would like to introduce some of the co-travelers from whom I have learned a few things about the undisciplined arts of translation, and about the embodied politics and pedagogies of hunger, hope, and knowledge making. Among these teachers are saathis of Sangtin Kisan Mazdoor Sangathan (SKMS), a movement of eight thousand kisans and mazdoors, most of them Dalit, working in 150 villages of Sitapur District.[4] The Sangathan, SKMS, fights for dignity and justice for its saathis or members and companions, and refuses what Joyce King, building on Sylvia Wynter's discussion of *néantisé* in the writing of Édouard Glissant, calls epistemological nihilation. Specifying that nihilation is not the same as *anni*hilation, King defines it as "the inherent denial or total abjection of one's identity and beingness."[5] For SKMS, a refusal to be nihilated means rejecting the discourse where Dalit kisans and mazdoors are reduced to the status of being the 'poorest of the poor' or as being on the 'margins' and therefore unable to produce and mobilize knowledge and politics to better their own situation. This refusal goes hand in hand with SKMS defining itself as a Sangathan of kisans and mazdoors who are Dalit—a term that literally means "crushed down" and constitutes an identity of dignity and self-assertion, "a democratic identity of the socially oppressed untouchable caste groups."[6] The Dalits in SKMS include about two hundred Muslims; in addition, approximately 150 members are from Other Backward Classes (OBCs) or Savarna castes.[7] The movement emerged from the writing of a book called *Sangtin Yatra*, or a journey of sangtins, that eight rural women activists and I undertook in Hindi and Awadhi between 2002 and 2004.[8] Since then the stories from the book, and stories of the book's aftermath, have traveled as translated texts in multiple languages, including English, Turkish, Marathi, and Bahasa Indonesia. Along with this dance of the text across locales and languages, the people's movement in Sitapur has become a crucial part of my life regardless of my physical location: I have worked with and learned from the saathis in my roles as a scribe, a coauthor, a theater worker, and a co-strategist from near and far. As I have wrestled with the intricacies and dilemmas of my task as a storyteller of SKMS in multiple languages and genres, my labor and passion as a member of the US academy have become necessarily centered on the interbraided praxis of ethical responsibility, situated solidarities, and authorship within and across borders and hierarchies in ongoing movement. This praxis grapples with how to continuously strive to do justice to the accents, melodies, and meanings of that which the singing, dancing, and rallying bodies offer to us, and which cannot be contained or conveyed by the languages and frameworks available to us. To develop this discussion, I share three moments from my journeys with SKMS.

Standing Together: Introducing Sunita and Tarun

Everyone who finds out about it in the village of Kunwarapur rushes to the SKMS dairy.[9] It isn't every day, after all, that the meetings of the Sangathan involve an actor from Mumbai. SKMS has invited Tarun Kumar, a theater artist who has been following sangtins' yatra, all the way from Mumbai to Sitapur to help create a play, and the energy that is emerging in the village is intoxicating.

The cold damp fog has been trying to take over the morning again, but today the sun has decided to bless this January day. This is an auspicious beginning of our theater work because many more people will be able to join us now. A cluster of nine people gather on a tiny coir khatiya, threatening to break the poor cot into pieces, while another six sit on the periphery of a rectangular wooden takht where Tama sets himself up with his dholak, next to Pita, Kamlesh, and Richa S. As people pour into the meeting ground, Reena and Shamsuddin rush inside to get two daris and spread them by the cot and the takht. This extra seating vanishes in seconds as enthusiastic young women of Kunwarapur, bahus and bitiyas alike, grab a spot wherever they can find it.[10] Outside this circle of seated people stand dozens of people, young and old. When children who try to peek in find their gaze blocked by adults, some men plant them on their shoulders while others bounce them up onto the seats of the bikes that the passersby have halted at the scene of the theater workshop on their way to the fields.

"But where is Sunita?" someone asks.

Sunita, an active saathi of SKMS, lives right next to the dairy. Those from Kunwarapur already know that she cannot join us because her young daughter is burning with high fever. Someone murmurs that the poliovirus might have attacked the daughter. There is a shared moment of pause, as if to collectively recognize the sorrow and dread that Sunita must be feeling, and then begin the vigorous beats of Tama's dholak, with Pita's voice reaching the sky, while Saraswati Amma claps and dances, and the perky glove puppet called Rani jumps around, causing commotion under the direction of one hand after another.

Reena with Rani, the puppet. (Photo by Richa Nagar)

Sunita can hear every sound of her saathis acting and singing while she tends her daughter; she finds it impossible to stay away from this scene of spirited activities. She asks a friend to take care of her daughter for a couple of hours and joins the group. Grabbing the dholak from Tama, she circles around the crowd asking for punishment for all the village development officers who steal the wages of the laborers and leave their children to die. Throughout the day, saathis have been poking fun at the dishonest development officials who corrupt the National Rural Employment Guarantee Act (NREGA).[11] NREGA aims to enhance livelihood security in rural areas by providing at least one hundred

Tama's beats match Pita's notes while Kamlesh and Sarvesh look on. (Photo by Richa Nagar)

days of wage employment in a financial year to every household whose adult members volunteer to do "unskilled" manual work. Sunita's arrival at the scene introduces a rage and rebellion into the performance. Yet, several of us cannot focus entirely on what she is saying or doing. Our hearts thud with fear about what awaits her at home at the end of the rehearsal.

As a brand-new visitor to SKMS, Tarun feels especially uncomfortable—perhaps even a bit guilty—about the circumstances in which Sunita has been moved to participate in the theatrical activities. At the end of the day as everyone begins to leave, Sunita comes to Tarun and takes his hand in hers to thank him and to say good-bye. Tarun is at a loss for words. He wants to do something to show his appreciation for the enormous contribution she has made to the group's work despite her dire circumstances. Not being able to come up with anything else, he sticks two currency notes in Sunita's palm and gently closes it into a fist. Sunita does not flinch or speak. Without looking down at her fist or at what has been inserted in it, she opens Tarun's palm, places the money back into his hand, and then gently closes his fingers just like he had done with hers. For a wordless second, she looks straight into his eye, then she says softly and firmly, "You keep this, Bhaiyya. Give us your dua by standing with us." Calling

Sunita takes the dholak. (Photo by Richa Nagar)

him a brother, Sunita asks for Tarun's blessings in a way that seeks his solidarity with SKMS, but without defining for him what that solidarity might look like.

"My Voice Rising in Your Chest": Introducing Tama

Suddenly, the sun comes out and brings a brief respite from another wintry day in Pisawan.[12] It is that time of the year when the cold, damp, and heavy fog rules for weeks at a stretch. Opening his left hand, as if to catch the sunshine between his palm and fingers, Tama pulls the dholak closer to him. His poor vision prevents him from clearly seeing the many pairs of eyes that are watching him, but his fingers gently explore every line, curve, and texture of that dholak. Watching Tama adjust his dholak with that familiar longing, the saathis at the theater workshop with Tarun immediately stop their discussion on what kind of play they want to create on the current status of corruption the villagers are subjected to under MGNREGA. They know that Tama wants to sing, and now.

In order to give special effects to the beats on the dholak, Tama begins to tie a thin stick to the index finger of his right hand with a nylon string. As the string continues to tighten around his finger, Tarun remarks: "Tama, why are you making it so tight? Your blood will stop moving."

Tama laughs as he wraps the string around his finger one more time—"So what?" he says, locking his gaze into Tarun's, "The string will only stop the blood from moving. It won't stop my voice or my dholak's dhamak from rising in your chest!"

After several hours of chatting, parodying, playing, and singing that day, Tama starts getting ready to go home before everyone else. A couple of saathis ask Tama to stay. "Why are you going home? Hang out with us in Sitapur tonight. It will be fun."

"My mother and I have guests visiting."

"We are also your guests," Tarun smiles at him. "Why not stay with us tonight?"

Tama is visibly moved by Tarun's affectionate insistence that acknowledges a special kinship between them. With a wide grin that lights up his face, Tama claps in his inimitable style, and building on Tarun's words, he immediately takes the exchange to a deeper level—"No, not tonight, Bhaiyya. Tonight, my mother will cook paraanthas. I promised to buy some oil for the paraanthas." Tama swiftly reaches into the left pocket of his khaki pants and pulls out a small glass bottle the size of Tarun's finger, and the two exchange a long glance. Among the things said and learned in the glance—not only by them, but also by anyone who witnesses that moment—are the complexities of the terrain on which all of us have decided to walk together as saathis of SKMS.

No Living without Nautanki: Introducing Prakash

We are meeting as a group by Skype after a long time. Kamal, Mukesh, Rambeti, Richa S., and Prakash have joined in from Richa S.'s home after sharing a meal in Sitapur at night while I am sitting alone with my morning cup of chai in my kitchen in Saint Paul. The sunlight from the window is gently tickling my back on this cold March day. Sitting on a slim Ikea chair next to the stove, I adjust the screen of my laptop and see my saathis spending another night talking and sharing and growing together under the same roof. I miss the closeness and feel impoverished in my physical comfort.

Usually we don't bother with Skype meetings; it is simpler to just connect by phone as needed, and wait for the face-to-face meetings until we can meet physically during my next trip to India. But the year 2015 has been different.

Saathis watch Prakash during the making of the play *Inquilab Hamre Dum Se Aayi*. (Photo by Tarun Kumar)

Sitapur, along with the rest of the state, has been hit by a severe drought, the likes of which the small kisans and mazdoors of Uttar Pradesh have not seen in a long time. Throughout the month of February, kisans—small and big—in village after village have put a match to their fields. Burning the crops down to ashes has been easier than dealing with crops rotting in the fields.

It is during one of these weeks when the fields are burning that Richa S. says to me on the phone, "Some of us would like to meet with you by Skype to discuss the future of our theater work." It takes us a couple of weeks to find a time when Prakash and Rambeti can travel from their villages in Pisawan Block to the SKMS office in Sitapur town, from where the group can Skype. When the meeting begins, we start with the ruined crop of wheat and mangoes. Hearts are so heavy that it is difficult to sustain the conversation. Then Prakash changes the subject: "Aren't we going to talk about nautanki in this meeting?"

"Sure," I say, "but it has been such a hard time. I didn't want to assume that what was important two weeks ago is still the most important subject for everyone at this time."

Prakash assures me that there is no reason for me to hesitate—"Ab khet nahin rahe," he comments matter-of-factly, "to natak-nautanki ki bhookh badh gayi hai." Since there are no crops left, the hunger for theater has increased.

Tama engages his audience during a show of the play *Aag Lagi Hai Jangal Ma.* (Photo by Tarun Kumar)

Kusuma and Prakash join their saathis to oppose the corruption in MGNREGA through theater. (Photo by Tarun Kumar)

Rambeti demands justice. (Photo by Tarun Kumar)

Saathis resist through melodies. (Photo by Tarun Kumar)

Prakash's words pierce me. Even through the hazy screens we all feel each other smile awkwardly; other languages fail us. I remember what Prakash once said to me: "Natak-nautanki make you an addict. Once you get high on them, you remain intoxicated for life. I can live without food, but without nautanki there is no living now."

From 'Hungry Peasants' to Refusals

Reliving Learning Moments

Sunita and Tarun have only known each other for less than the three hours that they have shared in the workshop, but the spark that connects them leads her to refuse his money in a manner that is inspiring and humbling. In calling Tarun "bhaiyya," and in daring to return his money with a familial insistence, Sunita in fact demands from Tarun a thicker and more enduring kinship than one of a distant visitor who offers monetary help and then disappears without an emotional entanglement. Tarun's acute awareness of the gulfs between Kunwarapur and Mumbai may have made him ambivalent about the terms of his relationship with Sunita, and it may have made him assume that the best help he could extend in that critical moment was to provide some monetary assistance for the medical treatment of her daughter. However, Sunita offers him a far bigger space and responsibility in her and her companions' struggles, one that he would have been too presumptuous to wish for in the absence of Sunita's generosity.

Sunita's intense participation in the action that was happening outside of the dairy in Kunwarapur embodies a hunger for politics through theater.[13] Her dynamic with Tarun, furthermore, demands from him a trust and an ongoing relationship with SKMS despite the uneven terrain that produces violent gaps between the social locations of Tarun and SKMS saathis like herself. Yet this demand for trust is one that simultaneously involves the work of touching and feeling the edges of the uneven terrain lest they are forgotten in a romance of solidarity.

This is precisely the work that Tama does when he shows Tarun the tiny bottle, which he hopes to fill with mustard oil so that his mother can cook para-anthas for dinner with their visitors. While Tarun tries to address the uneven terrain by inviting Tama to stay with the group that night, Tama's words and gestures extend that work by potently enacting a reminder of a terrain where our ability to learn from and grow with one another simultaneously demands an intimate recognition of all of that which separates us. Tama's actions demand that we recognize the hungers of the stomach that part us and put us in very different kinds of life's circumstances, as well as learn to respect the hungers for creativity and justice that bring us together in situated solidarities in the face of those separations.

This hunger for creativity and justice also comes to the forefront in Prakash's words in the Skype conversation. In expressing his addiction to an embodied creative engagement with politics and art, and in pronouncing his need for natak-nautanki as larger than his need for food, Prakash disrupts dominant understandings of the social that are ubiquitous in the landscape of academic research, teaching, and policy making. In a global context where hunger is repeatedly posed as the most basic consideration for the deprived and the poor, and where the origins of their hunger are always reduced to such knowable factors as underdevelopment, natural calamities, or political unrest, Prakash refuses to be reduced to a body whose needs can be measured and then met by a set of deliverable goods through expert interventions. Along with Sunita and Tama, he pushes us to confront at once the superficiality of the discourses that imagine poor mazdoors and kisans as hungry bodies, and the irony of bourgeois clichés that segregate those 'poor' bodies from that of 'the hungry artist' who is faithfully cast as an urban figure. His hunger for theater becomes a desire for critical solidarities against the unjust landscape that separates *and* connects us. This, for Prakash, is one of the fundamental meanings of politics.

Obliteration and Nihilation

Experts on the poor often have no trouble recognizing that those who live with the hunger of underfed bellies are also hungry for justice. However, the same experts participate in epistemic nihilation of the 'poor' by refusing to appreciate their hunger for justice as a nuanced creative and intellectual hunger governed by a social imaginary that is often unthinkable or unintelligible through dominant frameworks. In reducing that complex hunger to a hunger of the belly—the archetypal sign of poverty—that can be alleviated by income to buy food,[14] these dominating knowledges either shrink Prakash, Sunita, and Tama to bodies that must be fed, developed, or aided during humanitarian crises; or they simplistically celebrate them as uniquely dynamic actors on their local stages. In either case, such perspectives fail to acknowledge the fullness of the political vocabularies, visions, and lives of Sunita, Tama, and Prakash for whom neither fever, nor blood, nor a failed crop becomes a barrier in pursuing art *and* politics as a multidimensional experience of mind-body-soul that is simultaneously material and ideological, creative and affective, social and spiritual.[15] This raises the questions: if academics' inherited understandings of the social perform epistemic violence by obliterating, how might we learn to disrupt those understandings and recognize that which we have been disciplined not to anticipate or appreciate? Can we learn to learn from Prakash, Tama, and Sunita in ways that do not have the effect of nihilating them and anxiously bringing the focus back onto 'our' own disciplinary frameworks and debates? How might these saathis become our everpresent interlocutors so that those who write about politics in a "world of small rooms" might feel a hunger to do justice to the agitation of these saathis?

Quỳnh N. Phạm confronts the violence of disciplinary nihilation in the context of international relations (IR) when she asks: why aren't peasants visible in IR and how have the strategies of "willful oblivion" with respect to their knowledge "been enacted over and over, so methodically and imperviously?"[16] She connects her question with the provocative words of Toni Morrison, who wrote in a different disciplinary context: "the question should never have been 'Why am I, an Afro-American, absent from [American literature]?' . . . The spectacularly interesting question is 'What intellectual feats had to be performed by the author or his critic to erase me from a society seething with my presence, and what effect has that performance had on the work?' What are the strategies of escape from knowledge? Of willful oblivion? . . . Not why. How?"[17] As a subaltern figure whose presence and voice are ubiquitous, yet effectively foreclosed from a convention-bound field, the peasant reveals for Phạm IR's limits of intelligibility. At the same time, *peasant* remains a perpetual subject of crisis as well as an object of intervention.[18] Phạm notes: "Associating peasant with alarming problems such as backwardness, poverty, illiteracy, hunger, and suicide, the global machinery of development aims to elevate the peasant, the quintessential figure of underdevelopment, out of crisis into an improved life in its larger mission to improve the world."[19] She reminds us that, although peasants in the Western industrial contexts have been marginalized as either an economic minority or a historical figure, peasants in decolonization movements have been "contemporaneous political subjects capable of . . . resisting empires and building alternative political futures."[20] Rather than being equated with an essentialized identity or category, then, peasant should be seen as a political subjectivity that is profoundly constituted through processes that articulate "potent visions of self-determination" and "alternative, albeit subalternized, way of imagining, ordering, and inhabiting the world."[21] Through an insistence on an analysis of the *global peasant*, she systematically undermines the binary through which the spatially, intellectually, culturally, and politically restricted 'provincial peasant' is placed in hierarchical opposition to the border-crossing, culturally sophisticated, and politically open-minded 'cosmopolitan.' She demands that her readers recognize peasant politics as centrally engaged with the processes through which global structures constitute peasants' place in the world and shape the conditions of their living and their dying.[22]

Refusals

When the worldviews and principles that shape the unstoppable creative turbulence and intellectual yearnings of this global peasant cannot be adequately grasped by the "word-poor" realms of the epistemically disciplined, then refusals become an essential part of the political landscape.[23] In other words, those who share an alternative vision of ethics and justice may be able to order their everyday lives only by actively refusing to engage the structuring logics of the disciplined and disciplining minds. In addressing this politics of refusals, it is important to guard against slipping into a binary formulation of a reciprocal refusal where the dominant frameworks dismiss the poor, and the poor refuse a monolithic framework that overpowers them. As Duvall and Çıdam remind us, "there is no single structuring logic and no particular type of power that is determinative of the world in which we now live, nor of the world orders that are yet to come."[24] Indeed, we see in Sunita's way of returning Tarun's money in the face of her daughter's grave illness and in Prakash's expressed hunger for natak-nautanki in the context of a drought, that it is precisely the multiplicity of these structuring logics and sources of power that enable the peasant to articulate and effect a shift in values, concepts, and material life in the ongoing process of building a different world. The endurance and power of subaltern dissent from dominant logics and structures emanate from their embeddedness in life worlds that have been systematically marginalized. Such dissent, underscores Phạm, is a historically constituted living subjectivity; it has the capacity to reconstruct political relations and order by embodying alternatives and rearticulating collective values, ideas, and institutions. It has the ability to "break the frame" as well as "the capacity to (re)compose the fabric of life and world."[25]

The dominant understandings that erase the political subjectivity of peasants in IR are similar to the ones that nihilate the political subjectivity of all those bodies in the global south who are seen as 'hungry,' 'poor,' and somehow tainted with 'rurality.' Quite frequently, these same bodies are assumed to be readily available for the interventions of certified experts who are eager to help or rescue them, but whose efforts fail to acknowledge the ways in which the hungry actively create politics and knowledge by living and honing a dynamic vision of what is ethical, what makes the good life, and what brings hope. The hope of the hungry, then, is entangled with the creative praxis of refusal against imposed terms, languages, and frameworks.

Rather than implying that refusals are dead ends, however, I would like to linger with refusals through the concept of hungry translations, in the hope that the researcher whom Muppidi calls an assemblage of "so many words" might be inspired to "engage politics otherwise." Specifically, I want to draw attention to two different kinds of refusals. The first allows for a relation between self and other through a hunger for ongoing translations despite the unevenness of the terrain on which such translations take place. The stories through which I introduce Sunita, Tarun, Tama, and Prakash give us a picture of such uneven terrain where refusals remain open to the serendipitous ways in which politics and justice may be realized. The other form of refusal I elaborate on through a fourth story forecloses a possibility of such relationship. Both refusals involve dissenting subjectivity that seeks to not only break the frame but also reweave the fabric of life and world; however, while one hungers for a deeper ongoing relationship with the other, the second sees no hope for such an ongoing engagement.

Translating Refusal

Of the myriad people whom I bring with me when I write, one is my colleague and sangtin, Rambeti, a Dalit farmer, who is an important leader of SKMS. I share with you two interconnected moments of collective refusal summarized by Rambeti after a series of dialogues that she, another SKMS colleague—Richa S.—and I had participated in in April 2013 in Phnom Penh, Cambodia, as part of a CGIAR Climate Change, Innovation and Gender workshop. On the third day of the workshop, as we proceeded for lunch after a session on mitigating carbon emissions, Rambeti said:

> They say they want to learn from us, but our conversations tell me that we can never be partners as long as they keep talking in the same sentence about my cow's carbon emissions and the carbon emissions of global corporations.

We reflected on the dynamics and erasures we experienced during the day. It was hard for us to fathom how those seeking to learn from us could reduce saathis' cows, water buffalos, and goats to a count of carbon emissions. Then Rambeti summarized her final assessment:

> You can translate my words to them and theirs to me, but if they remain blind to our lives and truths, there can be no dialogue on this unjust terrain.

The CGIAR describes itself as "a global research partnership for a food-secure future [that] is dedicated to reducing poverty, enhancing food and nutrition security, and improving natural resources and ecosystem services." Highlighting its commitment to help "the world radically transform our collective approaches and strengthen operations to deliver on-the-ground solutions to the planet's most vulnerable," CGIAR sees itself as working in "close collaboration with hundreds of partners, including national and regional research institutes, civil society organizations, academia, development organizations and the private sector" to transform "the lives of hundreds of millions of people through tangible research outcomes."[26] Consistent with these goals, CGIAR's Climate Change, Agriculture, and Food Security (CCAFS) research program organized a Climate Change, Innovation and Gender workshop. The workshop was attended by representatives of small NGOs working in Bangladesh, Cambodia, Nigeria, Kenya, and Honduras, and by experts from Europe and North America who sought to encourage sustainable innovations among their partners in the global south by helping to reduce the carbon footprint. After reading Sangtin Writers' book, *Playing with Fire*, one of the workshop organizers had contacted me to say that they wanted to learn from our work. Over our fifteen years of working together in SKMS, saathis have co-devised a methodology for addressing situations where I, or other city-based supporters, are contacted by professionals or activists to represent the work of the sangtins: I consulted with SKMS saathis in Sitapur, who deemed it worthwhile for us to research the organization and to pose a number of questions from the perspective of SKMS. After engaging in this preliminary research, I invited one of the organizers to come to wintry Saint Paul so that we could arrange an in-depth Skype conversation across several thousand miles with several representatives of SKMS, each of whom had also traveled several hours through dense fog to get to a location from which they could Skype. The objective behind these arduously undertaken journeys was to make sure that, given CGIAR's history, SKMS could trust CCAFS's desire to learn from the saathis and if so, whether this trust was enough for SKMS to invest its energies in participating in the conference.

In the communications that followed over the next four months, I conveyed to CCAFS on behalf of SKMS that the trip had to be worthwhile for Rambeti to leave her standing crop in the fields for four days and to suffer the pains and humiliations necessary to get a passport and visa to travel from Sitapur to Phnom Penh. The incentive CCAFS offered was a promise of $5,000 to help Dalit women undertake farming innovations: if SKMS continued its "learning partnership" with CCAFS, then twenty-five SKMS women, including Rambeti, could use the money to grow drought-resistant crops to gain more food security. This was an exciting prospect for SKMS.

Getting to Cambodia was a difficult battle for Rambeti and Richa S., who joined me in Phnom Penh to jointly represent SKMS in the CCAFS workshop there. All the workshop participants tried to cross multiple borders to understand one another. Despite the organizers' well-intentioned desire to learn, however, the meeting was simply not set up for a just dialogue. Although Rambeti, Richa S., and I were invited as a "unique" group representing a rural people's social movement, one that was led in large measure by Dalit kisan and mazdoor

Richa Nagar, Richa Singh, Rambeti, and Marvin Gomez Cerna after the CCAFS workshop in Cambodia. (Photo by David Edmunds)

women, there was no time or space in the workshop to contextualize or explain SKMS's work to other participants, most of whom worked in an NGO format. Nor was there much room for the translational labor that could allow SKMS participants to better understand the sociopolitical contexts and priorities that had brought the other attendees to the workshop. The workshop remained entrenched in dominant ways of communicating through slide presentations, research reports, statistics, and goals that also tended to fit within budget categories and donor-recipient equations, and that were debated and discussed in English. The actual labor of unlearning and relearning across borders—with humility, care, and persistence—that would have actually begun to create a learning partnership between CCAFS and SKMS was missing from the agenda and processes of the conference. In retrospect, a genuine commitment to build a space for retelling and receiving stories—about how workshop attendees had lost or found trust in development and empowerment projects—would have gone a long way in seeding a productive partnership. Such exchange of stories may have allowed the participants to help co-devise the agenda and to develop the questions, critiques, and languages that grappled with the incommensurabilities that mark the everyday landscapes in which the politics of 'climate change, innovation and gender' are played out.

The turbulence generated in Phnom Penh only grew as we talked informally with other workshop participants in the days immediately following the work-

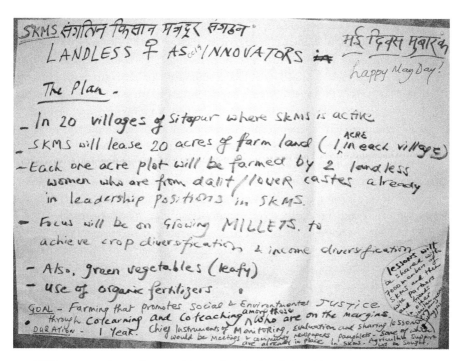

SKMS संगतिन किसान मजदूर संगठन
LANDLESS ~~¥~~ AS^{oc}/INNOVATORS ~~in~~ मई दिवस मुबारक
happy May Day!

The Plan.

- In 20 villages of Sitapur where SKMS is active
- SKMS will lease 20 acres of farm land (1 ACRE in each village)
- Each one acre plot will be farmed by 2 landless women who are from dalit / lower castes already in leadership positions in SKMS.
- Focus will be on Growing MILLETS. to achieve crop diversification & income diversification
- Also, green vegetables (leafy)
- use of organic fertilizers
GOAL - Farming that promotes Social & Environmental JUSTICE through Colearning and Coteaching among those who are on the margins
DURATION - 1 Year. Chief Instruments of Monitoring, Evaluation and Sharing lessons would be Meetings & computing, newspapers, pamphlets - Some of which are already in place in SKMS. Agriculture Support

SKMS representatives outline our vision at the CCAFS workshop. (Photo by David Edmunds)

shop. During this time, we also consulted by Skype and phone with other SKMS saathis in India. On the day of our departure from Cambodia, Rambeti, Richa S., and I met with our host. In this meeting, SKMS politely withdrew from future conversations with CCAFS because of what Rambeti had previously summed up as an "unjust terrain" that was "blind to the truths and lives" of our saathis, despite the workshop's expressed desire to build partnerships through dialogue. The inability of the experts to grasp the incommensurable world of SKMS, a world where a cow's carbon emissions are not comparable to a corporation's carbon emissions, had made it clear to Rambeti that CCAFS's desire to support Dalit kisan and mazdoor women like herself was tainted by the very terms of the terrain that makes such a desire possible in the first place. She declined to engage with CCAFS's offer. Her refusal, in turn, gave SKMS the collective courage to turn down the $5,000 that could have proved critical in launching an important initiative for Dalit women in the Sangathan.

In a context of environmental degradation and food insecurity where most members of SKMS make less than $2 a day and get fewer than a hundred days of work in a year, and where Rambeti, in particular, had to endure much pain and sacrifice to come to Cambodia, she may have deemed it entirely ethical to take the money as a compensation for what she in particular, and what we as a group representing SKMS, had already contributed to CCAFS's learning process, and to leave open the option to refuse the partnership later on. If Rambeti had made such a decision, SKMS would have supported her decision despite our shared analysis of the uneven terrain on which the exchange was taking place. However, Rambeti embraced the difficult decision to refuse the money that was contaminated by epistemic nihilation that she as an individual and we as SKMS collective experienced during the conference.

Let us use this event as a lens to revisit the exchange between Sunita and Tarun in Kunwarapur. In both cases, what was at stake was an unequal landscape where the very incommensurability of locations from which people were engaging with one another made the terms of transaction unacceptable to members of SKMS. Here in Phnom Penh, however, CCAFS's mode of engagement with the lives and knowledges of SKMS saathis had decisively foreclosed any possibility of our hosts becoming a bhaiyya in the way that Tarun was drawn into a circle of kinship and responsibility by Sunita. SKMS had made a leap of faith in making a trip to Cambodia in the hope of enabling genuine co-learning, and perhaps this was exactly what a couple of our hosts wanted to achieve. However, given the structure of the workshop, this hope turned out to be wishful thinking. Sunita invited Tarun to deepen his involvement with SKMS by continuing to search with the saathis for translations that seek poetic and social justice, but Rambeti's courage pushed SKMS to develop a political analysis and a stance that refused to participate in any translational exchange with CCAFS. In the latter case, the meanings of justice were compromised by the very terms of translation.

Although the refusals of Rambeti and Sunita are separated by miles, moons, and contexts, both underscore some fundamental truths. To begin with, the political geographies of subaltern struggles are increasingly configured in ways that necessitate encounters with difference, inequality, and hierarchy, and these encounters involve simultaneous translations across uneven terrains. When these translations are read as inherently 'unjust' by any of the parties, there is little hope for dialogue. In a global context of intricate diversity, intensifying conflicts, and increasing violence, how might we reconceptualize the responsibility of translating multiple, and often conflictual local diversities in the context of incommensurable lives and struggles? Far from being a scalar or territorially defined concept, the 'local' here includes the regional, national, and sociocultural, as well as specific articulations or 'vernaculars' that emerge from scientific or theoretical expertise.

If, following Merrill, we do not reduce translation to simply "a carrying across" of meanings but rethink translation as "a telling in turn"[27] where the tellings must be passed along and negotiated afresh in each round, then what possibilities for justice can be created by rethinking translation as an enterprise of ethical and ever open mediation across space, time, and struggle? Can the unevenness of the terrain be addressed in ways that allows systematically marginalized and erased local conceptions of justice to receive a fairer hearing in global dialogues of the certified experts, so that those local articulations are not epistemologically nihilated or obliterated? What might it take to reimagine translation as a dynamic, multidirectional process of ethical and politically aware mediation among otherwise impermeable local diversities—a process that always hungers for new political possibilities that we may never have imagined before?

Sunita's refusal opened up precisely such a possibility for a local conception of justice to emerge. Her way of returning Tarun's money reduced the unevenness of the terrain by shifting his status from a Mumbai-based acquaintance who could afford to give her some cash, to a bhaiyya or brother whose involvement in the workshop had now made it his duty to stand with Sunita and her saathis in their collective struggle. In sharp contrast to CCAFS hosts, whose already fixed definitions of 'food (in)security' and 'gendered gaps' as well as of the roles of 'the donor' and 'the recipient' foreclosed the possibility of hungry translations, Sunita's affective imagination craved justice for herself and her saathis through the possibility of ongoing translations despite being aware of that which distanced Tarun from the Sangathan.

What authorizes me to excavate these specific meanings of different moments of refusal from a range of possible and similarly imperfect interpretations? Far from being authorized by a research project, or a commitment to a field-site or to a category defined as "ethnographic subjects," the translations I offer and refuse here are enabled through long-term relationships and analyses developed with SKMS saathis and specifically through my entanglement with the learning moments in which those of us who walk with SKMS are able to agonize together over the meanings and implications of the events and exchanges that transpire at different junctures.[28] It is this commitment to advancing the movement by rallying, fighting, reflecting, speaking, and writing together as saathis from unequal locations—co-travelers who will also inevitably commit mistakes in the process of walking together—that gives me the courage to connect the two hungers: one that my saathis live in their bellies and bodies every day, and another that underscores, on an unjust terrain, a collective yearning for sociopolitical and epistemic justice.

We learn to translate, or to tell in turn, through yatras that do not seek a conclusive interpretation of the moments in which we walk together but that long to continue the journey and the relationships in order to keep struggling for justice. The yatra becomes a nonstop dance between worlds and languages where it is impossible to define an origin or a destination. The impetus to entwine the apparently divergent hungers—one of the belly that is seen as reality and the other of the mind that is regarded as metaphor—then, comes as much from conversations with academic colleagues about lessons learned with and from my SKMS saathis, as it emanates from reprocessing and refining those conversations with SKMS saathis on an ongoing basis. It is this dance that enabled me to participate in the making of the January 2018 issue of *Hamara Safar*, the community newspaper of SKMS in Hindi, where the entanglements of these hungers are explored. Below, I offer a translated excerpt from this newspaper:

> Many saathis of the Sangathan [SKMS] live and know acutely the hunger of the belly and the pangs of material deprivation, in much the same way as they know how our saathi Kamlesh died of acute anemia in the bitter cold of this January. Or, how saathis such as Rekha accept as an intimate part of their bodies the unimaginable swelling of legs due to a disease such as filaria and toil year after year doing manual labor. However, when we claim that the Sangathan has become a part of our existence, then we are also saying that the relationships and journeys of this movement have enriched us immensely. They have planted a deep desire inside us: for all kinds of rights and justice, for all sorts of knowledge, and for living our lives in our own ways. We yearn deeply for the freedom to put forth our thoughts in our own ways on every platform; for powerful ideas, slogans, songs, plays that can move hearts, for all of that which can give us the tools to live a full life with respect and dignity.
>
> What an amazing thing would it be if such a desire can engulf each saathi who walks with the Sangathan in the form of an insuppressible, nonstop bhookh—a hunger akin to fire that burns our stomachs. A hunger that can fire us to plunge ourselves in the work of extinguishing it every day with the same desperation that we feel for satisfying the hunger of our belly—a hunger that we know comes daily and can never be obliterated.
>
> And what an amazing thing it would be if that same acute desire can feed the soul of every companion who walks with us, whether that saathi is breathing in our own village or very far away from us, so that they can feel and live this continuous hunger for justice and dignity in and through their words and deeds. Only then will our chants, our arguments, our campaigns, our lives, our actions, our spoken and written words, commingle and become strong enough to help each one of us advance in our struggle for truths.
>
> In order for this hope and commitment to continuously invigorate our mode of living and our existence, we must remember to nourish our collective processes, even as we fight to address our own personal needs and the pains of our loved ones. The gulfs and poisons that are fed to us right from birth; or the knots and distances between us that get transformed into unbridgeable faults due to history, geography, politics, religion, and rituals; or the desires and habits

that we absorb amid the loot and corruption of our corporate world and self-ish politicians—we should never shy away from honestly confronting the ways we find ourselves stuck in and defeated by these endless swamps. We should never avoid the difficult work of continuing to dissolve our egos and admit our mistakes and weaknesses before one another. Rather, we must remember that it is only through these thick collective efforts and journeys that we can find the insights and courage to identify the next turns and halts in our ever-unfolding journey. It is only these collective energies that can give us the strength to fulfill the responsibility of turning our desire for justice into a hunger for justice.[29]

The grounds from which I can retell or refuse to retell stories from these journeys are constituted, then, by a long-term shared commitment to abide by the vision of SKMS that allows me to be part of the 'real-life' drama staged in the theater of that movement. This 'abiding by' aligns with the spirit in which Qadri Ismail and Tariq Jazeel also invoke it: 'abiding by' the places in which we labor entails the injunction to "'wait, stay'; 'pause, delay'; 'tarry over', . . . 'to stand firm by . . . hold to . . . remain true to . . . '; to 'endure . . . encounter, withstand, or sustain'; and . . . to 'suffer,' even."[30] It is equally important not to contain these words in a discursive realm that is chiefly academic, and to give them meanings through the messiness of doing that is at once intellectual, embodied, strategic, and aesthetic. It is this requirement, responsibility, and longing for continuing to journey together with SKMS that makes it possible for all the saathis, including me, to participate in these hungry translations.

• • •

So what makes a translation hungry?

Every translator tries to do justice by coming as close as possible to a truth of what they are translating. In this sense, the translations generated by the development apparatus or human rights machinery or prison industrial complex may seek to be just as ethical as translations that might be guided by feminist, Marxist, or similar other sensibilities. However, when a project of translation assumes that it can render transparent the meanings of complex lives or struggles, it not only consumes the other, it also annihilates that which has been othered.

A hungry translation, by contrast, is distinguished by its insistence on a collective and relational ethic of radical vulnerability that refuses to assume that it can arrive at a perfect translation. It recognizes that the meanings of justice, ethics, or politics can emerge only in the shifting specifics of a given moment in an ongoing struggle—a particular convergence of subjectivities and articulations that is itself located at a unique confluence of time and place. This impossibility of arriving at perfect translation, furthermore, keeps the relationships hungry for continuing to grapple with fluid and unresolvable sets of incommensurabilities. In other words, even as a self comes together with an other, both remain alive in and after translation. The political potential of such engagement lies in this yearning to keep the retellings, as well as the relationships that energize and authorize those retellings, open and flowing.

This kind of hunger in a translation cannot be demanded or achieved through mechanical protocols. It can only emanate from an intense relationality and co-ownership of dreams among those who occupy different locations in predominant epistemic hierarchies; it involves cultivating what María José Méndez poetically terms as "a disposition to listening to incommensurable worlds where rivers tell stories and call upon us."[31] Such relationality inspires a situated solidarity where our minds and bodies, our hearts and tongues can always be open to diverse ways of knowing and cocreating in a world where the humans alongside the land, forests, rivers, and nonhuman animals can become our ever-present teachers and interlocutors.[32] An intentional and shared search to continue learning how to breathe, to flow, and also to refuse, relationally, is what makes a translation or retelling hungry. Such hungry translations can dare to fight and interrupt projects that seek to educate, modernize, or emancipate certain categories of bodies—including 'the rural poor' and 'women'—through globalized vernaculars that reproduce a landscape of intellectual enfranchisement and dispossession.

In resisting formulaic modes of defining citational architectures or methodological approaches, and in radically reimagining the temporalities and meanings of knowledge-making partnerships, these translations demand a collectively embraced radical vulnerability in which the individual ego must surrender to a politics of co-traveling and coauthorship that involves difficult refusals.[33] In this formulation, radical vulnerability cannot be an individual pursuit; indeed it is meaningless without collectivity. Yet, this collectivity does not seek to erase the singular by subsuming everything in a larger whole; rather, the singular relearns to breathe and grow differently in the plural. While this praxis may be reminiscent of Butler's idea of vulnerability as a necessary condition for an ethical relationship,[34] it builds from lessons learned in and through the ongoing work of fiercely alive collectives that define the conditions for solidarities within and across borders. This praxis of radical vulnerability opens up the possibility of a togetherness "without guarantees":[35] it does not seek to know prior to the journey where the shared paths will lead us but it commits to walking together with the co-travelers over the long haul in the struggles and dreams that we all have chosen to weave, unweave, and reweave together. Such coauthorship is guided by a belief that the risks and dangers of learning and growing together through radical vulnerability are worth the enrichment and meaning that the journey will give us.[36] In forgoing the very category of a "subject" in the form of a singular, autonomous self, and in actively co-constituting an intersubjective space, such a praxis does not look for corporeal or moral protection of one individual from another. It recognizes that each of us is limited by our locations and languages, by our pasts and presents, by our desires and complicities.[37]

A relationality embedded in radical vulnerability strives to internalize that our self is intensely co-constituted and entangled with the other. Whatever we learn, whatever we come to be, becomes deeply contingent on what each one of us is prepared to give to the collective journey that seeks to unite the I and we with the you and they. By disrupting such categories as writer, educator, activist, artist, kisan, and mazdoor, these ever-evolving solidarities enable the formation of multiple interpretive communities so that people in the so-called margins cannot become raw materials or suppliers of stories. Each saathi or co-traveler wrestles with unlearning, relearning, and negotiating which stories can cross which borders, in which form, when, and with what intentionality. Such storytelling moves across contexts and sociopolitical idioms and vocabularies, across forms and genres, and it recognizes how different forms of labor that constitute protest must shift with every staging according to context and audience, each time pushing for new forms of co-constitutive retheorizing, restrategizing, recalling, and retelling.[38]

In this translational praxis, the meanings of the political cannot be learned in a straightforward journey. Rather, this praxis is a complex choreography among and across multiply located discursive sites. For the one who participates in this praxis as a writer, a responsible grappling with this dance asks that the page become a stage where the saathis located in each site can come alive as co-critics and co-performers who co-own authority, insights, and courage. Together, we shape and refine the narratives that emerge in the dance. Theatrical and political positions as well as storylines and rules of narration must coevolve as every encounter or movement in one site leads to a new round of revisions in the next retelling. This storytelling—where words, effects, and affects are always in continuous and critical creative motion, and purposeful and collective revision—fundamentally complicates our received ideas about 'the expert.'[39] Such storytelling can acquire the ability to poke, pinch, and play pranks. It can unsettle the cultural and material economies of intellectual and material enfranchisement and disenfranchisement that are embedded or entangled in dominant conceptualizations of expertise and the accompanying authori(zi)ng practices. It can instill laughter and sanity amid unimaginable hardships. It can create spaces to evolve modes of being and becoming in and through a continuously unfolding politics without guarantees.

For those of us in the academy, a desire to partake in, and contribute, to such hungry translations requires that we do not merely travel *to* the Other*ed* worlds that form the basis of our knowledge claims. Rather this desire comes with the responsibility to embed ourselves in the relationships and hopes that form our entwined worlds, so that that which has been Othered in dominant imaginaries may emerge differently in our consciousness and conscience and in our ways of being. Here I find affinities with Jazeel's recent "manifesto for incomparable geographies" where he calls for a passionate and poetic insistence on "singularity," which can only be realized by "sticking with, attending to, and thus making oneself part of a particular problem space" while simultaneously querying "just how compatible this patient attention to the singular is, where not much may change over long stretches of time, with the temporality and scale of the large grant funded research projects that promotion and reputation are increasingly dependent on in the corporate university today?"[40] The responsibility I argue for requires us continuously to strive to retell stories with an acute awareness of the tones and textures, memories and feelings, logics and poetics—of people, places, and times as well as the seemingly mundane truths of life that remain distant or insignificant in the imagination of mainstream academia. It is through this possibility of dwelling, breathing, touching, and creating between and across worlds that hungry translations can become productive of alternative worlds, and where academic intellectuals can participate not merely as detached analysts or do-gooders of the world but as active political beings who labor to cocreate just worlds by sharing epistemic agency with those we accompany.[41] In such dwelling, furthermore, the academic as narrator cannot always be the principal teller who controls the story; at times, the narrator is merely a conduit, a passage, through which the stories of a breathing, throbbing world peopled by our saathis are received. These stories interpret and theorize the narrator as much as the narrator theorizes the content and cast of the stories.

A desire for a deeply aware relationship between the imperfect translational acts of academics and the collective labor of world making is not reducible to a longing for improving the quality of our research, or for producing better critical ethnographies. It is also not an argument for greater caring for the Other. Nor is this yearning driven by a romantic notion of 'activist scholarship' where we do our activism outside the academy and then return to the academic mode to narrate or theorize the subjects and objects of that activism. Instead, this is a shared hunger for an intense transformative engagement with social worlds that can inspire intellectual and political agitation by remaking *how* we locate ourselves in relation to the bodies, battles, wisdoms, and worlds we move among, and that we represent and reimagine. It is an insistence on building abiding trust and reciprocities between incommensurable regimes: those that produce the big and small rooms studded with books, reports, and case studies, on the one hand, and those that refuse the norms, frames, and expectations of what is spelled out in those pages, on the other.

Such collectively claimed hunger for full-bodied engagements and translations in academic engagements must refuse comfortable closures or transparent renderings of meanings. It must strive to narrate and theorize the conditions of the incommensurable terrains, and it must have a provincializing effect on our knowledge-making paraphernalia—our terms, concepts, theories, and methods. In reconceptualizing knowledge making as a shared, simultaneous, and unending labor on an uneven terrain that makes perfect translation impossible, hungry translations must destabilize our inherited meanings of the social and make our knowledges more humble, more tentative, and more alive to the serendipitous creativity of life. If social justice seeks tangible gains in the immediate political and historical context and poetic justice is that which provides consolation and courage in an imaginary realm,[42] then our translations must fearlessly search for ways to interbraid poetic justice and social justice without compromising the singularities that constitute each community of struggle. They must ensure that the collective labor of weaving dreams, words, and tunes for a better world can keep moving, without believing in preannounced arrivals or legible definitions of justice, empowerment, or the good life.

Hungry Translations on Three Stages

Hungry Translations has emerged from yatras undertaken with thousands of co-travelers in what have become three deeply interrelated and interlayered realms of learning for me: movement building, political theater, and classroom. In entangling these varied worlds of unlearning and relearning, the rest of this book is organized into four parts. Part 2 comprises tales and diaries of protests and campaigns that have formed SKMS's battles with the Indian state, its development apparatus, and the painfully intimate and violent hierarchies of caste, class, religion, and gender within and against which saathis live every day. Significantly, these stories are simultaneously about articulating a vision of solidarity through the continuous work of evolving and deepening complex relationships and political analyses among SKMS saathis, including a Savarna writer like myself who is not a kisan or mazdoor and who earns her living as a university professor in the United States.

Part 3 revolves around a collective effort undertaken with Parakh Theatre in Mumbai in 2014 to interrogate Hindu brahmanical patriarchy, casteism, hunger, and death with twenty amateur and professional actors.[43] This six-month process focused on reinterpreting Premchand's last story "Kafan," and transforming it into a play in Awadhi called *Hansa, Karo Puratan Baat* (hereafter *Hansa*). That work sought to extend the epistemic labor of SKMS through political theater, albeit in a location far away from Sitapur. The twenty team members who came together to create *Hansa* are migrants from seven Indian states who now work in Mumbai as domestic workers or as aspiring or underemployed film actors. In the process of wrestling with complex sociopolitical, geographical, and linguistic hierarchies, these actors articulate a situated solidarity with the worldviews of those who are dismissed as rural, Dalit, uneducated, and poor. This collective creativity reimagines the aesthetics of artistry through an embodied immersion in the politics of casteism, communalism, patriarchy, uneven development, and poverty in India.

The interlayered journeys of SKMS and Parakh Theatre pushed me to explore how the ways of knowing and being codeveloped with saathis in these two sites might be shared and reworked pedagogically with students in a public research university in the United States. This exploration birthed Stories, Bodies, Movements, a combined undergraduate and graduate course at the University of Minnesota that grapples with possibilities and impossibilities of embodied learning by reimagining the classroom through theater. The syllabus of Stories, Bodies, Movements that constitutes part 4 of this book unfolds in the form of fifteen weekly Acts over the course of an academic semester. In reading and absorbing texts and political analyses of such thinkers and writers as W. E. B. Du Bois, Suheir Hammad, June Jordan, Naeem Inayatullah, Viet Thanh Nguyen, Beaudelaine Pierre, Nina Simone, Eve Tuck and K. Wayne Yang, the course poses two fundamental questions. First, what of ourselves must each member of the class offer in order to become an ethical receiver of the stories we are reading? Second, how might this commitment to ethically receive stories translate into an embodied journey that seeks to transform the self in relation to the collective? Finally, the book's "Closing Notes" are coauthored with Siddharth Bharath and Sara Musaifer, two of the twenty-seven participants who immersed themselves in the first two semesters of Stories, Bodies, Movements.

Below I elaborate on the ways in which the next three parts of *Hungry Translations* locate the work of making knowledges in an unending process of building and sustaining long-term relationships that search for sociopolitical and epistemic justice. In working to internalize the complex and fluid co-constitution of the *i/I* and *we*, of here and there, of past and present, and of human and nonhuman, these relationships long for modes of connecting and trusting, living and being, troubling and creating that are often ignored in the dominant forms of scholarly inquiry. This commitment resonates with writings of a number of scholars, including M. Jacqui Alexander, Gloria Anzaldúa, Patricia Hill Collins, Saidiya Hartman, and Leanne Betasamosake Simpson. At the same time, it breaks from a familiar citational infrastructure on which much academic production and performance rest. The knowledges enabled through journeying with SKMS and Parakh-Mumbai, and through Stories, Bodies, Movements become inseparable from the moments, processes, events, and encounters through which knowing across multiple histories, geographies, languages, and axes of difference and power happens. Such retelling becomes a part of the ongoing labor of learning how to "refuse citational practices that fragment the bodies (of knowledge) which constitute our consciousness and conscience and that reduce modes of creating knowledges to recognizable, nameable individual sources while erasing the necessarily complex collective processes from which we all come to know and be known."[44]

First Staging: SKMS After *Sangtin Yatra*

Sangtin Yatra began as a journey of nine women—six of them hailing from families of poor kisans and mazdoors in rural Sitapur—who built a partnership with one another and with me to write their stories in a collective voice. This coauthorship sought to present an intimate and constructive critique of the practices of NGOs that tend to reduce complex processes and experiences of empowerment and disempowerment to narrow identity-based or issue-based categories without addressing the violent epistemic hierarchies that constitute the subjects and objects of empowerment. Equally, it encouraged rural people to seek a different vision of happiness and well-being than the one handed down by those eager to save them.[45] The Hindi book, *Sangtin Yatra: Saat Zindigiyon Mein Lipta Nari Vimarsh*, and its English version, *Playing with Fire: Feminist Thought and Activism through Seven Lives in India*, resulted from this collective yatra. These books sparked important debates around NGOization of rural women's empowerment and around the interbraided local and global politics of knowledge production. Key elements of these debates continue to anchor the vision of SKMS saathis, as reflected in the following words from a speech that Prakash delivered at a SKMS rally in December 2010:

> When we can fight and take the unemployment allowance that was due to us, when we can take the hundred days of work [promised to us by law], then why do we need the support of [these contractors and NGOs]? We are not lame that we need their crutches. If the Employment Guarantee law is made for the mazdoors, then the drivers of that law will also be mazdoors. There will be no NGOs, no contractors, no mechanization.[46]

Here, SKMS saathi Prakash, whom we met previously as a passionate nautanki artist, protests against NGOs that wish to ensure that the hundred days of work promised to the rural poor by MGNREGA will not be endangered by the corruption of the development bureaucracy. In pointing out that the struggle against the corrupt development officials is a struggle owned by the mazdoors, and in refusing to be subjects in need of help by either NGOs, or contractors, or machines, Prakash and SKMS continue the political commitment first articulated in *Sangtin Yatra*.

To give a quick sketch of SKMS's birth, the collective journey of the nine coauthors of *Sangtin Yatra* changed its course after we successfully fought the attack launched against us by the director of the NGO that employed seven of us.[47] The victory of the Sangtin Writers transitioned into an unplanned and gradual process in which thousands of new saathis—adult women and men as well as youngsters—became sangtins in an emerging movement that defined its own quest for empowerment through an alternative vocabulary. Yet, while the spirit of the journey called sangtin yatra propelled SKMS, most new saathis could not read the book by the same name due to lack of access to formal literacy. In fact, the movement began where the written word paused and only three out of nine women who participated in the writing of *Sangtin Yatra* were able to continue their participation in the political agitation that subsequently became SKMS.

SKMS is a movement of bodies in struggle. It requires living, laboring, fasting, and protesting together. Those saathis who stand with the Sangathan but who are unable to move with the collective in person on a continuous basis must become deeply cognizant of the ways in which their place in the movement cannot be the same as the place of those who live, sacrifice, and fight in the villages of Sitapur. This is only one of the crucial lessons of the movement making that unfolded after the battle over *Sangtin Yatra*. In a context in which the majority of the saathis have not been schooled to read and write, profound questions have emerged in relation to knowledge making: what kinds of languages are needed for SKMS saathis to learn and grow in the new phase of struggles around state-sponsored development and empowerment in the villages of Sitapur? What artistic and political practices can enable a different social imaginary that generatively challenges prevailing logics and ways of thinking and being in the world?

It is in this context that theater as an embodied creative pedagogy allows SKMS to explore the links between the dramas of a violent development bureaucracy and the Sangathan's own labor as a producer of alternative vocabularies that seek to do justice to the saathis' worlds and visions. Theater becomes intellectual and political labor that refuses the dominant languages and frameworks, which often make rural bodies into an Other who is acted on by formally literate experts. It pushes us to face the limits of formal languages and to learn from imaginaries of justice that do not emanate from assumptions about a shared lexicon that exists prior to the collective creative process. In searching for new expressions through the gaps and fissures that exist in our own abilities to know and enunciate, theater becomes pedagogy. This pedagogy emerges organically from the shifting needs of the struggle and it is grounded in the soils and bodies of those who make the struggle possible. At the same time, it seeks solidarities that can allow critiques, theories, and visions to remain stubbornly undisciplined and always in motion in order to actively converse with other sites of struggle.

Part 2 retells several key moments and events that make sangtin yatra or the journey of sangtins an ongoing relation among the saathis who have chosen to walk together in the aftermath of the political controversy generated by the book, *Sangtin Yatra*. Saathis embrace the pedagogies that unfold in the course of walking together and collectively we theorize with and through those pedagogies. This embracing involves working against the antagonists that are the developmentalist state and the casteist and capitalist patriarchy while also confronting the antagonists that live inside each one of us. Unlearning the hierarchical differences between the mazdoor, kisan, reader, writer, actor, theorist, teacher, and leader implies delving into the very structures, understandings, and languages that shape our everyday desires and identities; it asks that we confront without resolutions the predictable and unpredictable paradoxes that make us.

Learning moments from this coauthored journey of several thousand people have informed my work with Tarun Kumar of co-building theater with saathis of SKMS. Over the last decade, this work has slowly evolved as an effort to do justice to the hungers and refusals of saathis, including Prakash, Tama, Sunita, and Rambeti, and to share the Sangathan's critical analysis and its retellings of the apparatus known as Development to more and more people in the streets, lanes, farms, and courtyards of Sitapur. In dismantling the walls that separate critique, play, and protest, this work shreds those definitions of literature and art that suffocate the possibilities of learning from the dynamic political theater of people without formal scripts. At the same time, it is constituted by the everyday dramas in which saathis' epistemological resistance reveals not only the violence prevailing in the government offices but also in the minds of fellow saathis and supporters who may erroneously wish to interpret or judge that violence as if we are outside of it. The Sangathan and its movement, then, become living pathshalas, borderless sites of learning, whose lessons must be internalized by all of us who commit ourselves to learning and growing through them.

Second Staging: Parakh's Journey with *Hansa*

When theater is consciously shaped in conversation with modes of being and learning that embody epistemic resistance, then the ethics, poetics, and aesthetics of protest and drama become interwoven. This recognition of theater's potential as a site for building solidarities through embodied collective pedagogy is what led to the growth of Parakh. Parakh or critical eye[48] emerged as an approach from the work Tarun and I first embraced with SKMS saathis in 2006 and then continued to explore sporadically with amateur and professional actors whom we subsequently helped bring together for different durations of time in Minneapolis–Saint Paul (2008), Lucknow (2013), and Mumbai (2014). This approach also informed our work as co-facilitators of the Stories, Bodies, Movements course at the University of Minnesota in the spring and fall semesters of 2017.

The Sangathan's pathshalas have been teaching us that transformation does not happen simply by bringing into the same space bodies who desire change. The real movement begins when the bodies enter into intense embodied journeys in order to wrestle with incommensurable gaps in lived experiences and in theoretical and political positions through radical vulnerability.[49] A necessary component of building situated solidarities across uneven locations, radical vulnerability is inspired by relationships of trust and critical openness that allow for serendipitous and playful co-learning. Yet, this trust and surrender cannot be demanded, nor can such opening up be regarded as a sign of weakness. Vulnerability becomes radical only when it is becomes a collectively embraced mode in search of the shared creative power it has the potential to enable. This collective creativity—which is never fully attained and always in progress—emerges slowly as we learn to let go of the threads of stories that we have inherited and that have made us, and as those threads get entangled with the words and worlds of our saathis or co-travelers. In such letting go, narratives about our childhoods and our ancestors, our relationships and our losses, our fears and our dreams become collectively owned narratives that enable a hitherto unknown awareness of spatialities and temporalities. Fragments of our journeys reemerge as pangs and evoke new hauntings; they allow us to discover new accents and moves we could not know otherwise; we stumble on unforeseen melodies and languages through which to sing and read our shared fragments within the structures of the sociopolitical, cultural, and affective fields that constitute us relationally.

The tentative questioning that initially inspired this work gained increasing clarity through repeated efforts: if saathis including Prakash, Tama, Rambeti, and Sunita must be reckoned with as sources of profound knowledge that are nevertheless dismissed by the prevailing common senses of experts, then how might we form diverse collectives to challenge those erasures and dismissals? How might we bring together into the same space bodies that may never otherwise meet in a mode of radical vulnerability? What can these differently located collectives learn through encountering, reliving, and rehearsing stories that delve into literary and other representations of the subaltern[50] while reflecting critically on ourselves and our social imaginaries in the process?

These questions, in turn, have led to new ones: can we responsibly encounter the bodies represented in the stories, even as we learn to re-tell and re-present them through the creative process we coauthor with one another? In what ways can we devise playful and serendipitous learning that also inculcates an insuppressible hunger for undoing the scripts and languages that trap us? The different collectives who have constituted Parakh in different places have worked to deromanticize the idea of border crossing by conceptualizing solidarity work as a responsibility to learn how to ethically read, think, rehearse, play, and *embody* positions in ways that can allow us to internalize the non-separation between the protagonist and the antagonist within ourselves, and that can enable hard conversations across locations and epistemes that we neither regularly encounter, nor have the tools to adequately comprehend. In so doing, the co-travelers and co-actors begin to recognize, and at times yearn for, hitherto unforeseen definitions and possibilities of justice.

Part 3 of *Hungry Translations* presents several entangled scripts that emerged during one such exploration by Parakh: the theatrical adaptation of Premchand's last short story, "Kafan," into *Hansa, Karo Puratan Baat*. A group of people who have left their villages in various parts of India to look for a better future in Mumbai—either as actors in Bollywood or as domestic help in the homes of film and television stars—come together in this work to radically reinterpret prevailing ideas about the 'rural poor' and to interrogate commonly held beliefs about who and what makes a good actor or artist. The group learns through each other's experiences what it might mean to be generous to those we have been taught to see as antagonists[51] and to grapple with the complex structural and psychological processes that have constituted them. The making of *Hansa* is neither guided nor informed by the controversies that have surrounded Premchand, and specifically his story "Kafan," with respect to politics of caste. In retrospect, however, Parakh's process of reinterpreting the story births new hungers for embodied solidarities in search of justice. Playing the story and its characters, dead and alive, becomes organically entangled with the lives of those who are playing it. Through improvisation and cocreation, the director becomes a facilitator whose instruction can only emerge through the lived stories and embodied interpretations of those who are enacting the evolving script.

At the same time, *Hansa* reveals a difficult contradiction. Despite the audiences' praise and despite the desire of most participants to continue working together as a loosely formed 'repertory,' this labor cannot continue. While the workshop that created *Hansa* offered alternative ways of exploring the meanings of artistry and critique, the professional actors who became involved in it cannot continue learning from the domestic workers who became involved as actors. In some cases, it is the resistance that the domestic workers face from their employers that makes continued collaboration impossible. One can say, then, that the very success of *Hansa* is trapped in an oppressive and hierarchical social order; this reality is a poignant reminder of Da Costa's insight: "Stigma sticks, but not congenitally. It is made to stick."[52] I enter into these themes by narrating key moments from the six-month process of making *Hansa*, and by sharing fragments of the multiply translated diaries of several participants.

Third Staging—A Syllabus in Fifteen Acts

If retelling stories is one of the key ways in which justice is negotiated, then how might the classroom become a space to internalize the need for an ongoing critical praxis of ethically receiving, retelling, and restaging stories? Can such praxis help us reconceptualize the classroom as a place and as a stage for collective movement, one that enables a rescripting of one's own situated stories in relation to the journeys, narrations, and refusals of other bodies who inhabit the classroom? Can this praxis rest on the basic principle of learning what it takes to build trust and collectivity? What might we learn about the incommensurabilities of our own histories and geographies by working on letting go of our own stories, formed and unformed, so that we might learn to receive others' stories in the same ways that we would like our own fragmented tales to be received?

Stories, Bodies, Movements is one such effort to remake the classroom. Far from envisioning a syllabus as a fixed text and pedagogy that can travel in disembodied and placeless manner from one classroom to another, I rethink the syllabus as a dynamic vision and political text that seeks to move us in unanticipated ways. Through playfulness and performative doing and undoing by those who inhabit the classroom, the syllabus offers a pedagogy for confronting the unevenness of the unjust terrain and the violent histories and geographies that breathe through our words, our accents, and our skins.

Undergirded by the ethics of responsibly receiving stories and telling them in turn, Stories, Bodies, Movements demands ongoing reflection on the work that the traveling of a story does. It asks that the bodies who inhabit the classroom co-develop a critical awareness through which our reception of a text or tale can trouble or displace the disciplined eye and *I*. Rather than theorizing the complexity of an other in disembodied ways, such political pedagogical sensibility engages an other's (hi)story as well as our socially imposed embodiments through feeling and playing that are grounded, dynamic, and anti-hierarchical. This commitment requires unlearning and relearning *together* from the intellectual labor of those who occupy marginal spaces, while helping to forge new publics that seek politically vibrant processing of stories through anti-definitional analytical spaces. It asks us to be mindful of the painful contradictions that emerge in this process, especially when the displaced words of those inhabiting the locations deemed as 'margins' might be enacted by those who form the mainstream.

Merging Stages: Pedagogies of Fractured *We*s

> I cannot use the old critical language to describe, address, or contain the new subjectivities . . . I scrutinize my wounds, touch the scars, map the nature of my conflicts, croon to las musas (the muses) that I coax to inspire me, crawl into the shapes the shadow takes, and try to speak with them. . . . My job is not just to interpret or describe realities but to create them through language and action, symbols and images. My task is to guide readers and give them the space to co-create, often against the grain of culture, family, and ego injunctions, against external and internal censorship, against the dictates of genes.
>
> —Gloria E. Anzaldúa, "Preface: Gestures of the Body—Escribiendo para idear"

> Fire can kill, but without it we *will* die. Can we see that a lotus can bloom in the furnace without losing its freshness? We would need to learn to make peace with contradiction and paradox, to see its operation in the uneven structures of our own lives, to learn to sense, taste, and understand paradox as the motor of things . . . Still, we know that living contradiction is not easy in a culture that ideologically purveys a distaste for it, preferring instead an apparent attachment to consensus. But we know, as well, that living contradiction is necessary if we are to create the asylums of identification and solidarity with and for one another, without which our lives will surely wither.
>
> —M. Jacqui Alexander, *Pedagogies of Crossing*

In *Transformation Now!*, AnaLouise Keating points out an urgent need for scholars to explore paths that can lead us toward a post-oppositional politics of change because oppositional consciousness usually traps us in arguments that are grounded in the very systems, frameworks, and worldviews that we try to transcend.[53] She echoes Bruno Latour's lament that scholars and intellectuals are drowning in "So many wars. Wars outside and wars inside. Cultural wars, science wars, and wars against terrorism. Wars against poverty and wars against the poor." And she reiterates Latour's poignant questions: "Is it really our duty to add fresh ruins to fields of ruins . . . to add deconstruction to destruction? . . . What has become of the critical spirit? Has it run out of steam?"[54]

Readers of this book may have felt similar sentiments at some point or another. I certainly have. Yet, it was not until the beginning of sangtin yatra in 2002 that some of these questions became defining points of my universe. The concerns of sangtin yatra did not center so much on the "critical spirit" of academic scholars, however. Rather, in focusing on the "NGOization of grass-roots politics," the sangtins came to be concerned with a general category of experts—including but not restricted to academics—who are entitled to become thinkers, writers, activists, artists, trainers, policy makers, and leaders, and who aspire to fight for justice for the less privileged others. These others, furthermore, are almost always deemed nonexperts, except perhaps as narrators of stories that can confirm the ways in which the nonexperts' own lives are marked by violence, inequality, disempowerment, and injustice—thereby reinforcing the need for expert interventions.[55] In articulating a dream to dismantle this dichotomous landscape of those who can emancipate and those who must be emancipated, sangtins' storytelling struggles for situated solidarities that necessitate multiple i/Is from uneven and diverse locations to come together as wes while also recognizing that every blended we will also be an intensely fractured we. Mapping the words of Alexander and Anzaldúa from the opening epigraphs onto sangtins' journey, then, I can say that the hope of turning an asylum of solidarity into a continuous movement resides in a collective commitment to scrutinize the fault lines and fractures, to map the nature of our conflicts in ways that the fragments forming the we can feel inspired to continue walking together.

The idea of situated solidarity in the form of a "blended but fractured we" is one of the foundational principles of SKMS, the movement that emerged from the political battles summarized in Playing with Fire and that animated Muddying the Waters: Coauthoring Feminisms across Scholarship and Activism. Arguing against the common sense that mastery of certain theories and methods can enable well-meaning academics to bring justice to those they pronounce to be the "marginalized," Muddying the Waters translates the methodology of Sangtin Writers and SKMS as "radical vulnerability"—an essential requirement for journeying together as coauthors in a political landscape disfigured by nonstop epistemic violence. This coauthorship hinges on sharing authority through a situated solidarity that continuously strives for radical love through the dissolution of egos. Hungry Translations extends the concept of coauthorship as a relation of translation—one that is always hungry for journeying together in search of justice while also recognizing that there will always be faults in both the relation as well as in the search. Moreover, it is in the impossibility of arriving at completion and of knowing the destination with certitude that the hope for the journey resides. The possibility of justice, too, is contingent on the shared need to continue journeying together; for, the end of such need is the end of the ethical relation that is hungry translation.

Hungry translation, then, is a forever evolving entanglement—a relation of radical openness, a politically-aware submission that also struggles to overcome intense bitterness, hatred, or suspicion at times. As an embodied mode of co-living that co-constitutes its own aesthetics and politics, it is as frequently marked by tears of joy and frustration as it is by silences of trust and distrust. In this co-living, spiritual activism becomes one with political activism, and theory and epistemology become inseparable from pedagogy. It is in learning to breathe, sing, dance, and break together, it is in feeling the wordless pangs of fasting, rallying, mourning and celebrating together that the possibility of discovering and living alternative rhythms and movements lies.

By naming and lingering with the simultaneous presence of connection, disconnection, compassion, and intolerance in journeys of co-making theory and pedagogies, hungry translation struggles with the contradictions of radical vulnerability. Radical vulnerability is not a one-way street of endless generosity and openness; it is equally about understanding the simultaneous coexistence of inhumanity and humanity within each one of us. It is about reminding ourselves and one another of the violent histories and geographies that we inherit and embody despite our desires to disown them. Confronting these realities and contradictions implies working through the specific moments in which resistance to collectivity emerges as well as the significant lessons that those moments may carry about context-specific meanings of ethics, aesthetics, and justice. Such grappling with the simultaneous presence of the protagonist and antagonist in all of us is necessary for *just* translations—that is, for modes of retelling that agitate against the structures and epistemes invested in guarding the binary of 'the emancipators' and 'those in need of emancipation.'

The following pages of *Hungry Translations* retell stories where countless people have worked to surrender to the serendipitous meanings of all that evolves in the poetics of moving together. In narrating these embodied knowledges across the spaces of community theater and movement building in Mumbai and Sitapur District in India on the one hand, and the classes—chiefly located at, but not restricted to, the University of Minnesota on the other, I interrupt the idea that we do research or community engagement in sites that are separated from the university, while the teaching happens in our formal classroom spaces.[56] These ever-unfolding political pedagogical sensibilities and commitments, moreover, are not motivated solely by instrumental gain. At times, the co-travelers hunger to hear another's sorrows and hopes, validate another's insights and experience, and forgive another's fallibilities and inhumanity in search of a situated solidarity. At others, the co-travelers become part of a journey by accident without subscribing to its goals, yet choosing to remain with it. These threads form connections—sometimes through hard knots—not to produce the institutionalized practices that social scientists or policy specialists typically examine, but to produce tenuous pathways toward resisting everything that prevents our lives from attaining fullness and dynamism. These knotted threads animate an ever-unfolding unlearning and relearning that does not seek out totalizing knowledge, but that dwells in moments of imperfect resonances and wordless refusals that escape familiar registers of comprehension. Such moving moments are shaped by hopes that humans everywhere harbor in our hearts for ourselves and our loved ones who live; for the unfulfilled promises we may have made to our ancestors and to our human and nonhuman relatives; for the neighborhoods, villages, rivers, forests, and lands that are essential parts of us.

An embodied pedagogical praxis that braids and untangles such threads must strive to translate at some points, while refusing to translate at others, each time recognizing the limits and paradoxes of our retellings and refusals. Each retold story, furthermore, must remain grounded in its experience of knowing, even as its very translations and nontranslations must migrate out to other bodies and sites of struggle in order to find echoes so that the struggles may continue. These braided strands find their strength, not merely from the back-and-forth motions and journeys across time and place but also from movements within, across, and beyond the borders of languages: languages that bear scripts and official status; languages that exist only as bolis or utterances; nameless languages that can sometimes be played, felt, and heard *without* spoken or written words; languages that push our imaginations beyond what has already been defined for us in dictionaries, thesauruses, and textbooks.

· · ·

In *Acting Up: Gender and Theatre in India, 1979 Onwards*, A. Mangai writes about bodies on stage, and the ways in which they relate to, reflect, subvert, and remake social bodies. She tells us about the manner in which moving bodies create new scripts and make new meanings as they read and reread familiar stories and texts from yesterday, and as they respond to the present political concerns by taking over today's tales and refashioning them on their own terms.[57]

The situated solidarities whose explorations have birthed *Hungry Translations* are, in many ways, shaped by a similar set of concerns, albeit with a more expansive notion of the *stage*. If a significant part of politics is constituted by whether and how we tell a story, then this book's stories long for contextually specific meanings of justice and ethics through performing retelling. The stories I retell are equally about the scripts, strategies, repositionings, and performances that evolve when people come together to form campaigns, struggles, and knowledges in collectives and movements. In this rethinking of moving, performing, protesting, playing, and refusing, the stage is not merely a site for creating spectacle; it becomes a negotiated pedagogy that wrestles with the aesthetic and political interbraiding of poetic and social justice.

Such entangling of bodies, stories, sites, and stages allows us to explore the creative labors of movement as theater, and theater as movement. It interweaves questions of translation and political engagement in critical creative and pedagogical work—a point made in the "Closing Notes" coauthored with Siddharth Bharath and Sara Musaifer. These last pages offer a meditation on how in each of the above-mentioned contexts—movement building, theater, and university—it is a combination of the strategically designed performances *and* serendipitous embodied encounters that open up hitherto unforeseen possibilities for collective critical reflection, reinterpretation, reimagining, replay, and reaction. These possibilities, in turn, enable a *oneness*—what some might call a planetary consciousness—by molding relationships that demand emotional and embodied surrender in a shared journey of life. By enabling a continuous and deeply difficult process of unlearning and relearning, such a process can become a politics without guarantees that is dedicated to continuous becoming. This openness to continuous unfolding of politics is key in disrupting preformed proposals about 'the social' as well as formulations that compartmentalize research, writing, art, engagement, and activism.

In *Hungry Translations*, pedagogy becomes inseparable from a praxis of *strategic retelling* that undoes any straightforward narrations of what happens 'out there' in 'the community' inhabited by Othered bodies and epistemes. The politics and poetics of teaching, embodied theory, and living resistance unfold as a thoroughly entangled journey of translation and movement. By decentering 'the product' of pedagogy and by replacing it with an evolving struggle, such an approach asks us to suspend our prior assumptions about aesthetics, ethics, and protest. It allows us to provincialize the discourses of hunger that are scripted by a range of expert projects and institutions and to reimagine hunger as an episteme, a relentless hope, and a collective drive for social and poetic justice.

• • •

For the reader who still remains skeptical of the idea of radical vulnerability because we are all vulnerable in unequal ways, or because the institutions we breathe in are hostile or dismissive of such a mode of being, I offer a few last thoughts as we enter "Movement as Theater." To begin with, if hungry transla-tion is the only relation through which one can search for justice with those one has encountered as one's Others—and if that journey must continue without arriving—then it is solely by offering pieces of oneself that one can hope to enact hungry translation. Moreover, it is the continuation of the hunger in the relationship that gives all co-travelers the courage to continue offering new layers of themselves to one another.

Second, in this continuous cycle, where radical vulnerability and hungry translation make and remake one another in search for justice, the terms of the relationship—or the nature of offerings—cannot be demanded in accordance with any predetermined formula or recipe: the journey of this entanglement must remain an organic process—a long yatra that unfolds serendipitously to realize a shared goal; a yatra in which not everyone may choose to remain together until the next halt or turn. Third, even though such a journey asks for sacrifices, the stories I retell in this book attest to one common truth: that the joys and lessons of moving and creating together in a radically vulnerable mode are often deeper than the sacrifices made by individual travelers. Last but not least, one always must be prepared for the impossibility of realizing radical vulnerability as well as hungry translation: after all, these are part of a politics without guarantees.

The hungry translations I offer in this book, then, can never attain comple-tion. Rather, I hope that every page can also become a stage where you, the reader, can arrive at each retelling as an audience and as a protagonist who processes the stories in relation to your own embodied entanglements. Or to use another analogy, far from serving a fully cooked meal before you, I invite you to step into my kitchen restless to add the ingredients from fragments that constitute your own journeys. So that you can join me in the ongoing labor of trying to do justice to the stories I tell. So that together we may struggle with the contradictions and possibilities of situated solidarities that dare to stand with hopes to create just worlds within and across borders.

PART TWO

Movement as Theater

*Storylines, Scenes, Lessons,
and Reflections*

Walking Together

The Work of a Likkhaad

We are in the final days of December 2003. This has been a particularly cold winter in Uttar Pradesh. In Richa S.'s small rented home, the one large hard bed guarded by a tiny room heater serves as more than just a shared sleeping area—it's also the office, the living room, the eating room, and the playroom for seven of us: Richa's nine-year-old son, Parth; my six-year-old daughter, Medha; Richa's mother, whom we call Amma; Richa's brother, Appu; our friend and colleague Mukesh; and of course, the two Richas. With wool shawls drawn close to our heavily clad bodies, and with our legs slid under two weighty cotton razais, the whole herd of us is huddled together on a foggy winter night. On top of the razais, we have spread a newspaper on which Appu has poured a full kilo of warm peanuts that we are cracking out of their shells and rubbing in rock salt before popping into our mouths—a well-tested method of gaining comfort during the imprisonment this freezing night has imposed on us.

i read aloud a section i have just finished drafting in the last chapter of sang-tins' collective book in Hindi, which is yet to be titled. It focuses on the experiences of village-based NGO workers with the trainers who come to teach them, but who end up violating the trust of those they are trying to help. The material is serious, but the ironies presented in the story are so familiar that even Amma cannot help laughing. Mukesh pats my back approvingly while also affectionately poking at my academic credentials, "Waah, Professor Sahiba. Sundar likha hai."

Richa and Richa: sixteen years of writing together. (Photo by David R. Faust)

By now, i have become used to Mukesh's relentless teasing when he shifts from "Richa" to "Professor Sahiba" to distinguish me from Richa S. He similarly switches to "Didi" when he sometimes talks to Richa; Didi, literally older sister, is the reverential title by which Richa S. is referred to by everyone in the villages where Sangtin works. An experienced activist dedicated to radical pedagogies, Mukesh has come up with great nicknames in jest; "Professor Sahiba" suggests that i may be a sangtin, but i am also a globetrotting professor—a status and privilege that other sangtins do not share with me. Yet his teasing never fails to convey his firm belief in the labor i am contributing to the dream we are all weaving together. i am touched by his words, but before i can thank him for his compliment, Richa S. interjects, "Don't praise her like that. She is a likkhaad. This is the least she can do."

Likkhaad, in Hindi, means a writer who writes profusely, but there is something about the way Richa S. uses that term to interrupt Mukesh that perplexes me. On the surface she seems to be saying that because i can write abundantly my labor does not merit his compliment; is there something else that she is trying to get at?

It is hard to tell whether it is the sudden slowing down of the speed with which we have been cracking the peanut shells, or if it is an expression that has just come on my face, but Richa S. immediately senses that something has not

Writing *Sangtin Yatra*. Clockwise from left: Shashi Vaish, Reshma Ansari, Surbala, and Ramsheela with Ramsheela's son, Sachin, in the center. (Photo by Richa Nagar)

Shashibala holds her son, Sarthak, while reviewing a draft chapter of *Sangtin Yatra*. (Photo by Richa Nagar)

gone right with the exchange. She wants to bring the mood of the conversation back to where it was—"Don't misunderstand me," she says matter-of-factly. "To you written words come easily. Writing is your privilege and your passion, but when we are moved by your writing it is not necessarily because you write well; it is because you can write in our language in ways that make our stories matter. You can write as if we have written those stories ourselves. Because you can and we can't."

Since that foggy, damp December night more than fifteen years ago—when a group of nine women had barely begun to imagine an organization that approached empowerment in a form that was liberated from NGO-dominated imagination—i have never stopped thinking about that conversation. What does it mean to be a likkhaad in the context of being a saathi of SKMS? What does it mean to write the stories of SKMS in ways that those stories can come to matter in the lives of my saathis as well as in the different locations they and i occupy? Can i write these stories without exploiting my saathis—so that my own purposes for retelling their stories do not unintentionally contradict or undermine their struggles for epistemic justice and the work they want these and other similar stories to do? What joys and burdens come with the responsibility of writing those stories as someone who has the tools and privilege to be able to write in ways that many of my saathis cannot?

Like a shuttlecock in a badminton court, the stories of the struggle move between different sections of the court; i have to keep switching places to make sure i can hit them right with my words, so that stories of struggle can do their work. In this strange game, there is no singular teammate and no singular opponent. The shuttlecock, too, becomes a player whose movement depends not only on how i hit it, but also on the contours of the court where the game is unfolding. It is as easy for me to slip, as it is to drop a shuttlecock.

Like the endless page that is also an unbound stage, this game of hitting stories with the most apt words, tenses, pauses, and silences cannot conclude. For, concluding the game is the end of learning.

My training as a likkhaad continues.

> Movement   Sangathan
>   in togetherness with
>   bodies, breaths, emotions, wor(l)ds
>   traces that
>   walk   fight   stretch
> expand   deepen
>   pull
>   in different ways

hungry
        journeys of loosening bodies
passions visions words in remaking
        in concert
        andolan.

        Movement
            shifts   *agitation passage*
            (e)motions of saathis that trigger
      actions affects effects
                tireless
      dreams screams responsibilities
      for justice
      unending lessons heeded in the soul
            before the next utterance, halt, turn
                in the journey
                in the sentence

        Movement   *Move heart and mind*
        in response to another's   *Movement*
translations
        forever struggle to write responsibly.

Living a Critique

One year later. It's another freezing night at the end of December. Nine bodies of women who, in crucial ways, have become one as 'Sangtin Samooh' after the publication of our collective book, *Sangtin Yatra*, are scrunched together in shawls and quilts around a kerosene lamp in a dark room we have rented in a dharmshala, or inn, in Mishrikh. Our hearts beat tonight with a strange mixture of pain, anger, fear, joy, and excitement. The publication of *Sangtin Yatra* and the controversy around our critiques of NGO-driven empowerment have drawn the attention of people throughout Uttar Pradesh and the world to the oft-forgotten textures and tunes of the sangtins' lives and wisdom. All this has led to events we could have never imagined. At different junctures during the penning of their stories, several authors faced serious opposition in their homes for writing about their bodies and desires or about conflicts in their homes. As sangtins' ink started flowing on paper and intimate truths gushed out in intense conversation with one another's words, some family members felt threatened. In one or two instances, the husbands and relatives accused the sangtins of selling away their honor by writing their stories.

Each author persisted, however. Like pillars at floodgates, we stood alongside one another, fighting every wave that threatened to sweep our collective truths away.

That drama now seems miniscule in comparison with the postpublication attacks that came from the NGO that employed seven out of nine authors. The NGO director reprimanded the writers for reflecting on their experiences of elitist, anti-Dalit, and anti-Muslim attitudes that abound in the same Savarna-dominated workplaces that seek to "uplift" rural women. Even worse, she proclaimed the rural activists intellectually incapable of expressing these truths as part of their own political journey in the absence of an "outside mind."

The attack and its effects have been unforgiving. They have left each one of us traumatized in different ways even after we emerged victorious in our fight to protect the rights of each author to pen herself.[1] How could a feminist organization ask the authors to apologize for *writing* their wish to be regarded as experts on their own lives? For refusing to be parts of projects that separate "poor women" and their culturally designated "enemies"—their fathers, brothers, husbands, sons—from such issues as caste politics, water politics, political massacres of people labeled as "minorities," and global imperialism? Furthermore, the manner in which the blame for "inciting this trouble" was extended to Richa S. and me as Savarna and formally more educated members of the group, who helped with scripting editing, publishing, and distributing the book, mocked everything the collective's labor stood for.

Since the launch of *Sangtin Yatra* more than nine months ago, we have won many battles. There has been significant support in the media from intellectuals and political activists for *Sangtin Yatra* and for the authors' rights to express their views without fear of the NGO that employs them. Richa S. resigned from the NGO, several members of the Minnesota Chapter of the Association for India's Development (AID-MN) studied the book, and AID-MN stepped in to support Richa S. in advancing the next phase of sangtins' work. We have also heard that the chapter of the book that focuses on our childhoods will be included in the Hindi curriculum of the Central Board of Secondary Education. As a result of active transnational petitioning against the attacks that targeted the authors, the education minister of India asked the NGO's director, who was leading the attack against us, to resign from her position. Last but not least, all the diary writers employed by the NGO were promoted in their jobs.

The attack made us recognize more sharply than ever that the journey has barely begun. We must now show the world that the critiques we articulated on paper are not empty rhetoric to be read, then celebrated or trashed, before moving on to the next fashionable project. Our critique must become part of a breathing, growing world; otherwise the words that form our speeches,

Sangtin Writers resolve to continue their journey. (Photo by Richa Nagar)

slogans, manifestos, and books bear no meaning after they have served their instrumental purposes in our fields and careers. The vision achieved through the writing of *Sangtin Yatra* and *Playing with Fire* must now be transformed into an ongoing fight to change the ways in which the so-called poor, or materially underprivileged, are repeatedly mistreated—in our villages and cities, in our development bureaucracies and funding agencies, in our political institutions and cultural organizations, in the school textbooks and in novels and films.[2]

First and foremost, this fight involves surviving with no guarantee of funding and not becoming too moralistic about this matter. How many of us are willing to embrace a new path that comes with no fixed honoraria, salaries, or stipends? Can those who are able to do so also learn to accept, without being judgmental, the decision of those who cannot?

Living our critique must become a collective state of being: one where we can live with our eyes and I*s* opened—in our homes, workplaces, neighborhoods, and fields; in our many lives and locations. Justice and injustice both await us everywhere—not just outside of us but also inside ourselves.

How do we make this journey an ongoing awareness that also sustains us over the long haul?

NGOs
photocopiers drivers accountants jeeps
air conditioners generators internet per diems
typists sweepers hotels receipts
accounting
pilots projects preplanned self-proclaim innovations
budget lines wedded to infrastructure staff projects
accounted.

NGOs
a common sense almost
mode of thinking and doing
a ruler of imaginations.
a takeover communities, dreams, battles for justice.
Journeys—complex, entangled, messy
torn apart, labeled, despirited, sanitized
            reconceptualized, segregated
lives turned into projects.
NGOization, NGOs alive, academic jargon.

NGOs
suffocated by secured knot donors-funders
time bound jobs with promised stipends
continuous cycles of activities.
forever remain in business.

But Not all not all of them
suffocate and crush
            NGOs
modes of Critique lived
breathed
everyday parts of ourselves.
Regardless of budgets, staffs, infrastructures.
Open to its own revisioning   Liberated
from moralistic positionings and posturings.

Translating Critique into Struggle

In the weeks and months that follow the Sangtin Writers' meeting in Mishrikh, three women in Sitapur—Richa, Surbala, and Reena—fling themselves fully into the task of imagining what social and political transformation from their own soil might look like. Even after years of speaking about decentralization, transparency, and collectivity, they find it hard to realize the deeper meanings of these terms as they embark on their new mission in the villages of Mishrikh Development Block in Sitapur District. The uncertainties of this path make their hearts fearful, but the relationships they have formed through their past work give them faith: if they truly commit themselves to the all-consuming journey of building a movement, people will surely come together to fight against the injustices that are suffocating them.

Fueled by the critical energy of *Sangtin Yatra*, the political battles in its aftermath, and the courage of their hearts, these three sangtins step into a territory that their previous work in the NGO never prepared them for. Radically distancing themselves from 'women-only' consciousness-raising meetings, they spend night after night around fires with men and women, old and young, talking about the issues they deem most critical. Without a doubt, the government's policies, Hindutva politics, and the presence of political musclemen in the state have deeply hurt the neglected and humiliated sections of the society. Yet, a different kind of thinking is emerging in these nightly discussions. People say that the responsibility to fight against social and economic injustices cannot be carried out by the government, the parties, or the do-gooders who sing songs about the 'upliftment of the poor.' When so much damage has been done to the rural poor by constantly labeling them as stupid or indifferent, the poor themselves will have to take active control of what is said about their needs and upliftment under such grand labels as development, democracy, human rights, and social justice.

In order to get there, however, the sangtins must first create a strong people's movement. We need to identify a set of issues around which hundreds of people can coalesce in Mishrikh. To do this, sangtins are organizing meetings in village after village. Everywhere people list the countless problems they face: the missing roads, the unseen water, the undelivered pensions, the housing schemes run in their names that never provide roofs over their heads. They underline the value of all that their difficult lives have taught them. They remark on the pointlessness of the education their children receive in the terribly under-resourced schools, only to remain locked in webs of exploitation and servitude that continue to suffocate the Dalit communities.

During one of these nightly meetings around a fire, a young man remarks, "We didn't get a chance to study in a building but . . . haven't we made ourselves? Haven't our lives already given us the education that we need to fight these systems?"

"That's true," another man responds, "but any so-called educated person occupying an official position in a city—no matter how green in age or experience—never hesitates for a second before preaching to us about anything under the sun. To say that poor make themselves is one thing; to be able to feel this truth is quite another."

The sangtins present their view: "Issues such as roads, pensions, water, and primary education are serious, but what is the one major concern that can bring together large numbers of people in Sitapur's villages to understand, strategize, and struggle for a cause *now*?"

One set of recurring concerns centers on bringing water to the Islamnagar distributary canal. This irrigation canal has not seen water for sixteen years. About forty villages are severely affected. People have heard stories from older women about the miracles of the canal. A woman talks of Sabelia: "There was a time when my village had so much rice that people from the surrounding villages wanted to marry off their daughters there! With plenty of rice for both meals, the parents knew that their daughter won't starve. As the water disappeared, so did the possibility of a belly content with rice!"

The issue of the irrigation canal is also surrounded with grave political risks. In recent years the contracts to clean the canal have been allocated to politically well-connected and corrupt persons who simply pocket all the money without doing the work. A direct challenge to these thugs will be risky; at the same time, an organized collective can make demands of the government. It is the state's responsibility to provide water to its people, so even if Sangtin does not have the means to confront the thugs directly, it can still wage a determined battle for more equitable access to irrigation by focusing on the state's failures to deliver water.

Many people have lost hope that a canal that has been dry for more than a decade and a half will ever see water again. Sangtins are trying to convince them that even if a fraction of them pour their collective energies into the task, the impossible can be directed toward the possible. Kilometer after kilometer, people living in villages on both sides of the irrigation canal are coming together to form Nahar Sangharsh Samitis, or committees to lead a political agitation to bring water back into the canal. The women and men who are emerging as leaders in their own villages are meeting with organizers in the other villages to form a solid core, dubbed the pakke saathis of the emerging struggle. These pakke saathis include Shivram, Raibahadur, Santosh, Sunita, Kamala, Pramod, Shamsuddin, Saraswati Amma, Rajpati, Sobran, and Hasnain. Along with dozens of other women and men, these saathis are undertaking padyatras to spread their message along the entire length of the irrigation canal. Hundreds of people are merging their energies to build an atmosphere of shared struggle and hope.

With all of this arises the political question of how to name the struggle emerging in the villages of Mishrikh. It all begins one afternoon when Shamsuddin, also called Shammu, of Aant village astounds everyone by posing a crucial question. While signing a petition against the corruption of the Irrigation Department, he asks, "Why are we still signing petitions as representatives of Nahar Sangharsh Samiti?"

The sangtins present at the scene are perplexed—"Why? What's wrong with signing the petition as a representative of the committee that is leading the agitation for irrigation water?"

Shammu teases, "Will someone explain why I don't qualify as a sangtin?"

This question stuns everyone. Shammu is dissatisfied that the organization called Sangtin exists as a separate entity from the movement that is emerging around the issue of irrigation water. Sangtin, which literally means a woman's closest woman companion, was established in 1998 as a registered body that would continue the work of empowering women after the time-bound NGO program that once employed Reena, Richa S., and Surbala would no longer receive the support of the state and external donors. A growing number of men who have joined the struggle for irrigation water feel that even if the registered body called Sangtin was initially created by women to address women's issues, it is time to rethink the definition of a 'sangtin.'

Shammu's words echo the core of the collective critique of NGOization that sangtins have launched in *Sangtin Yatra* and *Playing with Fire:* if empowerment cannot happen by trapping people's existence in identity-based or issue-based ghettos, shouldn't the meaning of 'sangtin' include all those men who are accompanying women at this revolutionary moment?

One year after this incident, this matter resurfaces as a burning issue in the emerging Sangathan. At the monthly meeting in Kunwarapur, the pakke saathis ask: "What does it mean to recognize the power of kisans and mazdoors in Sangtin without compromising our commitment to fight against brahmanical patriarchy?" It is collectively decided then that the registered body called Sangtin whose membership initially included only women would still remain an important part of the organization and its history. However, the people's platform emerging from the revolutionary notes of the saathis will now be known as the Sangtin Kisan Mazdoor Sangathan, or SKMS, an organization of farmers and laborers who also see themselves as sangtins. The dream of forming a different kind of political trajectory and social struggle through the writing of *Sangtin Yatra* becomes real through the birth of an organization where all those who walk with the Sangathan come to be known as saathis of SKMS, regardless of their gender, caste, class, ability, or location. This development revitalizes the vision and energy of SKMS. In the conferences and meetings, women and men feel comfortable with one another. While the women's NGOs working in the area always take strict measures to ensure that no men come near their meeting venues during their overnight gatherings, in SKMS it becomes normal for women and men to confer late into the night and then to fall asleep wherever they find a spot in the shared halls. Saathis see this coming together of women and men to lead discussions on the processes of sociopolitical change as a foundational step in giving substance to all of our talk about equality.

> *Living critique*
> *a yatra*
> *a journey*
> *slow train ride of co-travelers:*
> *ascending, descending, re-ascending*
> *the train*
> *sometimes leaving the ride altogether*
> *on our unfolding journey*
> *of life*
>
> *critique permeates*
> *bones*
> *politics become*
> *journeys interbraided*
> *conclusion-free, unscriptable, everflowing*
> *currents*
> *critics must learn to be*
> *currents,*
> *without compromising the core of critique,*
> *owned by all*
> *who surrender to the cumulative force*
>
> *An organization registered as NGO*
> *can still live critique,*
> *creatively refuse—*
> *institutionalization*
> *flow with currents*
> *gain meanings from*
> *tides*
> *rising and falling*

Women Lead a Sangathan against Scheming State Machinery

To stop people from gaining access to resources promised to them on paper, the state machinery invokes bureaucratic procedures and demands that proper paperwork be on file. As the enthusiasm to bring water to the distributary canal peaks, the saathis resolve not to be defeated in the game of paper trails. Even as the saathis confront the state by getting countless signatures and thumb impressions on documents and petitions, the government officials spring non-stop surprises on them. First, the Irrigation Department randomly launches the work of silt cleaning in the distributary canal under the auspices of its new Kaam ke Badle Anaaj Yojana (KBAY, or National Food for Work Programme) and slyly hires mazdoors through contractors even though the government's rules explicitly forbid operationalizing KBAY through contractors.[3] After long arguments between the Sangathan and the Irrigation Department, mazdoor saathis are hired to clean the silt. These saathis are from villages where the canal is completely dry or where very little water is reaching. For them, water in the canal would mean freedom from the brutal expenses of diesel engines and fuel to pump groundwater.

The saathis' happiness is short-lived, however, as the Irrigation Department prematurely releases water into the canal before all the silt can be cleaned. This deprives the saathis of the cash and grain they are getting from silt-cleaning work, while also reducing the chances of water reaching the tail of the canal. Angered by these tactics, Reena, a saathi from the Kunwarapur village, confronts the junior engineer (JE) and proposes a different approach to the Irrigation Department on behalf of SKMS. Entirely unaccustomed to being approached by a village woman thus, the JE refuses to listen.

"Fine," Reena warns the JE. "You sit comfortably in your chair. We ourselves will stop the water that you have released ahead of time; we grant you our permission to take whatever steps you must to stop us." Reena storms out of the JE's office with this warning, but on that bitterly cold December evening in 2005, Shamsuddin is the only saathi who agrees to accompany her to help turn her threat into reality. As Reena climbs on to the back of Shammu's bike, she feels abandoned by her other saathis; disenchantment starts trickling down her face in the form of tears.

After covering some distance on the bicycle, she hears some sounds and turns around to look. A dozen saathis are marching toward her and Shammu with sticks and hoes. Walking proudly in the front, Sobran Dada, the oldest of the lot, declares—"Arey, when our bahuriya, our daughter-in-law, has fearlessly embarked on this trip for all of us, how can we lag behind?"

Saathis of Kunwarapur village, along with another 150 women and men from the surrounding villages, arrive at the head of the canal. Descending into knee-deep water in the freezing cold, the people dam the canal. Three employees of the Irrigation Department set out to stop the saathis, but with dozens of fiercely determined people staring in their faces, they flee. The next day, about three hundred saathis gherao, or surround, the Irrigation Department and force it to hire SKMS saathis for cleaning the silt of another three-kilometer stretch of the canal.

Now comes the turn of the big Savarna kisans in the head area, who have seized as much water as they possibly can by constructing private ditches into their own fields, which also causes considerable leakage and water waste. Under the leadership of Surbala and Reena, twelve saathis labor in the shivering cold of January 2006 to close those ditches. Water advances another kilometer up the canal.

While the enthusiasm among the saathis crests, a new commotion begins inside the homes of women saathis. Surbala's husband brings up the same old question: what kind of work is this, after all, that requires her to spend entire nights walking along the irrigation canal in the name of bringing social change? The women who are emerging as leaders in the campaign are encountering tensions like this every day. Ironically, the people who raise these questions also realize that it is only because of the fiery leadership of these same women that hundreds of mazdoors have been able to secure their payments in cash and grain in the same Sitapur District where more than 1,200 quintals of grain from the KBAY have been sold on the black market due to state corruption.

As SKMS removes full plates of food from under the mouths of the greedy, the Irrigation Department deliberately overpays some saathis and underpays others to try to break the Sangathan. For saathis whose roti is in jeopardy every day, this becomes a sensitive matter, but strong women saathis such as Rajpati help sort out such messy conflicts. The Sangathan decides that the cash received in overpayment can remain with the saathis who have received it in error, but all the grain they have received should be distributed among those who have been underpaid.

• • •

It is March 2006. Water is supposed to be delivered to the different parts of a canal system on a schedule, or roster, that channels the water equitably to various parts of the system. However, the Irrigation Department's refusal to supply water according to the roster is causing the fields to dry. The standing crop of wheat is being stressed. SKMS finds it necessary to escalate the battle again. Approximately four hundred saathis gherao the district magistrate (DM) of

Sitapur. Dalit women such as Madhurani who colead the gherao are increasingly clear about one thing: it is the officers' responsibility to serve the mazdoors and kisans; therefore, saathis must not be silenced by the state's arrogant and bullying attitude toward them. This fearlessness does its work. The DM delivers an ultimatum to the executive engineer (EE) in the presence of SKMS representatives—"Your security now lies in the hands of the mazdoors who are sitting outside this office!" With tears shimmering in his eyes, the EE assures the four hundred protesting saathis that their demands will be met.

The next day, the EE works with nine mazdoor saathis to turn the water's course toward the tail and promptly pays them at the legally approved rate, but without asking them to sign any receipts. If it were government money, they would be signing receipts. The saathis ask, "Wouldn't an officer who is paying us from his own pocket today find ways to refill that pocket from elsewhere tomorrow?" The issue of contractors being hired to do the silt cleaning in the minor distributaries also keeps resurfacing. In open defiance of the JE, the saathis publicize the information about the silt-cleaning work through letters and phone calls, and dozens of mazdoor saathis assemble to perform silt cleaning in the canals under the government's newly launched NREGA, which entitles each adult person living in a village to one hundred days of paid labor.

With silt-cleaning work in full force, water moves farther up the first stretch of the dry canal. However, neither does the water budge past the first five kilometers, nor do the mazdoors get paid, even though the rules of NREGA spell out that payment must be made out within seven days of work. The Sangathan also learns that wooden planks had replaced the iron planks that were once hung from the pillars at the head of the canal. Gradually, the wooden planks also disappeared and the pillars were destroyed. During silt cleaning the saathis place pressure on the assistant engineer (AE) and JE to get the pillars at the gate repaired, but the planks are nowhere to be found. Without the planks, there is no hope for water in the distributary. Exhausted from the continuous indifference of the Irrigation Department, the Sangathan warns: if the planks are not installed and the payments not made to the mazdoors for their work immediately, SKMS will gherao the Irrigation Department in protest.

• • •

It is November 25, 2006. One hundred and fifty saathis gather at the Irrigation Department. Even as the strong gusts of wind cool down the weather, the mercury of the saathis' heads rises with every passing hour. By 4 p.m., angry saathis close the three gates of the Irrigation Department so no staff member can enter or exit the premises. The administration fears that the mazdoors will set fire to the place, so five screaming policemen reach the protest site banging their sticks and boots, pushing the saathis away from the dharna site. As the mazdoor saathis cautiously begin to descend from the veranda where they had been sitting, three women saathis loudly confront the policemen. This energizes the remaining saathis; Tama and Pita break into a soulful song with all the protestors joining in: "Mazdoor kisano ne ladne ki thaani hai, sarkar ke khate mein daana hai na paani hai." Mazdoors and kisans are determined to wage a war against a government whose coffers have neither food nor water to offer!

The policemen worry that, if the saathis refuse to budge, the policemen will also have to spend the night in the cold. A sub-inspector discusses the matter with the officers, and soon the EE and the AE step outside, guarded by the police. Saraswati Amma laughs—"Look at these scared officers. They need police protection to face us!" Eager to see an end to the dharna, the EE verbally promises to replace the planks and to pay the saathis promptly. However, when he refuses to give the same assurance in writing, the saathis spend the night in the open and mobilize overwhelming support from Sitapur's journalists as well as from the chairs of the Board of Trade and the Municipal Corporation. Eventually, the EE and AE extend a written promise to pay the mazdoors by November 26 and to place the planks on the canal by December 2.

In this way, silt is cleaned in the Islamnagar distributary canal and water released for the first time in sixteen years. The victory establishes the centrality of women's leadership in every aspect of SKMS. Even in the realm of nautanki, where men traditionally play the parts of women and which is often termed as an inappropriate and vulgar arena of entertainment for women to participate in, the women saathis make it essential for their communities to rethink their norms and values. As Santoshi argues, "If nautanki is not an appropriate form of performance for me as a woman to act in, then it is not an appropriate entertainment for the men to watch either." We all reflect further on this point: maybe we need to redo nautanki, maybe we need to redo entertainment. We must redo everything unjust that we celebrate in the name of culture, just as we must overhaul everything unjust that is celebrated in the name of democracy.

> a community in struggle
> takes power and creativity
>   of coming together
>   of giving and suffering together
> battling loving losing
> isolated souls becoming
>   resilient   together
> no egos nor proclamations

—feminist marxist nationalist liberal—
        tags dissolve in storms
        entangled we excavate, rebuild for ourselves
        flourish in our soils   find
        fuller languages of politics
        encompassing all life
        energies of all who rise with us, around us
        unstifled by singular identities.

        an intimate enemy
                brahmanical capitalist patriarchy
        analyze it, personalize it, challenge it   intimately
        The Developmentalist State
        uncover hungry breaths bellies howls dreams
        tangled with its moves
                        manipulations
        oppose by engaging
                its discourses policies,
                souls of those who do its dirty work
        you and i are capable of the same greed, of
                corruption   violence   we oppose
        create spaces to feel-theorize-tell
(y)our complicities
        sharpen movement   Move
ever open to all
all that throbs and beats in me, in you.

A Long War

Diary of a Battle: From Job Cards to Unemployment Allowance

28 December 2005—The villages are resounding with the news that the government has launched NREGA, which entitles each adult person living in a village 100 days of paid labor. To implement this scheme, the state requires each mazdoor to have an identification card, also known as a job card. Anyone without a job card would be ineligible for paid labor under the program. Some saathis already smell the red tape. Mazdoors are worried they will be excluded if they do not hurry to get their job card.

19 January 2006—The work of taking photos for the identification cards has begun in earnest in the block development offices. Today is the first of the three dates allocated for taking the saathis' photos. Endless rows of people have filled the premises of the block office. Three policemen are roaming around, banging their batons and calling people names. A pradhan who is a thug is standing at the gate as watchkeeper, while other pradhans and block office staff are busy scolding the mazdoors. Not a single line advances because the office has hired only one photographer, with a malfunctioning camera no less. Saathis demand that the block development officer (BDO) hire one more photographer locally from Mishrikh but he refuses. Saathis go to the next level above the BDO and advise the DM to organize the photography according to the membership in the nyaya panchayats. The DM orders that the plan be implemented.

14 May 2006—The government changes its mind: instead of the previously announced individual identification card, the employment guarantee scheme now asks that each household have a single card. All the resources spent on the photographs go to the dumpster. There is a renewed uproar. Middlemen appear in a number of villages to guarantee family job cards for 10 to 20 rupees. While mazdoors in the state of Rajasthan have seized 50 days of work in February and March, here in Sitapur District of Uttar Pradsesh, saathis are still trying to obtain their job cards! Saathis decide to publicly register their disappointment with the state machinery.

21–25 July 2006—The heat sparked by SKMS in Mishrikh spreads to the neighboring block of Pisawan. Rambeti, a woman mazdoor from Allipur village, organizes Sangathan's first meeting in Pisawan's Inspection House; mazdoors from four villages of Piswan, all of them Dalit women, attend the meeting and join SKMS. With both Mishrikh and Pisawan Blocks now involved in the struggle, the saathis decide to gherao the subdistrict magistrate and demand that he call the development officers of both blocks before the people. Preparations for the rally begin in full swing. The goal is not merely to secure job cards—it is to hold the state development administration responsible for its negligence and corruption. The Sangathan publicizes the reasons behind the state administration's failure to deliver job cards, while appealing to thousands of mazdoors and kisans to advance the struggle for their own livelihoods by joining the rally and gheraoing the subdistrict magistrate in unprecedented numbers.

15 September 2006—The guidelines of the National Rural Employment Guarantee Act specify how to disseminate the information about the job card camps to as many people as possible, but the administration of Mishrikh and Pisawan Development Blocks has taken no steps in this direction. Taking upon themselves the state's work of implementing the right to information, saathis paste copies of the formal notification all over the villages. The bazaars of Kutubnagar and Aant become the centers of publicity, as drivers of three-wheeled carts and tempos embrace the role of SKMS's messengers in village after village.

The secretary illegally charges 5 rupees per job card in the Kutubnagar nyaya panchayat, but the saathis force him to return the money. In a number of nyaya panchayats job card applications are duly filled out, but no cards are delivered. Moreover, the secretary fails to arrange for a photographer.

People who provide their own photos for the application form get no reimbursement for the expense of the photographs that should be borne by the government. In some camps, saathis are asked to deposit their photos for the job cards and many of these photos are subsequently misplaced by the pradhan or the secretary. Photos are retaken but their expenses are borne out of pocket by the mazdoors. As if this is not enough, Secretary Sahab "forgets" to put the registration number on some cards and fails to stamp others.

Relearning in Situ
23 August 2006

In sweltering heat and humidity, approximately 1500 mazdoor and kisan saathis join the rally to the tehsil and surround the office of the Sub-District Magistrate. Dozens of supporters from Sitapur and from other cities and towns of Uttar Pradesh and Uttaranchal travel hundreds of miles to join the saathis' satyagrah.

After four hours of the gherao, the subdistrict magistrate of Mishrikh, the block development officer of Pisawan, and the additional development officer of Mishrikh Panchayat reach the site of the dharna. Faced by thousands of angry people, the BDO nervously declares—"We'll immediately set up counters at this site to deliver your job cards."

From the ocean of people, Sarvesh's sharp voice rises—"BDO Sahab, we know you will make them now, but why weren't they made until now?"

None of the officers ever dreamed of being questioned by a Dalit mazdoor like this. Their brows go up in unison in bewilderment and disapproval.

Saathis recognize the political value of this historic moment. A Dalit saathi sitting in the front row stands up and chants her lungs out: "Hum apna adhikar mangte, nahin kisi se bheekh mangte." We demand our right, we don't beg for mercy!

A storm of arms swing in the air with raised fists. Within a couple of minutes, the officers begin to sweat nervously. Stabilizing his grip on the microphone, the BDO announces—"Your job cards should have been ready by now, and, regardless of who is at fault for this, we know that it will be seen as our mistake." To get a statement like this on a public platform from the mouth of an officer who is always demeaning the economically weak Dalit kisans and mazdoors and blaming them for their own misfortunes is no small feat for the Sangathan.

A few minutes later, the BDO repeats his point about setting up counters to deliver job cards. Several supporters who joined the rally from Lucknow and Uttaranchal suggest to SKMS representatives that the Sangathan should welcome the BDO's proposal: getting their job cards on the very day of the rally would give the saathis a sense of concrete accomplishment after a difficult battle. A couple of mazdoor saathis express concern about the proposal. Sarvesh states angrily, "We haven't come today to get our job cards. Our gherao is to make the administration accept its mistake and to help plan the delivery of job cards."

At first, Sarvesh's fierce opposition to the BDO's offer baffles me also. Several thousand people are sitting in the scorching sun and the BDO is offering to deliver the job cards immediately, so why not take what he is giving under pressure now, when the government is notorious for its delaying tactics? Sarvesh gets frustrated as this conversation among a group of SKMS saathis and supporters unfolds. Then it dawns on everyone that Sarvesh is making a critical point: SKMS must ensure that the block development administration does not collapse its public apology for engaging in corruption with an instant delivery of the job cards. For him, the significance of this political moment resides in the opportunity to challenge the insolent attitude of many well-intentioned people that if you hand something to the angry poor to pacify them instantly, they happily return to their homes. There is a practical issue also: it is already the end of the day, and no matter how many counters the BDO may open, trying to make 1,500 job cards instantly would only result in chaos. The attempt is likely to fail miserably due to its sheer impracticability, but all the blame would be piled on the so-called indiscipline and idiocy of the poor and Dalit mazdoors.

In confronting Sitapur's rural development administration on that hot, muggy afternoon, everyone present at the dharna site also grapples with our own assumptions about what is at stake for each one of us, and what do those stakes imply in terms of concrete strategies. Fighting with those who are seen as poor and hungry does not mean merely ensuring the supply of goods or amenities they may in fact desperately need. It requires unlearning what we have been taught and relearning new lessons together in situ at every step. It requires that we take the time and heart to process and internalize those lessons with humility.

In the end, SKMS representatives embrace Sarvesh's critique and propose that the block administration arrange special camps for making job cards, and that the cards be made according to the records of the nyaya panchayats in both blocks. The administration consents to the proposal.

It is well past 5 p.m. by the time the rally ends. With hoarse throats and bodies layered with dust and sweat, people greet one another with countless smiles, hugs, and handshakes. As saathis begin a long trip home to their villages, a cluster of us approaches the nearest dhaba for celebratory chai and samosas. A strange peace is radiating within and around us. As our cluster of six sips chai from the kulhads and talks about the events of the day, one saathi remarks, "This joy we feel is not merely about the hope of attaining job cards. It's about what changed today in our ways of thinking about the world."

How true! Today's rally has signaled a shift not only in the thinking of the block development administration but in the thinking of all of us—the kisans, the mazdoors, and the saathis and supporters of SKMS. Each of us feels the emergence of a powerful collective creativity that does not hesitate to embrace disagreements. The Sangathan has become a place of transformative learning for all who have stepped into its orbit.

15 January 2007—The job card has become subject to the same kinds of misdealings as all other cards issued by the government in the name of people's welfare. Mazdoors work and receive payments in several villages, but the pradhans and the secretaries refuse to loosen their clutches on the job cards. In some places, mazdoors do not even ask for their job cards, while in others they are given excuses about why the job cards are not ready. In a village in Godlamau Block, 80 percent of cards have more days of work entered on them and the extra money is pocketed by corrupt staff. Saathis confront this corruption while also agitating on the matter of unreimbursed photo expenses. Through letters, pamphlets, and meetings, saathis mobilize hundreds of people in the villages of Sitapur. When a supporter asks a mazdoor saathi, "What's the point of fighting for 15 rupees?," her response unsettles his cost-benefit approach: "We won't give up our right even if each one of us has to spend 50 rupees to win the fight."

The job cards! (Photo by Richa Singh)

Negotiating Dramas
14 February 2007

More than 1,500 saathis gather in protest at the tehsil intersection. The subdistrict magistrate (SDM) tells them to go to the block office because all the records for the job cards are placed with the BDO. The flood of protestors sets out for the block office only to find it surrounded by a massive security force. When no officer appears at the block office even after two hours, saathis begin a loud chant:

"Return the money we spent on photos! Return our job cards!"

The SDM and BDO hear the chants and arrive at the scene. The block pramukh follows under the protection of his security guard. The SDM sends the word, "If you want your problems solved, send your representatives to talk to us inside." The saathis, however, demand a public conversation with the officers: "We resist the corruption that openly happens behind your closed doors!" The administration calls this demand an unwarranted defiance of its authority, but the saathis do not yield.

Negotiating Dramas (continued)

By the time all three officers come out, the saathis are angry. "We have been standing here waiting for hours," one saathi says to the officers, "and now it's 4 p.m."

"The whole day has gone by," another chimes in, "so we will just spend the night here and talk to you tomorrow."

The saathis want to sensitize the administrators to the inhuman ways in which they engage with Dalit mazdoors and kisans, but the block pramukh keeps digressing from the subject of job cards and interrupts repeatedly with the same question that targets the women saathis: "Why do you all create such a drama each time you want something from us?" Two women saathis respond in quick succession: "When poor and Dalit mazdoors come together to demand their rights, the event becomes a drama," says the first. The second finishes the point: "But when the entitlements of the same mazdoors disappear mysteriously, no one wonders about the dramas that go on behind closed doors!"

Even in this tense atmosphere, the coordinating committee of SKMS reaches an agreement with the administration about specific dates for village-wide reimbursement of the photo expenses and the distribution of job cards. The administration is incensed at the political critiques launched by the members of SKMS in the dharna. However, SKMS saathis return reenergized from the power of collective learning. They reflect on how certain kinds of Savarna heteropatriarchal styles of deliberation are given authority, but when the mazdoors and kisans claim the same authority in the public spaces dominated by Savarna male bureaucrats, they are denigrated as complaining, greedy, and dramatic. This becomes especially evident when the mazdoors who are challenging the bureaucrats are also Dalit and women. SKMS resolves to radically shift this terrain.

---

26 March–13 July 2007—The good news first: even with all the hassles and hurdles, the photo expenses are reimbursed on the set dates in all those gram panchayats where SKMS saathis are active. Now the bad news: saathis who were supposed to get 100 days of work by the end of March have barely worked for 15 to 20 days. Claiming the right to livelihood requires escalating the fight. Saathis have

Basic Truth
13 July 2007

All of us who stand with the Sangathan are baffled by the same question: why does the administration refuse to listen until saathis organize a protest or blockade for the smallest of things? And then, later, why does the same administration agree to meet the Sangathan's demands? One day a guard working at the Irrigation Department remarks to the saathis, "The officers here fear only two kinds of people showing up at their door: 10 goons with guns or 100 mazdoors with hoes! If you keep the pressure on, they will listen."

True, we say, but why does it become necessary to organize massive demonstrations and gheraos for schemes that have been passed by the government under its own laws? Why do the very officers who preach tirelessly about law and order defy the same order every day? Clearly, those in power want the Dalit mazdoors and kisans to be always begging and fighting for their right to live in dignity. A system that relies on this basic truth is a violent and unsustainable system that must be fought, crushed, and overhauled.

decided to follow up with the chief development officer (CDO) and district program officer-NREGA to demand that the mazdoors get work without delay. If the administration fails to respond, the Sangathan will launch a dharna on August 8.

8 August 2007—When the administration fails to respond to the saathis' notice, 2,000 people surround the Vikas Bhawan in Sitapur. The CDO avoids the saathis entirely, but the DM meets with them and comes to an agreement that on a trial basis, mazdoors will be paid through direct deposits in the banks in five gram panchayats. It is also decided that work will be provided within 15 days of application; muster rolls will stay at the worksite to prevent tampering; and women and disabled mazdoors will be given preferential treatment in the work assignments. In the Piswan Block, the DM intervenes to ensure that the application of 600 mazdoor saathis is duly received so that they can begin working.

15 November 2007—Despite the DM's intervention, saathis from only a handful of villages have gotten the work they had applied for. Even in places where the saathis have managed to submit applications, there is no hope of actual employment. If no work is granted to an applicant within 15 days of the receipt of that worker's application, the applicant is entitled to unemployment allowance under NREGA. Saathis begin strategizing about demanding the unemployment allowance: "Are we strong enough to sustain an indefinite strike to fight for the unemployment allowance?" As they ponder this question, they remember the realities they already live in the cold January nights and in the harsh summers and monsoons; the imaginary pains of the dharna begin to pale in comparison.

28 November 2007—The Sangathan's written notification to the CDO demands that

- unemployment allowance be given to every mazdoor who has not been granted work within 15 days of receipt of that worker's application;
- a clear plan be outlined to provide 100 days of work and timely payments;
- maximum work of NREGA be done through the gram panchayats;
- women and disabled persons be given work according to the act's provisions;

- a social audit be conducted in all the development blocks for the work done under NREGA.

The CDO declares that it is impossible to give unemployment allowance. Adhering to the Sangathan's notice is now the only way to respond to the deep humiliation meted out by the district administration to the saathis. SKMS decides to commence an indefinite strike on 5 December.

5 December 2007—Approximately 400 saathis declare an indefinite dharna by surrounding Sitapur's Vikas Bhawan. When the city magistrate sends a message from the CDO's office that he is prepared to receive a petition from SKMS, Saathis respond: "The CDO already has a list of our demands. We have no further petitions to deliver. We refuse to move until all our demands are met."

7 December 2007—Four saathis enter the Vikas Bhawan at 9:30 a.m. and announce their intentions. The staff members leave the premises without resistance, and four clusters of saathis take their positions at each entrance of the building. When the circle officer of Sitapur City arrives with his security force around noon, saathis stage an argument with the administration for 90 minutes before relinquishing their control.

Tasting Protest
6 December 2007

Outside the Vikas Bhawan encampment, the saathis feel their bones freeze. With almost 600 protesting bodies, the 50 quilts loaned by a supporter are nowhere near enough. After a few confrontations, the administration supplies wood to light a fire. Sharing, discussing, and singing, the whole night passes in a flash. However, more action is needed to draw the attention of the administration, the media, and the people of Sitapur to the issues of Dalit mazdoors and kisans.

Early in the morning, more than 500 saathis march around the Vikas Bhawan singing the prayer, "Raghupati Raghav Rajaram, Adhikariyon ko buddhi do bhagwan," and the premises of the entire Vikas Bhawan echo with their voices. Passersby on the streets laugh, and some join the saathis in this prayer, which plays with the words of Gandhi's favorite bhajan and asks god to instill some sense in the heads of the officers.

As soon as the singers reach the first story of the Vikas Bhawan, the CDO arrives in his office and the singing transitions into loud chanting. When the CDO's orderly commands SKMS members to go inside and talk to him, Bitoli, a Dalit woman mazdoor saathi, yells piercingly from the edge of the crowd: "So many people are sitting outside your Sahab's room to talk to him and he is ashamed to come out?"

Multiple notes blend into Bitoli's: "Tell your Sahab to come out. We will not talk behind closed doors."

The CDO steps outside to say: "Your demands will be met. Just give them to me in writing."

Saathis are angry: "You already have our written demands. We won't leave until they are met."

"The chief minister's review delegation is coming to Supauli. I must leave urgently. I'll speak to your representatives upon my return," the CDO promises as he flees the battleground in his car. The next day, the administration completely ignores the mazdoors and keeps preparing for the chief minister's delegation by decorating the village of Supauli in Reusa Block.

Every grain that saathis had brought from their homes is now gone. Some saathis have a brainstorm: "So many people from Sitapur City promised their support to us. Why not reach out to them at this crucial juncture in the strike?" No sooner than SKMS makes its appeal, hundreds of new supporters from the city, including media people, small shop keepers, and the chair of the municipal corporation spring into action. "Don't worry about feeding yourselves anymore," they announce. "We'll support you no matter how long your strike."

The Sangathan's courage doubles. Many saathis come in the morning, spend the whole day at the dharna site, and leave in the evening in order to eat and sleep at home before returning the next day. At least 500 people are present at the dharna at all times. To simplify the logistics, they eat only one meal a day, and 15 women and men assume the responsibility of cooking. Roti with boiled potatoes, green chilies, and salt has never tasted so sweet.

Cooking rotis at the dharna site. (Courtesy: Sangtin Archives)

In the midst of today's meal preparations, exciting ideas emerge: why not show up in Supauli village of Reusa Block, where all the district officers are preparing to greet the chief minister's delegation? Plus, this is also an apt time to bring the work of Vikas Bhawan to a grinding halt for half a day. Shutting down the Vikas Bhawan means shutting down the work of 50 government departments.

For the first time in the history of the district, a Sangathan of chiefly rural Dalit mazdoors, many of them women, openly challenges the meanings associated with the building that symbolizes "Development." The entire city watches in awe.

Meanwhile, as one group of saathis manages the Vikas Bhawan shutdown, 60 others discreetly find their way to the bus arranged for Supauli, where thousands of people from Sitapur's villages have gathered. In Supauli they blend into the crowd and ease their way into the front row under the marquee.

One saathi, Richa S., approaches the stage at the first opportunity and begins speaking into the microphone about how millions of rupees under NREGA are being inappropriately distributed throughout the district and about the several thousand protesting saathis in Vikas Bhawan. As she exposes the true colors of the district's development apparatus before the top officers, the state delegation, and thousands of people, the mazdoor saathis sitting in the front row add details and nuances to every statement she makes.

Protesting with Humor
8 December 2007

With all of Sitapur city abuzz with stories about what SKMS had accomplished in Supauli and through the Vikas Bhawan shutdown, saathis are hopeful the administration will invite SKMS to dialogue. But the morning turns into afternoon, and still nothing happens. Undefeated, saathis prepare two boxes; on one they write: "Support the CDO with your bribes," and on the other they write: "Support the mazdoors in the struggle for their rights." Marching with the boxes, several hundred saathis barely leave the dharna site when a man comes running to say that CDO Sahab is inviting SKMS for deliberations. Rather than pandering to the arrogant administration's fickle-mindedness, saathis state sharply, "This is no appropriate way to invite an organization for dialogue. Tell the CDO that our representatives will see him at 4 p.m.!"

Resuming their march, saathis playfully ask people to choose whether they want to support the mazdoors' struggle or the development machinery's corruption. Holding a rotating megaphone, they make their way to Lalbagh and the municipal market, educating the people of Sitapur city about the reasons for their protest. The box for

Protesting with Humor (continued)

bribes amuses people; some roar with laughter. Dropping a 500-rupee note into the mazdoors' box and a 100-rupee note in the bribe box, one man announces, "the CDO won't do anything for less than this. . . ." Sometimes people carelessly drop money in a wrong box and the saathis joke with them about how the contribution they made to serve the mazdoors' cause has accidentally gone into the corrupt CDO's pocket. One saathi points out how educated townspeople sometimes drop their money without reading the writing on the box. Another saathi elaborates on how the "educated" people who make such mistakes belong to the same section of the society that congratulates itself on being 'socially aware' and that blames the conditions of the rural mazdoors on their lack of formal literacy.

The deliberations between the CDO and SKMS begin at 4 p.m. and continue until 10 p.m. The CDO agrees to four demands but refuses the unemployment allowance; SKMS refuses to concede. In the end, the CDO and the district development officer agree in principle to give unemployment allowance and to inform the SKMS about their final decision on this matter after investigating the evidence and the mazdoors' applications. With no faith left in verbal assurances from the officers, SKMS demands a complete written agreement from the administration. The dharna continues.

10 December 2007—At the CDO's invitation, area panchayat pramukhs, BDOs, pradhans, and secretaries from several blocks of Sitapur reach the Vikas Bhawan, along with an impressive gang of armed security guards. The saathis see how collusion among administrators and elected officials protects those in power: in the meeting held in the CDO's suite that evening, several saathis report that the pradhans, secretaries, and panchayat mitras in their villages have pressured or bribed people who are not active in SKMS into forging documents of false evidence against the Sangathan. The entire governmental machinery is dedicated to the mission of falsifying the mazdoors' eligibility for unemployment allowance. To stop all the forgeries and lies, the Sangathan demands that all the applications and documents associated with NREGA be brought from the relevant gram panchayats to the headquarters and then be sealed.

Protest as Pathshala
11 December 2007

The dharna becomes a revolutionary pathshala, a school where we learn critical lessons in how to fight and sustain a long battle for a just and dignified life of our saathis. How do we learn to grow into ideas that may not match our initial positions? What strategies must be devised and implemented, how, and when? What skills do we need to navigate an unpredictable political terrain together? The saathis are continuously teaching and learning from one another. Those who tended to remain shy in the city are boldly playing and speaking. Those who could not memorize any chants or songs are now composing and singing songs that people of Sitapur will sing for a long time. Those who once hesitated to confront their caste privileges and discriminatory practices now cook for one another, share meals, and spend cold nights under the same blankets.

In this same pathshala of the Sangathan, some saathis propose the ideas of launching a hunger strike and of continuing the strike until the demand for unemployment allowance is met. SKMS has no prior experience with such a strike, so the first question arising in response to this idea is "Who would sit on a hunger strike?"

Ten hands go up in a flash.

"How many days can we sit like this?"

"As long as the struggle needs it!"

This courage and determination boosts the Sangathan confidence: the experience of hunger strike will enrich the saathis for life, regardless of the outcome. All the saathis throw themselves into the strike.

12 December 2007—Based on the reports of BDOs of Mishrikh and Pisawan, and without any systematic investigation, the CDO declares the mazdoors ineligible for unemployment compensation. On receiving this news, one saathi announces through the megaphone, "The CDO may be the program officer for this scheme, but we, the people, can refuse to accept an order that violates the rules of the program. If our eligibility has been deemed invalid on the basis of the report of the same BDO who has failed to do his work, then we can also declare this order to be invalid."

Procedures require that the whole matter be investigated. SKMS representatives demand before the DM that the investigation be carried out by a committee that also includes saathis from SKMS. The dharna and sequential fast continue.

13–14 December 2007—The DM is unwilling to include any saathis in the investigation committee, but the Sangathan persists. The files associated with NREGA are brought in from the gram panchayats, sealed in the presence of the additional district magistrate, and placed in the treasury. Correspondence from two gram panchayats is missing, but the saathis have been assured these would soon be handed over to the investigation committee. The people of Sitapur have begun a signature campaign to extend their support to the Sangathan.

The DM issues his order: chaired by subdistrict magistrate (SDM)-Mishrikh, the investigation committee will include Richa S. as the representative of SKMS. Richa S. also has the right to nominate two additional members as SKMS representatives; she brings the matter to the Sangathan and saathis unanimously choose Rambeti of Allipur and M. R. Sharma, a journalist who formerly worked for the *Hindustan Times*. Rambeti's presence on this committee is a major achievement.

A Dalit mazdoor woman saathi is sitting at par with the SDM!

As the 10-day historic dharna concludes, the Sangathan warns that the saathis will strike again if there are any attempts to corrupt the investigation process.

16 December 2007–16 February 2008—At the first meeting of the investigation committee in Vikas Bhawan, the members determine their process. Both BDOs claim the mazdoor saathis were working elsewhere during the period for which they are demanding unemployment allowance. One committee member states that if a mazdoor has worked anywhere under the sun, technically they cannot be eligible for unemployment allowance. The SKMS representatives disagree: "Suppose a woman is divorced from her husband and her relatives step in to take care of her expenses. Should that woman give up her legal right to ask her husband for maintenance just because she has the support of others? Similarly, if a mazdoor does not get work promised under NREGA, she will have to work somewhere else to light a stove in her house. The question at hand is whether the work she had applied for under NREGA was given to her or not."

With such skilled argumentation by SKMS, the committee establishes the saathis' eligibility for unemployment. However, the block level governmental machinery does everything it can to invalidate their claim for benefits. There are continuous reports of SKMS saathis being harassed or verbally abused by their village pradhans. Rumors are being spread against active saathis so that their attention would be diverted from the investigation. For the Sangathan, however, the fight for unemployment allowance is not a fight for a few rupees. It is a battle for the basic rights, dignity, and integrity of the saathis.

3 April–24 May 2008—On 14 March, the committee submits its report confirming the SKMS saathis' eligibility for unemployment. Now, the report must be forwarded from the district level to the state level, but the BDOs stall the process. They incite the pradhans by misrepresenting the mazdoors' fight as SKMS's public condemnation of them. Incensed, the Pradhan Sangh of Sitapur threatens to begin a dharna in opposition to the investigation. The DM now reels under the pradhans' political pressure.

In order to determine the amount of compensation each mazdoor is eligible to receive, the committee must have access to all the documents pertaining to NREGA. The committee had been charged to submit its report within a month, but after 34 days it is still await-

ing the documents. Despite three written requests from the committee chair, the SDM-Mishrikh and the BDOs of Mishrikh and Pisawan have not provided a shred of paper.

Saathis are hurt by the continuous flouting of the DM's orders by officials at the block level. In protest, SKMS begins its second indefinite strike in Vikas Bhawan on 21 May.

For two days in row, the administration turns a blind eye to hundreds of mazdoors sitting in the scorching sun. Enraged, hundreds of saathis and supporters surround the CDO and demand that all the documents be made available to the committee without delay. At 10 p.m. on 23 May, the dharna ends with the delivery of the promised documents. Now begins the work of counting the amount of compensation for each mazdoor.

7 June–26 November 2008—The investigation stretches over several months, as do the nonstop attempts to force, frighten, tempt, and fool the saathis into providing statements against the Sangathan. Aware of the risks created by the formal illiteracy of many SKMS members, saathis decide to not sign any document without first finding out what is written on it.

At long last, the committee submits its complete report to the DM in October. Now, the report must be sent onward to CDO and then to the commissioner of the Rural Development Department in Lucknow. The homes and offices of the CDO and the commissioner are located just a few steps away from each other's, but, even after eight days, the report fails to move.

Upon SKMS's interrogation, the report reaches the CDO on 19 October. When the saathis go to the CDO to inquire whether the report has been sent to the commissioner for further action, the CDO confesses that he has resent the report to one of the BDOs for further clarification. It is incomprehensible why the report needs clarification from the same BDO whose account has provided the grounds for invalidating the eligibility of the saathis for benefits. However, there is no option but to be patient with this endless red tape and the well-rehearsed bureaucratic obstructions that exist in the name of developing the poor.

On 26 November, a delegation of nine members of SKMS appeals to the commissioner to provide the unemployment allowance to the mazdoors on the basis of the investigation committee's report. The commissioner orders the CDO to send the report within 10 days.

18 December 2008—Twenty-two days later, the report has yet to reach the commissioner. Today, angry saathis launch a rally to warn the administration. As the rally approaches the CDO's office, a special messenger leaves the same office to deliver the report to the commissioner. If the administration fails to pay unemployment allowance, warns SKMS, the mazdoors will begin an indefinite strike on 16 January.

15 January 2009—The dharnas of December 2007 and May 2008 were marked by unprecedented support from the people of Sitapur city. However, a movement that is fighting for the rights of the mazdoors must sustain itself on its own strength. The same mazdoors—who are condescendingly called "lifafa chhap" by some because they have only enough money to buy each day's worth of grains in a lifafa, or packet—collect more than 20 quintals of grain to support 500 striking mazdoors for the January dharna. This includes the contributions of saathis who do not have any grain in their homes but who have purchased the grain with their daily earnings to donate to the dharna.

The movement cannot be stopped or defeated.

16 January 2009—Barely a few hours before the official beginning of the dharna, the saathis are shocked to read the main heading on the front page of the *Hindustan Times*: "The mazdoors of Sitapur

The victory rally. (Courtesy: Sangtin Archives)

have won unemployment allowance." When the reality sinks in, the whole Vikas Bhawan echoes with the mazdoors' victory cry:

"Ladenge, jeetenge. Ladey hain, jeetay hain!"

We will fight, we will win; we have fought, we have won!

24–28 January 2009—While the administration collects the bank account numbers of the saathis to pay them their allowance, the BDOs of Mishrikh and Pisawan suddenly decide to take the matter to the High Court. This brings the payment process to a grinding halt. Saathis are horrified by this move, but they are also confident that the outcome of their satyagrah cannot be reversed so easily.

Within days, the High Court places its official stamp on the Sangathan's victory by announcing that the commissioner should secure the payment of the unemployment allowance to eligible mazdoors.

New Beginnings
24 February 2009

Thus concludes a long battle, but challenges continue after the victory. With the passing of the order arises the question of why in a battle fiercely fought by a whole Sangathan, only 826 families are deemed eligible for the benefits. Saathis knew from the beginning that the majority of them would not gain anything monetarily, but difficult questions are inevitable. The Sangathan's responsibility is to nurture spaces where collective reflection and analysis can continue.

The struggle has not only imparted enormous lessons about life, it has also laid the foundation of new beginnings. Saathis recognize the power of their own solidarity, as well as the need for economic support to sustain the Sangathan. The families who have won the benefits commit 3 to 5 percent of their payments to the Sangathan and, with these contributions, SKMS establishes its own fund. In addition, the saathis create a grain bank. The 10 quintals of food grains leftover after the dharna and meetings are set aside so that no saathi goes hungry in difficult times. According to the newly formulated rules of the grain bank, the saathis must return the grain to the bank when they are in a position to do so. This way, other saathis in a similar situation can rely on the bank.

Collectivity as Work in Progress
14 March 2009

Solidarity and collectivity are always imperfect and in progress. In every village, at least a couple of saathis donate a share of their unemployment allowance to SKMS; others do not. Of those who chose to remain distant from the strikes, some now complain they did not receive anything. A number of new villages join SKMS, while a few villages with a strong presence in the past see a weakening of ties. Similarly, a number of new saathis assume leadership roles while others step away from active roles.

Despite these shifts and trials, SKMS's successful fight for unemployment allowance becomes a subject of discussion and celebration all the way from the district and state levels to the national and international conversations. As others in struggle recognize the Sangathan's work, vision, and methodology, new challenges continue to emerge. Saathis prioritize one question above all: how can the Sangathan make spaces for each saathi to grapple continuously with the ways the personal, the familial, and the organizational realms must breathe together in our ever-evolving thinking and doing? The struggle with this question continues along with the journey of sangtins.

The Journey Continues

Unlearning Caste

For nine women to come together and weave a dream is one thing; for several thousand people to build collectivity is quite another. A growing Sangathan wrestles with what it means to have a shared leadership where political analysis and strategy are not concentrated in a few heads and hands. If the Sangathan encompasses all of life and not merely a few compartmentalized problems in the form of projects, then every saathi must have an opportunity to evolve with respect to their sociopolitical analysis and relationships in the collective. If the knots the Sangathan wants to wrestle with are tightly wound up in caste, class, gender, and communal differences—and in the games between the powerful and the resource-poor—then what methodology can we deploy to deepen its growth in both numerical and analytical terms?

Saathis begin earnestly to ask these questions in 2007. It is a time of serious reflection on the next course of the struggle. Between March and June, members of the Sangathan travel far and wide. While a few of us grapple with these questions by building new dialogues with supporters in the United States, many more saathis organize and join foot marches in those villages from where people have come to the forefront to advance the struggle for the just implementation of NREGA. During one such march, Surbala, Reena, Richa S., and Brahma Prasad spend the night in the village of Sabelia in Pisawan, where Dalits form the majority.

A cluster of about fifteen families live under thatched roofs not far from the village. When the four saathis decide to stay with these families, the residents immediately welcome them with yogurt and water. Surbala, Reena, and Richa S. wonder whether Brahma Prasad, a Yadav designated as OBC would eat and drink with Dalits. During a previous stay among the Adivasis of the Samajwadi Parishad in Hoshangabad, his inherited rituals of segregated eating and drinking had prevented him from accepting water in a Dalit home. What will he do here? As the three women watch Brahma Prasad with nervous trepidation, he lifts the bowl of yogurt by his hands and starts devouring it. A little later when the whole village is immersed in a passionate discussion, a boy from a Yadav family suddenly appears and asked Brahma Prasad to come with him for dinner. It turns out that the Dalit families had themselves arranged for his meal to be cooked in a Yadav household. Bewildered, Brahma Prasad asks his hosts, "Why did you have my meal cooked elsewhere when I have already accepted your food and water?"

This incident and many others like it catalyze serious conversations on casteism. Why do Dalits feel burdened with the responsibility of maintaining the violent rituals of untouchability? What difficult contradictions must each of us wrestle with in order to begin disentangling ourselves from the intricate cobwebs of untouchability that we have helped to nurture at different times? While Savarna saathis often claim that they oppose casteism, the journey is never straightforward. For instance, a Savarna saathi who had eagerly signed up for the above padyatra, withdrew at the last minute when he found out that saathis will eat and drink with any and all. Even Reena's brahman husband, Ram Naresh, created a big fuss about her participation in the march.

The matter, however, is not simply one of Savarnas versus Dalits. Of the eight young men from Sabelia village who join the padyatra for three days that summer, one is a young man whom everyone refers to as the village idiot. This man is no other than Tama who, despite poor vision, walks miles and miles with the saathis, energizing everyone with his magical voice and songs. The same Tama initially refuses to eat food prepared in the home of a raidas, who are considered lower than his own paasi community in the caste order. However, Tama soon realizes that the true joy of making music in and for the struggle resides in re-learning to walk with the Sangathan over the long haul. This involves breaking the rituals of untouchability and segregation with every breath. Nothing in his life thus far has given him the tools to perceive this possibility, or the strength that comes from such collective resistance.

At the same time, the everyday practices of casteism are so deep that it is never an easy or one-way street. It is hard to predict how far any of us are prepared to go in this journey, and to fight everything that has been handed to us in the name of our pride, purity, aesthetics, traditions, and values. We remind one another of the ways in which casteism might creep up on us in moments when we are least equipped to address it adequately. For instance, what lessons are buried in the reality that whenever I consume whatever food or drink is offered in the Sangathan, my saathis worry that my body might fall prey to food poisoning and I will become a liability on them? The difficult journey of unlearning caste in our everyday lives, and in the intimate systems that include our bodies, continues for each one of us.

Balancing Acts

This system we inhale and exhale is a monstrous stepped structure that must be dug out from its base so that a new foundation can be created. This is no simple task: when the material from one place is dug out, it accumulates on the other side where it is dumped. The same saathis who selflessly throw themselves into major battles with the bureaucrats for a shared goal sometimes end up in conflicts with one another. Similarly, many women who give exemplary leadership to thousands of saathis struggle in their own homes to maintain their dignity. After every overnight rally or meeting, a woman saathi comes home to listen to one accusation or another that makes her feel that her body is owned by someone else. At times the Sangathan opposes narrow ideas of women's empowerment by involving hundreds of men as pakke saathis. At others, it intervenes in the domestic affairs of those same saathis to protect the women. The same saathis who bravely fight together against the abusive regimes of the development officers and pradhans, sometimes seem unbelievably fragile when it comes to dismantling the rituals of caste and religion, not only across Savarna-Dalit and Hindu-Muslim divides but also within the Dalit and OBC communities that comprise the Sangathan.

In these delicate balancing acts, the strong relationships among all of us work like powerful beams of support. In the narrow, filthy, winding stairs of the structures we fight, the hopelessness is so intense that any lonely person would want to flee. In these same dark places, however, the bonds among saathis keep the Sangathan lit with hope. The strength drawn from these bonds gives countless saathis—including Sunita, Rambeti, Reena, Surbala, Prakash, Tama, Bitoli, and Sarvesh—the courage to attack the steps of this laddered monstrosity, to turn their intimate pains of humiliation into the resounding notes of the Sangathan. The soul-searching critiques powered by these same relationships keep our hearts, dreams, and words entangled across thousands of miles, inspiring us to continue our collective journey. On confronting casteism, too, saathis draw hope precisely from these relationships. As Santram Dada once said to Surbala, "We know that we are wrong sometimes, but remember, it's easy to write on a blank paper. When a sheet of paper is already scribbled on and scrunched a hundred times, it is difficult to erase that writing completely. Sometimes, a forced effort to erase can tear the paper itself. Even so, each one of us is trying. Some things may get rubbed off quickly while others may take a long time."

Surbala felt Santram Dada's words: the differences we have learned over thousands of years cannot disappear by pressuring or lecturing people to change their behavior. On the day when saathis such as Santram, Brahma Prasad, and Ram Naresh will be able to lighten or erase casteism on the slates of their own life, that is when they will themselves write a new word that has emerged from their own journeys. Until that day comes, each one of our journeys must also be the Sangathan's journey. The Sangathan must bear the responsibility of addressing all that our uneven bonds entail—including the traumatizing rituals and burdens we have inherited in this brutal system of caste.

Where's the System? Let's Fix It First!

The saathis of SKMS greet the new year by dreaming what their villages would be like after ten years: villages where they can rightfully claim their livelihood and protect their pride and dignity, and where their children can look forward to a future. Then they pose an open question before everyone who wants ordinary people to continue dreaming: would our system allow us to realize our dream without turning every bit of our lives into endless wars?

In a meeting during April 2009, someone begins talking about the system: When a saathi goes to the pradhan, he hands her a standard reply, "I am trying my best, but what can I do? It is the system that is crooked." If one goes to the secretary, he also mumbles something similar to shoo her away. If she goes to the block office, the BDO also sings the melody of "this is how the system is," and the great officers of the tehsil also cry about the system. Interrupting the discussion, Kusuma suddenly said, "Tell me, where can I find this system? Let's fix it first."

Kusuma's few words said in jest actually carry the essence of all of the Sangathan's struggles. Saathis often say—"What all must we do and how to decide what we must do next? Wherever we turn, there is an endless field of struggle. If we go to the government hospital, there are no doctors for us; even if we find them, they don't have medicines for us. When we go to the police station, the police turn a deaf ear toward us. The block and tehsil level offices are even worse! To top it all, the poor are not even considered humans—wherever whomsoever wants shuns us in whichever way they please." To this day, a number of Dalit mazdoors take off their slippers before entering the offices of the officers: they cannot muster the courage to step on the shining floors in their dusty slippers. So many Dalit mazdoors cannot talk about their problems before the officials without folding their hands in respect. The walls of casteism and communalism are thoroughly entwined with all of this, and women suffer within these entanglements in especially violent ways. So many women saathis bite their tongues and accept the humiliation that is repeatedly meted out to them in their own families and communities.

Within these overlapping and never-ending circles of challenges, saathis are constantly exploring and living our journeys. The foul smells and exhaustion of a rotting system are not so easy to get rid of even if we ourselves are a part of it. No matter how much collective strength we muster to grapple with the hardest questions, we recognize our relatively powerless positions in the system. Like a bag of mustard seeds scattered on the pathway, countless hindrances greet us in every direction we turn. We push them away with our hands, but another set of obstacles slips out from somewhere else and spreads itself in our way. We barely take a breath of relief after battling one issue, when another matter stares in our faces. Whether it is the Vikas Bhawan, tehsil, or block; whether it is the police station or court, a gang of looters awaits the exploited kisans and mazdoors everywhere. The whole country knows that whenever one needs a date for a court hearing, the clerk requires the appropriate currency note as a bribe. Then how can those who are made poor hope for justice from that court?

Whether it is due to the lack of medical care after an accident, or for tuberculosis, or a fever, the simplest of illnesses become life threatening in this system. It took two years of war to win the unemployment allowance. We had hoped that the people's victory would improve the corrupt work practices, but the muster roll is nowhere to be seen at the MGNREGA work sites, implying that the looting carries on unabated.[1] We try to make small dents into old, rotting system with our many hands, but far from inspiring sensitivity from the administration toward the issues, our battles are eventually rendered ineffective by the pacts among politicians, officers, and industrialists.

• • •

Chaandu, a young man of Satnapur village in the Mishrikh Block, is returning home from Sitapur on the night of 14 July 2010. A couple of police constables suddenly arrest him without charges. Several saathis of SKMS from Satnapur protest. The issue heats up, and an investigation is undertaken. The police officer in charge of Sitapur's Sadar Chowki asks the protestors not to fan the flames on this matter; whatever he did was under the directions of his bosses. The investigation declares Chaandu innocent, and the officer is suspended.

On the same night the suspension is announced, the young officer kills himself with his own revolver. With tears in our eyes, we witness these developments in stunned silence. An innocent police officer is sacrificed on the altar of this system. Someone repeats Kusuma's words—"Everyone says what can I do, this is how the system is; so we in SKMS say, 'Let's fix the system first!' One step in the direction of fixing the system, and an innocent man is killed. Yet, nothing happens to the health of those who rule the system."

Saathis ask: What is the connection between the arrest of Chaandu and the arrest of Binayak Sen, who after working for years as a humanitarian among the Adivasis of Chhattisgarh, is thrown into jail on the charge of helping the Naxalites? No doubt Dr. Sen is an extraordinary man and Chaandu an ordinary young man who spends his days herding his family's animals. Yet, both are innocent. And so was the police officer who committed suicide. Arrests and murders are essential parts of the functioning of this system. To get rid of the Naxalites, Salva Judum was brought forward and the government tried to establish that it was being run by the Adivasis. When the opposition to the government mounted, Binayak Sen was arrested to teach a lesson to all those who are fighting for justice: "If you state anything that can be considered anti-government, you will be silenced."

Saathis have a shared analysis of this thing called our system, that is driven by greed for endless money. The politicians who run the state collude with corporate powers to make maximum profits and to steal the lands of the poor. They do not care about ordinary humans. They do not care that the amount of available food per capita in our country is decreasing. Their only concern is the vote. The politicians are guided by a set formula: corporate development is that which brings profits, profits buy seats in the parliament, which in turn buy more development and more profits. Ordinary people like us have fought very hard to gain the right to information so that this collusion between politicians and corporations can be checked. Those of us who fight the hardest to change the terms of this system are also the ones who have to confront the wrath of the winter, summer, and monsoon, along with the wars of the roti. In Andhra Pradesh and Maharashtra, people have had to give their lives just for demanding their right to information. The fight to fix the system in just one little area can drain, exhaust, and kill; then how can a movement like ours even begin to contemplate fixing the system of the whole country, or the whole world?

Let us return for a moment to where we started this diary: the struggle for irrigation waters. Is the work of silt cleaning merely a project of the central government? Proper silt cleaning results in watered irrigation canals and better crops. Does it not have something to do with improved agricultural productivity and food security? With the food grains that are given to us through ration quotas? With the cash crops and hunger of the belly that torments our saathis and makes them die from anemia? In fields where people grew rice and wheat and many fed themselves on the grain that was left over after the wheat crop had been harvested, there is only sugarcane for cash now. How do we understand these uneasy connections between past and present hungers and greeds, between bellies and cash, between irrigated lands, dry fields, debts, and farmers' suicides?

Working for social change means working with conflicting currents. One plunge does not do it. The opposition is fierce and recurring, sometimes from the more powerful, and other times from our own ideologies, aspirations, and values that bind and suffocate us. For the last four years, hundreds of women and men attend SKMS's monthly meetings and in almost every meeting, some discussion invariably centers on the ghoonghats that cover the heads and faces of many women saathis. Dozens have voluntarily abandoned the ghoonghat, but the reappearance of a few ghoonghats always revives the debate. The majority of SKMS saathis desire meetings where there is no gender segregation, and they succeed in achieving this goal, but if the conversations do not continue, women and men revert to sitting in their segregated clusters.

Saathis dream the big dreams of changing all of this. They also have their little dreams—of claiming their housing, pensions, and wages. As one little dream is realized, we move to fight for the next one. Although none of this is easy, people everywhere are organizing—from the Narmada Bachao Andolan, to the farmers' fights for their land in Singur, to the Adivasis' struggle to protect their forests in Sonbhadra. In these fights for big and small dreams, there is always hope; sometimes we win hope and at others we lose it. Yet, not having hope is never an option; it gives us the inner resources to look forward to the next day. The movement, too, becomes strong with every little victory; with the arrival of every new saathi who brings her hopes and energies to the struggle.

Failures also make us strong. A young woman is killed by her own relatives for their "honor" far away from Sitapur, and our limitations prevent us from intervening. However, we become more determined than ever to stand against such killing wherever it happens again. Every defeat gives us the strength to continue the fight a little longer. We have learned that no collective fight will ever be wasted.

Many saathis and supporters of SKMS, a number of them far away from Sitapur, are critical of what we have been calling "the system" while also enjoying a number of privileges that are bestowed on them by the same system. They, too, make it possible for us to grapple with what it takes to envision and sustain long-term bonds and solidarities among people who come from disparate but enmeshed locations. Such reflection gives us the courage to become vulnerable as fighters in a shared struggle. It pushes us to think more critically, to dream more daringly.

We also pause and turn around to examine the absences and faults in our work, and to reflect on what we could have done differently. We remember a book from our childhoods: *Abbu Khan ki Bakri*, written by Dr. Zakir Husain during India's struggle for independence.[2] Abbu Khan's mountain goat, Chaandni, knows that it is dangerous for her to step out of the security of Abbu Khan's fenced yard because there are wolves on the other side; she knows that she can lose her life if she jumps over the fence. Yet, Chaandni cannot resist her only chance to know liberation. When Abbu Khan lovingly calls out for Chaandni and asks her to come back, she hears him; she even turns around to let him know that she knows how much he cares. Then she moves forward toward the mountains even as she can feel the wolf's eyes staring at her. The longing for one's freedom and dignity, the yearning for the core of one's integrity, drive our journeys of struggle. They give us the same strength and hope they gave Chaandni.

Definitions of Revolution

Once Rambeti, one of SKMS's active saathis, goes to discuss a matter at the block development office. A well-dressed man there stares at her and remarks— "no one can guess by your appearance that you haul mud at the pond." Rambeti laughs. "Do you think we Dalit women will spend our whole lives wearing rags while we labor as mazdoors? Don't you know that one day's wages can now fetch me a new sari?"

Rambeti hints at the ways in which saathis fight for more dignified living conditions based on the values emerging from their own struggles. As the numbers of SKMS saathis continue to grow, they also learn to identify a range of issues and to strategize and fight together against all they see as injustice. When thousands of saathis in Mishrikh, Pisawan, and Maholi Development Blocks successfully claim their hundred work days under MGNREGA, some friends and critics pose a generative question—"Fighting for mazdoors' and kisans' right to livelihood under MGNREGA can fetch a few weeks of work for the saathis, but how successfully can SKMS transform the social structure by simply focusing on the state's policies. Is SKMS becoming a machine for better implementation of the state's policies?"

The Sangathan sees this picture differently. Since 2005, the continuous fights with the state over the silt cleaning and KBAY (National Food for Work Programme) have succeeded in securing livelihood for thousands of mazdoors and small farmers, most of them Dalit. More than half of these mazdoors are women, many of whom are devoting part of their earnings from MGNREGA to raising the productivity of their tiny plots of land. The people who fought successfully for work under MGNREGA are initiating and fighting other battles with the state, knowing full well that the policies of the state will never become the source of their liberation. Yet, advances in gaining their rights can, and have, helped to forge greater collectivity and strength for the saathis. For instance, saathis from Pipri village worked under NREGA for the first time in 2007. Before then, the Dalit kisans of Pipri used to go to the big Savarna kisans to get food grains on loan and were forced to work for them on exploitative terms. These mazdoors now save part of their earnings from MGNREGA to invest on their own farms and have become free of the forced labor on the land of upper caste farmers. Additionally, they do not have to migrate seasonally to work as domestic help or cycle rickshaw pullers in Lucknow, Kanpur, or Delhi. This has brought happiness and stability that can never be adequately assessed by the development agencies or scholarly tool kits. In many places, this stability has allowed people to organize collectively for the Panchayat elections so that they can get a pradhan who supports their struggles. In the Maholi Block, where the Sangathan spread through its work on implementation of MGNREGA, Dalit residents of Bargadiya village fight to retain possession of their ancestral land without being terrorized by the Savarna thugs who operate with the blessings of the powerful. In Gopalpur village, saathis successfully organize for their rightful access to hand pumps, houses, ration cards, and scholarships. In Roora, Dalit saathis fight against illegal cancellation of housing registration under the Indira Housing Scheme. Kailasha of Jagdeva village and Dwarika of Bargadia village save their ancestral lands from thugs and corrupt bureaucrats. Such collective work on multiple fronts is continuously sharpening and strengthening the saathis. From enunciating ideas and chanting slogans to giving well-argued and rousing speeches—every saathi tries to claim the opportunity to learn these arts and to forcefully communicate their ideas before others, while also becoming an attentive and respectful listener. Through this hard work, saathis express for themselves, and for one another, the thoughts, memories, feelings, and sensations that have been trampled on repeatedly. They powerfully articulate their tensions and conflicts with all the values and social expectations that have been heaped on them in this world.

SKMS has many friends from the certified intellectual classes who themselves receive comfortable salaries or generous grants for running the everyday affairs of their lives and careers and who enjoy all kinds of amenities, but who are also critical of the institutions that feed them. However, these same radically thinking professionals are often unable to appreciate that mazdoors and kisans can—and do—live similar radical politics and that their engagements with the state do not amount to their struggles being confused, or lacking in revolutionary spirit. Saathis of SKMS know clearly that fighting for the proper implementation of the state's policies is not their ultimate goal, but along with this clarity they question other assumptions as well. This includes the prevailing assumption that fighting for just distribution of land for all is the only real way to advance the struggle of Dalit mazdoors and kisans. When this argument once reemerges in a meeting, Prakash gives a deeper dimension to the discussion— "I support this position. Still, a Dalit mazdoor's life will not change simply by having our right to land. From the means of earning everyday livelihoods with dignity, to proudly living our full lives with our people, to just implementation of everything that is done in the names of the poor and hungry: all of this we must claim as part of our struggle."

In other words, enabling the emergence of ever-widening meanings of revolution is a fundamental part of evolving together in the Sangathan. Moving together implies a continuous commitment to learn from imaginaries of justice that do not emanate from assumptions about a shared lexicon or vision that exists prior to the collective process.

Safar Jaari Hai, the Journey Goes On!

More than seven years have passed by since the historic victory of mazdoors and kisans in their fight for unemployment allowance against the district development administration of Sitapur. Since then, governments constituted by different political parties have come and gone; NREGA has become MGNREGA, and SKMS has spread beyond Mishrikh and Pisawan development blocks to the blocks of Machhrehta, Hargaon, Khairabad, Maholi, and Ailiya, with seven thousand saathis working under MGNREGA. Of these seven thousand, about 20 percent are able to get work for more than ninety days, and another 75 percent are able to find work for fifty days or so. A large proportion of saathis are those who do the work when they get it but who do not protest when they fail to receive any work. In Uttar Pradesh, the Labor Department promises certain facilities such as a bicycle, solar energy, and housing to all the mazdoors who work for more than fifty days. SKMS saathis working under MGNREGA are trying to obtain labor registration cards so that they can get these facilities.

The lives of many mazdoor saathis have changed as a result of fights for fair implementation of MGNREGA. Rambeti and Ramdevi are among hundreds of Dalit women who now have their own bank accounts and spend money from those accounts according to their own priorities. In many families where men spend all their cash on legal and illegal liquor and gambling, SKMS's women saathis feed themselves and their children with the work they get through

MGNREGA. In the monthly meetings of the Sangathan, saathis analyze the relationships between the government revenues earned through liquor, the number of homes without roti, and the politics of how work and earnings from MGNREGA play out on the domestic front.

The state's attitude is quite different, however. Instead of grappling with these complexities, the state is killing MGNREGA. A massive bureaucratic infrastructure has appeared in the guise of implementing transparency, fostering coordination, and fighting corruption. The great fluency with which the written rules and codes of conduct are cited by officers and staff at the block, district, state, and national levels can gain one the impression that the work is happening in accordance with these well-memorized regulations. There are countless paper trails and documents. If anything is missing, it is the actual work and timely payment for work. In Sitapur District, millions of rupees are yet to be paid in wages to unskilled laborers who have worked under MGNREGA. In the Arthapur village of Mishrikh block alone, the government owes more than 500,000 rupees to the mazdoors. No payments have been made for five months. Births, weddings, illnesses, and deaths have greeted and tested the families of kisans and mazdoors, and angry and violated people have enacted one protest after another at the offices of district magistrates and development officers to try to get the government to respond to this injustice, but to no avail.

One day before Diwali, Bitoli, a mazdoor saathi of SKMS, was moved by desperation to pawn three pairs of brand new bichhiya or toe rings owned by her youngest daughter-in-law. After pawning her own anklet for 500 rupees and her older daughter-in-law's earrings for 700 rupees in previous weeks, the toe rings were the only remaining items of monetary value in Bitoli's family, and she was hoping to get 300 rupees so that her family could at least have one celebratory meal to mark the festival. In Bitoli's family, seven people have worked under MGNREGA and the government of India owes them 22,000 rupees. In Allipur village, Surendra pawned his bicycle for 200 rupees. Rekha of Makdera pawned her anklets for 300 rupees, while Ram Kishore of Faridpur had to pawn his wife's silver chain—which cost them 1,200 rupees—for only 500 rupees. As these people await payments from the government, chances are that many of them will not be able to retrieve these items because of the excessively steep interest rates. After the wheat is sown, the winter will become another battle and it will be impossible for them to regain their pawned valuables that they fall back on in times of grave crises.

Pawning is not the only site of exploitation. When one mazdoor saathi could not find a buyer for her kharif crop, she went to sell 20 kilograms of sesame seeds to a shopkeeper in another village so that she had the money to prepare for the sowing of wheat. The shopkeeper did not have the money to buy it, so she traveled to another shop 3 kilometers away. This shopkeeper agreed to buy the sesame seeds at the rate of 4,000 rupees per quintal if she agreed to receive the payment at a later date. Last year, the same saathi sold her sesame seeds at 7,000 rupees a quintal. With no money in her hands still, this saathi is in deep agony. The sowing of mustard on her farm is already delayed. Her granddaughter's wedding is about to happen. She feels helpless as all options seem to disappear.

Eid, Raksha Bandhan, and Diwali—all these festivals have come and gone, but the homes and villages remain unmarked by festivities. Many homes could not be whitewashed; the pooris, kachoris, and desserts that are cooked only on festivals remained unrealized temptations for many, and dozens of people who had been waiting for a festival as an excuse to purchase a long-overdue item of new clothing or footwear had to postpone the idea.

As fields are getting ready in Sitapur for the winter wheat crop, small kisans and farmworkers are scurrying to find ways to borrow money. During the last several years, the arrival of MGNREGA had significantly reduced the terror of traders who lend money on interest. While MGNREGA had brought the monthly interest rate down from 10 percent to 5 percent in some villages, the nonpayment of MGNREGA wages has allowed loan sharks to increase rates back to 10 percent.

In Uttar Pradesh, the state government has managed to pay the officers and staff associated with MGNREGA while the most vulnerable mazdoors, who have actually sweated for the state, are being cheated out of their earnings. In fact, these delays appear to be a systematic part of the administration's strategy of budget cuts in social welfare schemes. How ironic that the two political parties in power, Samajwadi Party and Bharatiya Janata Party, who never tire of making claims in the name of the poor, are participating in this complete mockery of the rural poor. Two women saathis of Ailiya recently died while their payments were still pending. Does the state have a language to even pretend that it cares for the aspirations of our saathis who died while waiting for their earnings?

The tricolored flag is being hoisted by the state over and over again—sometimes to spread the government's programs in the remotest village, sometimes to instill pride among the people through Swaabhimaan Yatras, and sometimes to protect the cow. How can a Dalit mazdoor saathi who has not received her payment and whose family is waiting for a bellyful of roti participate in the government's songs of self-glorification? The annual crop of wheat has failed for three years in a row. The farms that commonly produce three quintals of wheat produced less than a quintal this year. The better-off Savarna farmers who gave their farms to Dalit mazdoors on contract have already taken their share of money or grain. The hands of our mazdoor saathis are now empty. How does a Dalit mazdoor in a remote village reach the government of India? Our respected elected representatives become angry if the mazdoors appear at their door, yet they themselves only bother to come to the mazdoor's door when they need a vote.

There is another problem with the missing payments. The rules initially required the workdays and attendance of the mazdoors to be documented on the muster rolls, but the muster rolls are nowhere to be found. The administration now says that no more attendance will be recorded on registers, but what of the attendance that has already been recorded? Will the state trust the records the mazdoor saathis have kept for themselves? Will the money be taken from the pockets of the officers or staff who have mishandled the situation so that the mazdoors can be duly paid?

Meanwhile, the everyday difficulties continue. At the crack of dawn one August morning, Rajaram Bhai calls Richa S.: "Didi, when will the payments come? My wife is seriously ill," he says and slips into a long silence. Are those who are given the responsibility to 'develop' us prepared to listen to the meanings hidden in his long silence? These responsible people have so much work to do: they have to make sure their honoraria increase properly. They have to secure contracts for their favorite people. They have to ensure their closest relatives and friends can get a ticket for the next assembly election. They must guarantee the welfare of their own political party so that it constitutes the government during the next elections. After all, they have to oversee the development of our nation — by creating smart cities, by constructing highways, by launching bullet trains. The one thing that we from SKMS want to say to all the mazdoors is this:

Saathis, remember that this country can have neither food nor development without our contributions.[3] *Without roti in our stomachs, without our healthy bodies, without an education that is meaningful for us, there is no hope for this country. . . . Its true development can only happen if we make our voices heard by the ears of those who rule us. Unfortunately, the gulfs that separate their ears from our mouths are so wide, deep, and numerous that the voice of only one of us is never human enough for them. It is only through the sharpness of our collective voice that we can pierce their ears and minds. Even if they can never understand us, it is important that we make our collective anger and sorrow heard. That's where our hope lies, and hope is what makes this journey continue.*

Safar jaari hai

May Day meeting of 2017. (Courtesy: Sangtin Archives)

Our Tunes Must Become Sharper

In the numbing cold of January 2018, we sit down once again to voice our aspirations for the New Year. Even as we look forward to advancing our battles for the basic rights of Dalit and exploited mazdoor and kisan saathis, the memories of recent events drown our hearts in sorrow. The political forces are bent on making more distant the possibility of peace for those who have already been chased to the margins of the nation. It becomes our responsibility, and our necessity, therefore, to meditate on how we can deepen our collective thought so that the edges of our struggle can become sharper. Without such preparation, we cannot survive in this country and this world!

We cannot forget the chilling incident that occurred in July 2016 in Gujarat's Oona District, when some cow-saving men ruthlessly beat up four Dalit youngsters and an elderly man, accusing them of murdering a cow and smuggling the hide. One year later, even as the youth leader Jignesh Mevani gave us the powerful slogan, "You keep the cow's tail; give us our land," the politics of hate in the country crossed all limits of cruelty. In April 2017, Pahlu Khan was killed in Alwar District of Rajasthan. Then, on the eve of Eid in July, Junaid Khan was murdered in Harayana. After that came the barbaric slaughter of Afrazul in Rajasthan's Rajasmand District. To make matters worse, murderers are being turned into heroes: first came the glorification of Gandhi's assassin, Nathuram Godse, then the cow-terrorists who slayed Pahlu Khan were compared to Bhagat Singh, and now some are hero-worshipping Afrazul's merciless killer, Shambhulal Reger. With such intensified politics of hate surrounding us, it is impossible for a sangathan such as ours to fight solely for livelihood, education, health, shelter, or pension, or even against the big and small scams of politicians and development officers. We must become extremely alert as we analyze the meanings of the violent incidents happening around us. Narratives of our own history and geography are being twisted around to breed communalism: thus, Kutubnagar Inter College in Sitapur's Mishrikh Block has been renamed Parashuram Inter College, and Kutubnagar is now being called Kusum Nagar by some in accordance with the Hindutva ideology. As we confront members of our families and neighborhoods about the social effects of these developments and assess who is benefitting from them and how they are benefitting, we must also ask what the role of our Sangathan should be in the grave political environment that we are breathing in.

• • •

Let us switch to another scene from January 2018. SKMS's monthly meeting is to take place at the Pisawan Block, but when saathis wrapped in their shawls and blankets reach the meeting site in the freezing cold, they see a tent being set up there. It tuns out that an MLA (member of the legislative assembly) is coming to distribute blankets to five people of each village in the area, and the Sangathan's meeting site has been deemed the most suitable one for the event.

The dozens of saathis arriving for the meeting become scattered because of confusion over the meeting place. When they eventually gather in another open space in the bone-shivering cold, poverty arises as the first issue of discussion. Politicians who are this desperate to distribute blankets to the 'poor' are poorer than those whose poverty and squalor they feel entitled to define according to their own whims and needs. Far from enabling the conditions that can ensure education, health, livelihood, and fair and prompt wages for those designated as 'poor' due to underfed bellies, weak bodies, or lack of resources and information, our elected representatives show up to toss some blankets at our saathis. Like prosperous people toss their leftovers at stray dogs.

Tragically, this is not merely a drama of our politicians. The entire system of this country and this world is in infinite need of a figure of impoverishment whose stomach is forever hungry and who can be endlessly helped, protected, and developed. Saathis who walk with the Sangathan and who feel quite rich in our hearts, our relationships, and our thoughts are still declared poor so that the system that rests on the claims of uplifting and redeeming us can continue to thrive. In this system are not merely votes, but also knowledge, money, weapons, wars, and rapes. When this kind of endless violence has engulfed our world, the colors of our struggle must also intensify.

Interrogating Institutionalized Ethics

I am not your data, nor am I your vote bank,
I am not your project, or any exotic museum project,
I am not the soul waiting to be harvested,
Nor am I the lab where your theories are tested.

I am not your cannon fodder, or the invisible worker,
Or your entertainment at India habitat center,
I am not your field, your crowd, your history,
your help, your guilt, medallions of your victory.

I refuse, reject, resist your labels,
your judgments, documents, definitions,
your models, leaders and patrons,
because they deny me my existence, my vision, my space.

Your words, maps, figures, indicators,
they all create illusions and put you on a pedestal
from where you look down upon me.

So I draw my own picture, and invent my own grammar,
I make my own tools to fight my own battle,
For me, my people, my world, and my Adivasi self!
—Abhay Xaxa, "I Am Not Your Data"

Abhay Xaxa's words reflect the spirit of refusal that animates SKMS's engagements with the state officials in Sitapur and with CCAFS in Cambodia. My invocation of this poem through these resonances, however, is not inspired by a romance of resistance.[4] For me, a Savarna professionally-accredited scribe and translator, who is also contaminated by a history of institutionalized violence committed in the name of research and development, Xaxa's words echo a host of questions mired in the messy politics of building situated solidarities across unequal worlds.

What happens to established ideas about academic research when an *I* refuses to be the data, the project, the field, and the cannon fodder for a *you* that pronounces "judgments, documents, definitions" and imposes "models, leaders, and patrons"? What do ethical transactions between an institution and a translator look like in a scenario where the *I* finds its searing strength from a collective history of struggle around "my existence, my vision, my space," against "*your* words, maps, figures, indicators"? How might those of *us* who are part of the *you* begin unlearning and relearning from the grammar invented by that collective *I*, without the shadow of 'our' colonizing practices lingering over that learning process? What kinds of institutional diggings and dismantling might it take for that *I* and the *you* to become co-learners in this journey, and can those uneven diggings become part of our retelling?

My chief concern in *Hungry Translations* pertains to the practices of engaging and representing that which the academic world labels as 'research' and the possibilities of co-owning that knowledge by all those who enable its dynamic making and remaking in the course of everyday life. Sadly, the dominant institutional understandings and practices that seek to honor and promote ethical engagement with research subjects in US research universities do little to advance a genuine engagement with these concerns.

• • •

In fall 2002 i first fill out the forms of the institutional review board (IRB) of my university for official human subjects research approval to carry out the initial meetings with the NGO activists who later became the authors of the books, *Sangtin Yatra* and *Playing with Fire*.[5] For more than fourteen years, i diligently submit my continuing review reports with the same information every six months: That i have "recruited" no new subjects since the nine Sangtin Writers first wrote *Sangtin Yatra*. That the transformation of the writers' collective into a growing Sangathan of thousands of mazdoors and kisans is a result, not of the research design proposed in a project, but of a dynamic building and spreading of energies where the knowledge is being continuously produced through the collective journeying and analyzing of the movement. That all of this amounts merely to my "following the research subjects" no matter what the nature and quantity of the output of my research. That despite the bold and innovative nature of the knowledge that is being created through the "project" all the time, there is nothing "unexpected" about the "risks" and "benefits" of the work because, by its very nature, the outcome of the work in a movement of several thousand people can never be planned or predicted by a certified researcher. It is, in fact, "expected" to be spontaneous and serendipitous.

After having submitted almost two dozen reports with pretty much the same information, i receive an e-mail from the IRB in 2016: "During review of your study, we determined that IRB oversight is not required for oral histories with no collection of identifiable information. . . . Please note that you may continue to analyze your data for as long as you want to since there is no identifiable information. The reason for this determination is based on the regulatory definition of 'human subjects research.' . . . According to your application, you do not record any direct identifiers or collect any protected health information. Therefore, your study is considered to be 'not human subjects.'"[6]

When this e-mail arrives, i am in Sitapur working on a street play with SKMS saathis against the government of India's demonetization policy. Although my reports to the IRB about my adherence to its protocols bore no relationship with the actual ethical principles that guide my scholarly creativity or long-term relationship with SKMS, i cannot help sharing the contents of this news with my saathis. Despite the institutional jargon, saathis understand the meaning of the message as well as the ironies of our work being considered as dealing with "not human subjects." Richa S. laughs, "Hum sabko mubarak! This is good news." As far as SKMS is concerned, our work cannot be institutionalized in accordance with IRB norms, procedures, and protocols. For the saathis who fight the red tape of development bureaucracy every day, this freedom is worthy of celebration. Another battle has been won without overtly declaring a war!

This journey shall also go on.

PART THREE

Living in Character

"Kafan" as Hansa

Nourishment

Don't be scared of my bony arms
you look so worried about
the pale yellow of my dry dark eyes bulging out of
sunken sockets on
my fleshless tobacco-chewing face
            She says
            spilling guts out
            glass bangles cascading
            her laugh rumbling hail
                    mumbai monsoons
            coiling the thickest darkest knee-length hair
            into a loose bun,
            stirring the sauce,
            turning over the paraanthha
                    on the tava
            rolling the next ball of dough
                    on the chakla
            she holds my gaze with hers
            a pledge she demands
            softly
                    no riddles today
            she laughs barely breathing

These wiry fingers can
hold your face
without cracking
                    when you feel
            fatherless
            motherless
            loverless
            childless
they will feed you
nourishing hot meals that calm your
anxious soul
            your fight
                        my plight
Eat!
don't feel guilty I feed you
with my belly stuck to my spine.
i will feed your
mother, too,
if she will let me
if she will
remember
me a Budhiya
in a sari, in a bindi
a dying body that lived
loved laughed hungered fed
not in this everyday attire
i wear for the world
fidelities demanded of me
acting
living
laboring
without compromising
Hansa, the Soul
processing
            desires
un-possessing
            attachments
dis-possessing
                dreams
re-possessing
            spirit

my own terms
    kicking sacred books
claiming religion
    namelessly
        freely
            abundantly
    Hair bun waves
    wrists roast
    she smiles silently now
        Closing my eyes
    losing myself
        singing Hansa
        the Soul
            again,
            yet again.

Mumtaz and Budhiya

To Begin

The hunger that burns one's stomach must be extinguished, yet one's creative hunger seeks only to be fueled, and refueled. The ongoing possibility of creativity and critique through political theater is centrally entangled with the challenge posed by these two hungers. The stories I retell in this part of *Hungry Translations* seek to do justice to these intertwined and often contradictory hungers by focusing on the collective labor of twenty people who came from diverse locations to travel intensively for six months with one short story—Premchand's "Kafan."[1] The tireless efforts of the group transformed "Kafan" into Parakh Theatre's production, *Hansa, Karo Puratan Baat*, in Mumbai. My necessarily fragmented translations of this journey tap selectively into many lives, voices, scripts, and texts to grapple with how this transformation is realized through embodied praxis. In this praxis, creativity, ethics, aesthetics, and politics become inseparable from the ongoing searching and haunting of the unnameable desires of the spirit, even as all of these travel through our bodies.

Mumtaz

Mumtaz Sheikh does not remember which year she left her village in Karnataka and came to Mumbai. She does not like to talk about the tough circumstances in which she came, or about the challenges through which she raised her three daughters and one son, or about the difficulties she faced in navigating the adversities of being a single mother from the Dalit Muslim community of kasais. But if you interact closely with her for a few days, you can tell that her life has been unimaginably hard, not merely because years of relentless back-breaking work as domestic help in more than half a dozen homes per day are beginning to leave their permanent marks on her body, but also because she has chosen to live and to raise her children without following the rules of any particular religion or community.

Mumtaz rushes from one home to another in Juhu and Yari Road to clean, wash clothes, and prepare meals, mostly for single male actors who moved to Mumbai from distant places. Almost all of them come to see her as an essential part of their lives. At times, her cooking, cleaning, and caregiving services are desired by elderly people who cannot take care of themselves and who have no immediate family nearby. Something about Mumtaz's unusually meticulous hard work, and the way in which she takes full charge of each space in which she works, fulfills her employer's deeply felt need for 'home' and stability even when every essential piece of their lives is in flux.

Due to the reputation Mumtaz has earned over the years, she is in high demand. For every home she works for, there is at least one more waiting in line with an offer. Mumtaz believes in maintaining good long-term relationships with all her past, current, and potential employers who show genuine respect and appreciation for her. Life has taught her that one can never predict when one might need another's hand. She remains open to everyone. Her health is not always on her side, however. Years of eating poorly have contributed to a situation in which she feeds nutritious meals to others, while her own body handles little more than the never-ending doses of chewing tobacco and dozens of cups of strong chai.

I first meet Mumtaz in 2006 in Tarun Kumar's home, when Tarun and I start working together on theater projects. She cooks, cleans, and washes for Tarun and his nephew, Shekhu, twice a week in their tiny one-bedroom flat on Yari Road, sometimes even taking care of their pooja corner and lighting baked clay lamps and incense sticks in honor of the goddesses, saints, and Sufis whose pictures adorn that corner. During the afternoons when Mumtaz works, she and I share stories with each other about our lives and about raising children. Later, Tarun moves out of Yari Road and Mumtaz no longer works regularly for him. Nonetheless, whenever I am in Mumbai, she makes it a point to visit me every other day and to feed me and my daughter, Medha, a few delicious meals, no matter what the nature of her other engagements. With Tarun's help, we also talk occasionally by phone or Skype.

Mumtaz as Budhiya

Mumtaz is sad when Tarun has to leave his rental flat in the Yari Road area in 2010 and move into a newly constructed building in Jogeshwari. In this high-rise building, many working-class Muslim families from Uttar Pradesh, who once lived in homes made of wood and corrugated metal, with their vending spaces sprawled next to their jhuggi-jhopdis, are now housed, along with their goats and the many rats who run amok in the dumpsters on the open ground floor. Mumtaz's objections to working here have partly to do with the inconvenience of coping with the lack of running water and the bad sanitation in these newly 'developed' areas and partly with the instructions she receives about how to be a 'proper' Muslim woman whenever she moves in and out of the building. Nevertheless, she is drawn to the chahal-pahal of the children, and she listens with great interest whenever Tarun reads stories with teenage boys who bustle around playing cricket or hopscotch in the narrow corridors of his building, sometimes getting into trouble for breaking windows or for getting into fist-fights. Whenever Mumtaz visits Tarun, she is eager to hear about the latest round of work that Tarun and I are doing with theater in Sitapur, Lucknow, or Minneapolis. After listening intently, she always says with a big smile, "If you do something in Yari Road some day, I want to be part of it. You know, my children are grown up now. I want to act in this theater before I get too old."

So in June 2014, when Tarun and I embark on organizing a theater workshop in the Yari Road area, Mumtaz is the first to come forward expressing an interest not only in acting in a play, but also in helping recruit participants and looking for possible rehearsal spaces. This is how Mumtaz becomes a core member of a group of twenty people—including trained actors, domestic workers, and the family who serves as caretakers of the studio where most of the rehearsals take place—all of whom identify as coming from outside of Maharashtra.

With two months of dedicated work, Tarun and Mumtaz bring together a fluid group of about twenty participants that assembles every day to read works of Hindi and Urdu fiction of their choice. We read stories by eminent writers who span several decades—including Premchand, Ismat Chughtai, Ibn-e-Insha, and Kamleshwar. The discussions and emotions unfold in such a way that the group decides to theatrically explore Premchand's last short story, "Kafan." This deci-sion becomes an all-consuming process that culminates in a play in Awadhi, *Hansa, Karo Puratan Baat*. The title is inspired by a song of Kabir, a poet variously claimed and labeled as 'mystic' or 'saint' and whose work has contributed sig-nificantly to Bhakti and Sufi traditions.

Premchand, often lauded as 'katha samrat,' a king of storytellers, in the sphere of Hindi literature, wrote "Kafan" in Urdu in 1935. The story revolves around two men—Ghisu and his son, Madhav—who are identified in the story as living in a settlement of chamars in their village.[2] Many who have studied Hindi literature in Indian schools recall this story from their high school textbook with an indelible image of a father and son sitting by the fire outside their hut on a cold winter night, eating stolen potatoes after combating acute hunger for two days. As the two roast the pilfered potatoes and reminisce and philosophize about the good and the bad, Madhav's wife, Budhiya, screams in agony with labor pains and dies by the end of the night. Then the two men try to gain sympathy from everyone in the village to collect money for Budhiya's kafan, or shroud. They end up spending the money on liquor and delicious food. Once their bellies are satiated, they share their leftovers with a beggar and bless Budhiya for the good day she enabled them to live.

Often seen as a classic along with other works of Premchand, "Kafan" has been cited for several decades for its complex engagement with casteism, feudalism, religious hypocrisy, and women's oppression in rural North India. In recent years, however, the story has come under heavy critical scrutiny, often on the grounds that, as a Savarna writer, Premchand has been insensitive in his portrayal of Ghisu and Madhav. Critics also argue that Premchand's Dalit characters remain trapped in their position as victims of an oppressive system and this, in turn, obscures pathways to imagining alternative futures.[3]

• • •

When the group takes on the challenge of working with "Kafan," most participants have no idea about the controversy surrounding the story. Those of us who do know a bit choose not to discuss it in order to open ourselves to a collective and organic exploration of the story's layers: after all, the work of doing justice to any story lies in how we interpret and reinterpret it. Due at least partly to this openness, the collective process of creating *Hansa* becomes a poetic search for ways in which we could abide by the characters who make the story. Through continuous readings and improvisation, the journey becomes an intense sharing of life's experiences and deepening of personal relationships among the workshop participants over a period of six months. The play that evolves from this process defies the rules of forms and genres, and transports the story across strictly bound historical periods and geographical spaces. It embeds Ghisu, Madhav, and Budhiya in their place and time in ways that serve as a prelude to, and as an analysis of, the story of Budhiya's death and Ghisu's and Madhav's response to it. Through a collective reinterpretation of the story in Awadhi—the first language of the majority of the workshop participants—"Kafan" evolves into an aesthetically rich drama with color, texture, music, romance, humor, suffering, and irony. In blending Premchand's critique of caste-based violence with radical Bhakti poetry and spiritual questioning of humanity's material investments as well as with tunes that mark everyday ironies of ordinary life, *Hansa* complicates the definitions of hero and antihero, exploitation and suffering, celebration and bereavement, and life and death, thereby reimagining and reopening the meanings and political and spiritual possibilities of Premchand's story. In December 2014, the group performs four shows of *Hansa* before packed audiences, followed by long discussions between actors and audiences at the Bal auditorium in the Yari Road area of Mumbai.[4] Members of the audience rejoice, sing, and cry with the actors; they find themselves "mesmerized" and "disturbed" by this "unforgettable play."

The process of making *Hansa* is intense and unyielding. For each workshop participant, transforming "Kafan" into *Hansa* becomes permeated with recollections and reflections on dying and on accompanying those we have known intimately as they faced death. For me, the embodied journey of co-creating *Hansa* with the workshop participants in Mumbai commences a couple of weeks after the death of my beloved father in Lucknow. The creative journey of continuous improvising with members of Parakh Theatre becomes a way to uncover new layers of emotion and understanding around Babuji's hospitalization and illness, to confront and make peace with the difficulties surrounding his death, and to honor his life as a passionate theater worker and a lover of Hindi and Urdu literature and Hindustani music.

Almost every evening between July and December, the group gathers for at least three hours. Although the contours and composition of the group shift over the months as some participants enter and others exit, the one person whose commitment to the workshop remains unchanged from start to finish is Mumtaz. On the third day of the workshop, Mumtaz laughingly declares to Tarun and me, "If we decide to do 'Kafan,' then I will be Budhiya. Only I am frail enough to play the dying Budhiya. Plus, I won't have to memorize any lines. I will just need to groan with pain and then die!"

Tarun assures her, "You will be Budhiya if that's what you want!" Then he adds, "However, you may not be able to identify either the Mumtaz or the Budhiya that eventually emerges on the stage. Are you ready to open yourself up to the process?"

"Of course, Bhaiyya. I will be in this until the end. I will be Budhiya, no matter what form she takes."

Labor Pains

It is the month of August in Mumbai and torrential downpours are making such a clanging noise on the tin roof of Tefla's Studio that it is hard for us to hear one another speak. Yet, the energy of the group remains unaltered despite this ringing disturbance and the dampness of our clothes. Binod and Sumit just took a turn at improvising the opening scene of the story where Ghisu and Madhav are eating roasted potatoes, and now Alok and Bhagwan Das, aka BD, are working on the same scene.

Today BD and Alok have introduced a pretend chilam in the scene that is allowing them to bring out a different nuance in the intimacy and interdependence of Ghisu and Madhav. Mumtaz is a bit late, as usual, because she has to finish her chores in at least six homes before she can make it to the rehearsal. She quietly enters the rehearsal space, sets down her wet umbrella and her large shoulder bag in a corner, opens her damp synthetic dupatta and drops it down her right shoulder to hang over her chest and belly before tying both its ends around her waist. The young men in the room nod respectfully at 'Mumtaz ji' as she moves across the makeshift stage to the corner of the room, where she takes her position—half lying down and half sitting up—and makes moaning sounds of Budhiya, while all the attention of the room is on the new dynamics and nuances that Alok and BD are exploring today. When Alok and BD are done, it is Bhole's and Gaurav's turn to enact the scene as father and son. Suddenly, a sense of aggressive competition infiltrates the room as the men try to impress one another with their talented approaches to the text.

All this time Mumtaz is ignored. She is just an occasional moaning noise in the rehearsal space, the voice of the dying Budhiya, whose death is a necessary backdrop in order for Ghisu's and Madhav's story to begin.

As the men decide to show off their acting prowess today, Mumtaz, Yasmin, Medha and I, the four women in a room of thirteen men, become uncomfortable. Yasmin, the caretaker at the studio who has taken on the contract to serve chai to the group, and who also spends time with the group watching every rehearsal and giving her frank feedback, cannot resist remarking in her Hyderabadi andaaz, "Today, the men in the room are really hyper. I'm glad I don't have to be Budhiya in a corner."

Hearing Yasmin's words, Medha writes a few words in her notebook and shows them to me: "There is too much testosterone in the room today. What if the men were asked to play Budhiya for a change?"

I share the idea with the group and everyone decides to try it. The contours of the room shift. Alok, Bhole, Anil, Sajjan (alias), and Yasmin's nine-year-old son, Aijaz, decide to occupy the corner that Mumtaz has been occupying day after day.[5] Each of them takes a turn at enacting the labor pains and, as they try to grab the attention of the onlookers by showing they can actually do a good job of *being* Budhiya, the locus of the scene shifts from the site where Madhav and Ghisu are roasting potatoes to the corner of the stage where Budhiya is dying. As each of the men and Aijaz thrash about as Budhiya, the corner becomes the new center of the room and Mumtaz intently watches each of them portray Budhiya's labor pains. Although none of the men or boys can possibly know Budhiya's pain, they cannot help thinking of themselves as more refined actors than Mumtaz; each of them seems to be demonstrating to Mumtaz what to do with her body when she acts as Budhiya.

When the group breaks for discussion after working on the scene for an hour or so, Roshan (alias) asks the group in his usual self-conscious and critical style: "Earlier the story was about Madhav and Ghisu, but now that all the Madhavs and Ghisus in our group have become Budhiya, I no longer know whose story it is."

Neeraj raises the question, "I am not sure anymore if this story is Marxist or feminist? No one ever calls Premchand a feminist, do they? Do they even call him a Marxist?"

As we get into a conversation about Premchand's writing and who gets to label his stories as Marxist or not Marxist, feminist or not feminist, Mumtaz remains quiet. At the end of the discussion, she says to me, "None of these boys or Bhole Dada have ever gone through anything close to death, and not one of them has given birth. Yet, every single one of them, including that little Aijaz, feels like he knows enough to teach me how to die in childbirth. So far I used to think that I can't read the story and most of them can. But now I know what I must show them as Budhiya. I feel I know this story in a way that they can't."

Mumtaz's words sink in slowly and grab me. She is defining the power of embodiment. She is claiming her embodied knowledge. She is identifying and challenging the hierarchy of gendered performance that has colonized the space in which Budhiya is meant to die. Mumtaz has recognized that Budhiya must live before she can die, and she has been moved to embrace the responsibility of participating in the collective pedagogy through which this engagement with Budhiya's life and death can happen.

Justice to Budhiya

A month after this episode, I am back in Minnesota for the beginning of the fall semester, while the group continues the rehearsals in Mumbai. Tarun and I talk every day when the group takes a break during its rehearsals at Tefla's Studio and, post-rehearsal, we touch base again about the meanings of the story that are unfolding in the improvisations. As the group works intensely several thousand miles away, every single day I steal from other responsibilities at least a tiny piece of my day so that I can immerse myself in the poetry of Kabir, Ameer Khusro, Malik Mohammad Jayasi, and Nazeer Akbarabadi; this allows me to delve into new connections with the group and its journey with the story, and to also suggest pieces the group can explore in conversation with "Kafan." Yet, I have not seen a full-fledged rehearsal from start to finish since Medha and I left Mumbai at the end of August. On a Saturday morning in early October, Tarun arranges for me to see an entire run through.

So much has happened since Medha and I were physically with the group five weeks ago. At that time, the actors were internalizing the words of the story through repeated readings and interpretations. In the last six weeks that story has gradually enmeshed with several other stories, even as the group has become absorbed with each other's journeys. Their intimacy is powerful, and I feel it in my bones even through the computer screen.

I meet Meena for the first time. She is Mumtaz's friend, a mother of two who migrated from Gujarat, and who works full-time in Madh Island in the home of a well-known television star. Meena has just joined the group, and she is excited I can communicate with her in Gujarati. "I get tired of all these people showing off their Awadhi," she says, "I am acting with them in their language, but they can't speak mine!" There is both a pride and frustration in her voice; she wants to connect with her coactors in Gujarati.

Avi is a quiet young man on the surface, but a couple of his statements indicate a deep turbulence on the question of what it means to accompany death. Avi has returned to the rehearsal after five weeks. He had to leave Mumbai suddenly when his brother was kidnapped because of a feud in his village in Uttar Pradesh. It is hard to say when things would be normal again for his family, but everyone is delighted he is back with the group. Avi waves at me and smiles quietly. He still seems shaken from all that he has returned from.

The process of grappling with the story of Ghisu, Madhav, Budhiya, and the people of their village has led to the creation of a play where only the second half is Premchand's story. The first half contextualizes the relationships and realities that lead to the death of Budhiya, and to Madhav's and Ghisu's philosophizing about life, death, and the systems of injustice that inspire them to drink away the money that is given to them as a charity to buy a kafan for the dead Budhiya. This contextualization and reinterpretation are made possible by the cumulative political understandings evolving in the group. Each person's memories and journeys through life, death, intimacy, and violence are allowing them to enter the story through their own and through each other's stories, thereby creating a unique space where learning, unlearning, and relearning are happening through a continuous improvisation of a new shared vocabulary. This vocabulary includes words and accents, motions and gestures, sounds and rhythms, feelings and sensations across the borders of time, place, tongue, occupation, and generation.

Improvising each paragraph of "Kafan" has become akin to creating a polyvocal verse of a poem whose course is known but whose rhythms are continuing to emerge like fresh waves. As Tarun learns to blur the borders between the roles of facilitator, learner, and director, he draws on the everyday experiences participants bring to the rehearsal space from their own lives. The scenes that have become inseparable from the story are playful and vibrant, but with sobering implications. We see the everyday realities that lead Ghisu and Madhav to become apathetic about the world. We are pushed to grapple with the complex everydayness of caste in the story as a politics not of 'then' and 'there,' but of 'here' and 'now.' We realize that it is the violence of untouchability that teaches Madhav to appreciate the art of thievery, something that his father congratulates him for—subtly but proudly. We recognize how the exploitation of the Dalit mazdoors by the thakur, or landlord, inspires Ghisu and Madhav to detach themselves from certain material pursuits of the world that surrounds them. Any mention of wages, familial stability, or a desire for their own next generation provokes bitter critique or avoidance on their part. At the same time, they never forgo a chance to live in the pleasures of the moment, even if the specific pleasures that each of them is pursuing are sometimes separated by their age. Father and son are bonded by a more or less shared vision of life, which is also marked by tension at times. However, the threads that thickly connect them allow them to understand and forgive one another, and to remain each other's companions in joy and suffering. Thus, we see Madhav falling in love with Budhiya, and hungrily seeking the contentment of matrimony and a home with her, as well as Budhiya's and Ghisu's participation in that dream. This occurs despite Budhiya's hesitations and premonitions, and despite Ghisu's simply worded insightful warnings that echo systemic critique of the feudal and violent casteist and patriarchal traps that Madhav's desires would entangle them in.

As I watch Alok and Mumtaz act as Madhav and Budhiya, I forget all that separates them, including almost two decades in age. There are tender moments of raw connection and thrill between them, moments that stir a discomfort and pain in the audience when we later encounter Budhiya screaming with the pain of childbirth, while Ghisu and Madhav sit together remembering the glory of an unforgettable feast Ghisu ate years ago. This discomfort is not easy to categorize or name; it stirs us and it baffles us, even as it eludes our grasp.

The workshop participants are playing with the languages they either know most intimately, or are drawn to, in order to create a powerful voice that belongs to all. Mumtaz, whose native language is Kannada, and Meena, whose mother tongue is Gujarati, proudly recite sentences in Awadhi because that is the language of the place where Ghisu, Madhav, and Budhiya live. Binod speaks in a mix of accents that are reminiscent of rural Bihar and Bengal. Alok and

Gaurav introduce a particular style of speech from Hardoi and Shahjahanpur districts of rural Uttar Pradesh, while BD brings a touch of Chhattisgarhi into his dialogue. The entire sequence of dialogue is based on improvisations, since several people in the team cannot connect with a written script. Every round of rehearsal yields something different, inspiring the group to reflect on the new meanings that are possible to incorporate in the evolving play, as well as on the spontaneous reinterpretations that seem out of place at times, and completely appropriate at others.

The play is interspersed with powerful music, put to tune by a chorus that Neeraj leads. Each song and musical interjection animates the poetry, pathos, irony, and political intensity of the story. The performance ends with a hauntingly melodious bhajan of Kabir, "Hansa, karo puratan baat," a song that emphasizes the unpredictable journey and placelessness of the soul that leaves the body. It calls for freedom from the materiality of the body so that the soul can witness a new dawn that is free from doubt and sorrow.

At the completion of the run-through, the team members remark on how the process of working with the story, and making it their own, has allowed them to grapple with all the shades of life—love and death, hunger and greed, exploitation and empathy, hope and hopelessness.

"Every scene raises an issue that gives us pause; every scene pushes us to rethink what we had previously assumed about life and our everyday relationships," says Alok.

"Coming here fills me with joy," says Mumtaz: "Ham yahan alag-alag zindgiyan lekar aate hain aur use kahani aur natak mein mila dete hain. Imandari se acting karne ke liye poora jeena padta hai." Each of us brings unique lives to this space and immerses them in the story and the play. To act honestly, one has to live fully. Mumtaz realizes that what she brings to the play as Budhiya is not something just anyone can bring; one comes to immerse oneself in a role through one's own life.

The process of grappling with the politics of caste, class, and gender has become entangled first and foremost with a dialogue about people's own understandings of their present—in Mumbai and in the places where they have come from—and with the process of collectively living, reflecting, interpreting, and learning about the politics and poetics of location, language, and performance. The bonds emerging in the team are palpably moving. One after another, every actor says something to the effect that it is no longer possible for them to feel complete without the rehearsals. The rehearsals of *Hansa* ground them. They give them hope and community.

BD and Alok want to take the group to Shahjahanpur so that the theater can be experienced and critiqued by the people who live these realities everyday

Mumtaz Sheikh and Gabbar Mukhiya during rehearsals of *Hansa*. (Photo by Tarun Kumar)

but who cannot read these stories because they are not formally literate: "If we are trying to create theater that originates in the rural soil, then all of us have to learn to connect with the earth of the villages; those who live in the villages must be able to enjoy and critique what we create," says BD.

Meena wants to make sure she is included in the details of this co-dreaming: She shares that she has already made arrangements to leave her daughters with her relatives if she has to go outside of Mumbai on a tour of the play.

In that moment, Mumtaz suddenly announces that she has left one of her cooking and cleaning jobs because of the play. All these years, whenever I have asked Mumtaz to reduce her workload so that she can take better care of herself, she has insisted that she cannot drop any of the jobs because her children, and more recently her granddaughters, need her earnings; so I am stunned by what she reports during the Skype discussion. Mumtaz states matter-of-factly, "Working in seven homes was not allowing me to immerse myself in Budhiya, so I gave up one of the jobs. I want my performance to shake people. . . . I realized that if I couldn't do justice to Budhiya, the group couldn't do justice to *Hansa*."

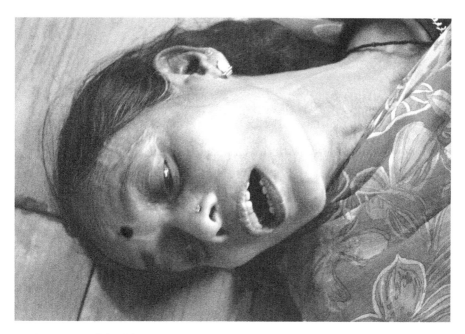

Mumtaz as Budhiya. (Photo by Tarun Kumar)

• • •

24 December 2014. Mumtaz and I are alone in Tarun's and Vibhoo's apartment in the Aman Co-Operative Housing Society, across the street from the Muslim Qabristan in Jogeshwari West. In this space of just over twenty-three square meters, Mumtaz makes rotis in the kitchen and I sit on the floor of the adjoining room about two meters away, folding the brochures for the shows of Hansa, *which begin in three days. The smell of puffed hot rotis stealthily slips into the fragrance of chane ki dal aur lauki-pyaz ki sabzi that is simmering in a cumin-powered tomato ginger sauce, with loads of dhania and kasoori methi. Every molecule of my body becomes one with this aroma that I inhale and exhale. As Mumtaz rolls the rotis, she rehearses her lines, and I give her feedback on the specific words and pauses she has difficulty with. As the cooking winds up, the conversation becomes more complex.*

MUMTAZ: Didi, I didn't like the way in which Shahina ji [alias] gave her merciless feedback yesterday! Bhaiyya [Tarun] invited her to engage with us so that we could be energized, but she did the opposite.

ME: Yeah, I know. She just started yelling at you and Meena about your dialogue delivery. I wanted to tell her to be quiet, but you stopped me. Why?

MUMTAZ: What would be the point of you trying to silence her? Meena and I were ignoring her, anyway. Shahina ji may think of herself as a great artist, but screaming in frustration at us because she thinks we are inferior actors is not such a smart approach. The boys did not enjoy seeing her coming after us, either. You don't gain anyone's respect yelling like that. I just let her words enter from one ear and exit from the other.

ME: But we could have just told her that it was unacceptable. Why listen to someone who was so out of line?

MUMTAZ: No, Didi. Live and let live. She needed to feel superior, so she screamed at us, but we know what we are doing, so we don't have to pay attention to her rage. I have learned so much from listening to the criticism that comes from within the group. We teach each other by loving and caring. Shahina ji doesn't understand what this learning has been about. She only sees the surface. Don't you think?

ME: What you're saying is profound, Mumtaz. It takes a lot of courage to forgive so generously.

MUMTAZ: Didi, can I ask something? Can you lie down and do the scene of Budhiya's death that Shahina ji was so unhappy with?

ME: That's a great idea. I will do it. Why don't you lie next to me and rehearse the scene also?

MUMTAZ: Yes, I will. You know, my body can't explore freely in that space. There are all those boys and men around me. I want to let my body go, but I can't. If we do it together—here, right now—we both can find something else . . .

In the very tight space of the apartment, Mumtaz and I lie next to each other at a ninety-degree angle so that we can be in each other's full view, even as we close our eyes to transport ourselves to the scene of Budhiya's death. We rise—moaning and crying with the most unimaginable pain that we can remember—then collapse, then rise with a new moan again. With every rise, moan, and fall we find a new energy and identify new muscles and angles in our body. Suddenly, Mumtaz asks me if I think it is okay for Budhiya to look beautiful in the scene where she is dying.

I was probably thinking the same thing but in different words. I say to Mumtaz, "Yes, I think so."

"I am glad you said that I can look pretty in death," says Mumtaz, eliminating the distance between herself and Budhiya, and between dying and death in the same breath. She loosens her bun, her thick hair falling like a heavy black cobra behind her skeletal frame, and her legs and chest moan with an intensity I have never seen before. I am struck by the beauty, grace, and honesty of her body. My own form seems a bit too oversized and pointless next to hers. I stop rehearsing the scene and continue watching Mumtaz.

Then Mumtaz stops, and looks at me: "Didi, I can do this now. Let's get a rickshaw. We are late for the rehearsal."

We both slip into our sandals and dash out the door.

Hansa, Karo Puratan Baat!
Based on
Premchand's story, "Kafan"

The lyrics of the songs created for this play are taken from *Kabir Granthavali*[1] and from Awadhi folk songs contributed by Neeraj Kushwaha

Workshop Participants on Stage
Meena Jitendra Bariya
Bhagwan Das
Gaurav Gupta
Neeraj Kushwaha
Gabbar Kumar Mukhiya
Alok Panday
Mumtaz Sheikh
Sushil Shukla
Sumit Singh Tomar
Satish Chandra Trivedi
Anil Yadav
Avi Kumar Yadav

Backstage Workshop Participants and Supporters
Ritwik Chowdhury, Medha Faust-Nagar, Aijaz, Mohammad Patel,
Purnima Kharga, Richa Nagar, Kaajal Singh, Munira Surati, Yasmin

Dance Choreography: Purnima Kharga
Music: Neeraj Kushwaha
Lights: Sujit Kumar
Workshop facilitation: Tarun Kumar

(Background noises announces the arrival of a new morning in the village.)

MAN 1: Hey Maiku. Where are you?

MAN 2: I'm here. What's up?

MAN 1: Arey, where is your head? Don't you see that water buffalo slipping into the field?

MAN 2: Hey, chachi, do you hear me!

WOMAN: What's the matter?

MAN 2: Look! That calf is sucking down all the milk.

WOMAN: Oh my god, here I come.

Scene 1

Ghisu, Madhav, village folk, Man 1, Man 2, Man 3, Budhiya
(Ghisu and Madhav are sitting in front of their hut.)

MADHAV: Dadda, I've been tossing and turning all night long. I can't bear this hunger anymore. Nothing has gone in my stomach for two days. I'm gonna die if we go on like this.

GHISU: You won't die.

MADHAV: What do you mean I won't die?

GHISU: You're alive, right? Not dead yet, are ya? I'll find a way . . .

(The two sit in silence, taking turns at a shared chilam. Then the voices of village men become audible.)

VOICE 1: Arey, O Chaituwa, move faster. Thakur Sahab has called for us.

VOICE 2: I'm coming, I'm coming.

VOICE 1: Hurry, hurry.

(A cluster of people talk busily with each other as they pass through the middle of the stage.)

MAN 2: Listen, should I ask Ghisu and Madhav to join us?

MAN 1: Why not! Let's ask them.

MAN 2: Bhaiyya, Thakur Sahab has begun a new project.

MAN 1: Yes, Ghisu, why don't you come along, too? There's quite a bit of work at the thakur's. He says it's a long project. Might keep us busy for months.

GHISU: Busy for months? What's this special project of the thakur's?

MAN 2: He's building a house. He's also digging a well. It'll take a lot of people. Holi is almost here. If you came along that would be good.

MAN 3: The regular farm work is there, too.

GHISU: That's all good, but when it comes to paying, the thakur makes us dance. (*Mutters softly.*) He makes us sweat hard, then fusses about paying the wages.

MADHAV: (*Lying.*) We're busy these days. We're loading and unloading the grain at the wholesaler's.

(*Ghisu listens attentively.*)

GHISU: He means to say that the work starts from today.

(*Now Madhav looks at Ghisu.*)

MADHAV: Yeah, it's just begun.

MAN 1: Forget about it, you two. (*To Man 2 and 3.*) There's no point messing with these two tricksters. Let's get going.

MAN 2: Right you are! These two have no shortage of work. Let's get out of here.

(*Another cluster of men and women mazdoors passes through. A young woman, Budhiya, turns around, looks sharply at Madhav, and crosses the stage with others. Madhav's eyes shine with excitement.*)

MADHAV: Dadda, I'll be right back. I have to go take a dump.

(*Madhav grabs the lota and dashes across the stage.*
A popular tune of Awadh plays in the background.)

La-la-la, laa-laa; la, la, la, laa, laa

Scene 2

Madhav and Budhiya
(*Madhav reenters the stage with a lota in one hand, and Budhiya's hand in another. Then they both squat as if sitting face to face in a sugarcane field.*)

MADHAV: Why do you stare at me like that whenever you pass in front of my home?

BUDHIYA: Bothered by my looking, are you? Aren't you going to marry me?

MADHAV: (*To the audience.*) Her eyes bug out as she ogles me right there in front of my Dadda! (*To Budhiya.*) Don't you know that makes me blush with shame?

BUDHIYA: You listen to me. My father is looking for a boy for me. And here you are, just lazing around, doing nothing. If you want to marry me, you'd better hurry. I have warned you a hundred times that my father will marry me off soon. Then you will just sit there picking firewood with your Dadda.

MADHAV: Budhiya, do you really want to marry me? You know, there is nothing in that home of mine—except Dadda and me.

BUDHIYA: Of course, I know all that. I can't bear to see you two wandering from door to door like beggars. The whole village talks nonsense about you and your father.

MADHAV: Arey, let them speak. I will deal with each one of them. Don't you worry.

(*As he puts his arms around her and tries to pull her close, a prankster screams, "Hear, hear, that water buffalo is poking her head into the field." Budhiya releases her hand from Madhav's and both run off in opposite directions.*)

Fade-out.

Scene 3

Pundit, Madhav, Ghisu
(*Singing a bhajan, a Pundit walks across the stage.*)

PUNDIT: Ajgar kare na chakri, panchhi kare na kaam, Das Maluka kahi gaye, sabke data Ram. A python serves no one, a bird does no work, Das Maluka has told us, it is God who gives to all.

(*After a few moments, Madhav traces Pundit's footsteps. He crosses barely half the stage, then spots something that he picks up stealthily and hides in his clothes. Just then, the Pundit retraces his steps looking hard for something he has dropped.*)

PUNDIT: Where the hell did it disappear?

MADHAV: (*Sneaking up.*) How are you doin', Pundit ji? Did you lose something?

PUNDIT: Get out of here, will ya? I'll find it myself. And listen, if you find something, don't you dare touch it. (*Hesitates for a second.*) But if you do see something, you can just speak with your mouth.

MADHAV: Pundit ji, if I touch it, it will become impure for you, wouldn't it?

PUNDIT: I told you, didn't I? If you find it, just tell me about it—don't touch it. Then why are you arguing with me?

MADHAV: (*Going aside and imitating the Pundit.*) "Don't touch it!!" Then go right ahead and look for it yourself. Ghusau! Go to hell!

(*Madhav leaves, then reenters the stage excitedly calling his Dadda's name. When the lights come on, Ghisu is sitting in a corner of the stage.*)

MADHAV: Here Dadda, look, what have I brought for you!

(Madhav opens the tiny bundle of paper that he had picked up when it had fallen from the folds of the Pundit's dhoti.)

GHISU: Quite the expert you have become, huh? Where did you get so much stuff from? This is enough for ten days.

MADHAV: Remember that Pundit ji from Gola? This had slipped from his dhoti. He was looking and looking for it. I found it before I saw him—so I hid it away. When I saw that Pundit ji was searching for something, I thought I should give it back to him. But when I asked, he started suspecting me and immediately began his talk about touching and not touching. Then I, too, said, 'Ghusau!' I mean, when he himself asked me to go away, I also told him, "Look, I am Ghisu's son"! Some big Pundit he thinks he is. I sent him home.

(Both start preparing the chilam.)

MADHAV: *(Taking over the shared chilam from his father.)* Now, let's purify the Pundit's impure material.

MADHAV: *(After inhaling a few times.)* Dadda, you should get me married now.

GHISU: Inhale this, my boy, inhale this. It will extinguish all your hungers. Forget about marrying.

MADHAV: Why? You also married, didn't you?

GHISU: Hmm, so I did! *(After a pause.)* What would come from marriage? I say, beg, borrow, and eat happily. Then curl up like a python and go to sleep.

MADHAV: Arey Dadda, marriage is a duty. How will our lineage go on otherwise?

GHISU: *(Laughs.)* Which lineage, eh? The lineage of beggars? Have you gone mad?

MADHAV: *(Closely watches his father as the latter laughs, then speaks.)* Nothing in this home looks like a home. No vessels, no chulha, no chakla, no belan. Whatever there is, is all on our bodies. Other than that, it's just you, me, and this chilam! *(After a pause.)* But Dadda, marry I will!

Fade-out.

(Wedding song plays heartily with beats of dholak.)

Mere banne ko koi mat dekho
Najariya lag jayihe
Sees banna ke kalgi sohe
Kalgi pe najariya lag jayihe

Mere banne ko koi mat dekho
Let no one look at my groom, lest they cast an evil eye upon him.
The crest on my groom's head is so becoming, let no one cast an evil eye on it.

(*The stage lights up as the song ends.*)

Scene 4

Ghisu, Madhav, Budhiya, Mazdoor
(*Madhav and Budhiya are now married. Some pots and pans are visible in the hut. Budhiya is cooking.*)

>   **GHISU:** Oh dear Madhwa, I say you've made a miracle! A chulha is burning in our home, and the smoke is rising as if gods are being summoned in a thakur's mansion.
>   **MADHAV:** The meaning of this life has changed, Dadda.

(*Budhiya pushes a plate with food in front of them. Both squat around the shared plate and eat.*)

>   **GHISU:** What has actually changed now are the days of landlords and big farmers.
>   **MADHAV:** Why, Dadda?
>   **GHISU:** Now you and I will have to work in their homes day and night. That's how this chulha will be lit. When you make a home, you also pay a price for it.

(*A farm mazdoor comes to their door.*)

>   **MAZDOOR:** Oh Bhaiyya Ghisu, eating a meal, are you?
>   **GHISU:** (*Sensing the sarcasm in the speaker's voice.*) Who's eating a meal? We're just lookin' at it.
>   **MAZDOOR:** Listen, Thakur has assembled a lot of work. There will be wages for at least eight to ten days. He'll pay three aanas a day, and even better, he'll pay us at the end of each day.
>   **GHISU:** Three aanas is too little. If he gives five aanas, then we'll see. Neither one aana less, nor one aana more.
>   **MAZDOOR:** Arey, ask for a wage that'll fetch you work. You just go berserk with your demands!
>   **MADHAV:** Why Dadda? What'll happen in five aanas?
>   **MAZDOOR:** The way you two are goin' on! One might think it's the thakur who has taken a loan from you and you're asking him to repay with interest. Think a little before you speak.
>   **GHISU:** Arey, why are you getting so angry? We aren't asking you to pay us.

Scene 5

Ghisu, Madhav, Taka, Thakur, the mazdoors
(With vigorous beats of the dholak, the mazdoors enthusiastically sing a song as they work, giving momentum and texture to the story's flow.)

Ta na na naa tanaa na na na naa ta na na naa na na na naa

(All the actors labor as farmworkers. In the middle of the work, Ghisu and Madhav sneak out for a smoke, and sit in a corner with their chilam. In the space immediately before them, Thakur's man, Taka Bhaiyya, is ordering the mazdoors.)

TAKA: Move those hands and legs fast, Thakur Sahab must be on his way. And what's happening there? (*Screaming at a mazdoor.*) Oye, Chaituwa, come here, can't you hear me? I will give you a hard one right under your ear, then you will hear. Look at these bricks here, can't you see them? Go dump them on that side. (*Imitating.*) "No, don't ask me to do any work but when the time comes to demand money, I will be the first." You won't improve, will you? (*Spots Ghisu and Madhav with their chilam.*) There you go again. You two only need the smallest excuse!

GHISU: Come, come, Taka Bhaiyya. You also take a drag with us.

TAKA: (*Looks greedily at them, and softens his tone.*) You want me to grow extra balls? Thakur Sahab will be here soon. (*Imitates them.*) "Take a drag with us." (*Extends his hand to grasp the chilam and almost drops it as Thakur enters the scene in that moment.*)

THAKUR: Arey Taka?

TAKA: Yes, boss.

THAKUR: How's the work going today?

TAKA: It's going well, boss.

THAKUR: How many mazdoors have you hired?

TAKA: Thirteen, boss.

THAKUR: And how many are there in the western farm?

TAKA: There the work already ended yesterday, boss.

THAKUR: (*Startled to see Ghisu and Madhav.*) What's this, Taka? You gave work to these two again?

TAKA: What work, boss! I asked them because we were desperate for hands. But father and son are both bad news. They barely carry four loads and sit down for a break.

THAKUR: Then why don't you send them home! They're just a waste of everything. Listen to me, give them two aanas each and kick them out. I don't want to see them here again.

TAKA: You, Ghisu, and you, Madhav! Come here.

MADHAV: Arey, I'm bringing the mortar there!

TAKA: Leave the mortar alone—just come here. Didn't I tell you earlier that you need to pull your weight?

(*Both come to Taka. The rest of the mazdoors stand around and watch.*)

TAKA: Here, take your two aanas each and get done! Vanish. Fast.

GHISU: (*With the coins in his hand.*) What's this? Are you kidding me?

TAKA: I'm kidding no one!

GHISU: (*Laughs a little.*) Don't play around, man, give us the right wage. Give us full six aanas—no less, no more. We have been breaking our backs all day. It's not coming out of your pocket, is it?

TAKA: Yes, it's not coming out of my pocket. As if your ancestors left a treasure for me! You think I'm your father's servant?

GHISU: Had you been my father's servant, you would have stood here where I am standing.

(*The mazdoors standing around them laugh.*)

TAKA: Shut your mouth. Don't you try to impress me with your smartass tongue.

GHISU: Then don't make me stand. Just pay and I will leave.

TAKA: (*Orders the mazdoors.*) Kick him out.

(*The men among mazdoors push, kick, and beat Ghisu and Madhav, and the two fight back.*)

GHISU: (*Screams in pain.*) Ouch, are you trying to kill us!? They need all the work from us, but when it comes to paying . . . (*To Madhav.*) Let's go. You're not hurt, right?

MADHAV: No, no. I'm fine. What about you? Didn't hurt you too much, did they?

GHISU: Of course, they did. Why would I have screamed otherwise?

Scene 6

Budhiya and Madhav
(*A scene without dialogue. Madhav impatiently waits for Budhiya to finish her chores in their hut. She needs to finish her tasks, but he ignores her protests. She gives in. As the chorus sings, the two melt into each other. The high pitch of music matches and absorbs their passion.*)

Chorus sings:

> Hiyan madan ban phool rahe hain
> Aaven sohan baas
> Man bhaunra jihn arujh rahe hain
> Sukh ki na abhilas
> A thick forest of desire has blossomed here. The bodies and souls become one.
>   The ecstatic souls are drowned in intense pleasure of unity. They do not
>   seek any other pleasure.

(*Madhav and Budhiya pull each other in their arms.*)
Quick fade-out.

Scene 7

Mazdoors, Ghisu, Madhav, Taka, Thakur
(*The music changes quickly. With fast-paced beats of the dholak, the mazdoors
sing.*)

> Ta na na naa tanaa na na na naa ta na na naa na na na naa

(*Thakur discusses accounts with Taka while another worker massages his shoulders. A number of mazdoors are working around them.*)

TAKA: Thirteen sacks have come. I've placed them there in the hay store.
THAKUR: Yes, that's fine.
TAKA: Four and two, six . . .

(*Ghisu and Madhav enter.*)

GHISU AND MADHAV: Good day, Sir!
TAKA: Boss, forty and fifteen, fifty-five, has to be paid to Chaitu.
THAKUR: (*To the worker pressing his shoulders.*) Move a bit. (*Then interrupts
    Taka.*) What's this? You've invited these two here again?
TAKA: You don't understand, boss, it's very hard to find mazdoors now. We
    need hands to do the work.
THAKUR: Yes, you need hands that can do the work, but ask these two to get
    lost. These wicked bastards will do less work, and more goofing off. Who'll
    run after them? Get some hardworking men who'll actually do the work.
TAKA: Maalik, we're putting the lintels on the roof today, so we need people.
    It's harvest time in the fields so hands are short. These two are pathetic, but
    they'll still help with something.
THAKUR: These two together will not do what one mazdoor will finish on

his own. They work for half an hour and then smoke the chilam for the next two and a half. I've never seen such lazyasses in the entire village.

GHISU: (*Mutters.*) If someone makes you do work, that's one thing, but if after doing the work you load us with ten more things to do, then how long will one work?

THAKUR: (*To Ghisu.*) What's all this mumbling?

TAKA: Hey, what are you grumbling about?

GHISU: Nothing, Saheb, nothing. You and I have known each other since we were little, that's why I take the liberty of speaking whatever comes to my mouth. That's all. It would be nice to get some work on daily wages.

THAKUR: I know you! You'll never work. All you'll do is cheat.

GHISU: (*To the audience.*) Even if a man peels his skin for him, it will not be enough.

THAKUR: What did you say? Can you speak a little louder! You're egging me on, you rascal. You think you're my relative? Why don't you come here— let me greet and treat you properly. Scoundrel.

(*Enraged, Thakur hits Ghisu and once he begins he can't stop.*)

GHISU: (*Trying to save himself.*) Stop, my lord, please stop! I am leaving, I promise!

Scene 8

Village men, Ghisu, Madhav, Taka, Girdhari, Hariya, Khilawan
Chorus sings:

Shram te hee sab hot hai, jo man rakhe dheer.
Shram te khodat koop jyon thal mein pragate neer.
It's the patient, unyielding labor that makes everything possible.
This labor digs a well, and makes the hard earth brim with water.

(*A clump of village men stands and chats.*)

FIRST: You know, that father and son! Both are made of some special clay.

SECOND: Hmm, they spew out whatever comes to their mouth. They fear nothing—not the work, not their bodies, not their bellies. They don't regret the beatings, and all the curses just roll off their backs.

FIRST: It seems as if some crazy ascetics have taken birth amid us. From somewhere or another, they find enough to live.

THIRD: They can go without food for two to four days at a time. They don't have proper clothes on their bodies, they're happy to wander about in rags.

FOURTH: Such people are made of a very thick skin. And then there're people

like us—we do bone-breaking labor day and night, but barely manage two
meals a day.

FIRST: Such mysterious souls trick the world. My brain stops working when I
see them. I start worrying, what does one do with such weird spirits.

(*Ghisu and Madhav enter.*)

MADHAV: Who are you worrying about? Who tricks the world? Tell me.

FIRST: (*Awkwardly.*) This, Hariya, he was saying . . .

GHISU: Arey Bhaiyya Taka. Don't you have some tobacco to spare?

TAKA: From where would I have tobacco! If you have some, let us know.

HARIYA: (*Teases Taka.*) His state is like this: "If I come to your place, what
will you feed me and if you come to my place, what will you bring for
me!"

KHILAWAN: (*Turns to Ghisu.*) Arey bhai Ghisu, it's hard to identify your
colors these days. When you both started growing your hair out like this, I
started wondering if the two of you'll become ascetics.

MADHAV: (*Laughs.*) Dadda, this Khilawan has gone mad.

GHISU: (*Laughs gently.*) Now tell me something, does one become an ascetic
just by growing one's hair? (*To Girdhari.*) Hey, you Girdhari, you're looking mighty pink with health. I heard you went to your mother-in-law's
house, haven't seen you in ages. No wonder you've returned with those
plump cheeks. Feed us something, too!

GIRDHARI: Who told you all this?

ALL: This one, and this one . . .

GHISU: Maan, why do you always whine and cry?

GIRDHARI: Who's whining, Bhaiyya?

KHILAWAN: Now that you two have appeared, we should sing and play a
little.

GHISU: Alright, so give us an impressive tune!

All sing:

Gagri sambharo, aho Banwaari, gagri sambharo
Aawat rahi Jamna jal bhar ke, kankar mare Girdhari
Gagri to phoot gai haan chunri to bheej gai, haan
Saas nanad hamka de hain gaari
Gagri sambharo
Watch that pot, O Banwari. I was returning from the Jamuna with a gagri full
of water, and Krishna began to hit it with pebbles. The gagri broke and
my chunri got drenched. Mother-in-law and Sister-in-law cursed me on
top of that. Watch that pot, O Banwari.

Scene 9

Ghisu, Madhav, Boy 1, Boy 2
(*On their way back home, Madhav and Ghisu dig up some potatoes and pluck some sugarcane from a field. In the background, people scream, "Look, look, some thieves are running away with the potatoes. Catch them!" Two boys chase Ghisu and Madhav, who run fast across the stage.*)

> BOY 1: (*Grabs the arm of the second boy and stops him.*) Now, where do you think you're going? The chamars live there. Do you plan to enter their neighborhood also?
> BOY 2: (*Stops immediately in horror.*) No, not really.
> BOY 1: You got it! We don't want to become outcasts.

Scene 10

Madhav, Ghisu, Budhiya, Dhankun
(*Madhav and Ghisu arrive before Budhiya with stolen potatoes and sugarcane and no earnings.*)

> BUDHIYA: I had gone to Thakur's kiln for some brickwork. I've cooked a little food. Wash your hands and feet, and eat. (*Pauses.*) Listen, I'll go to the pond tomorrow. Remember to give me your dirty clothes to wash.

(*The two look at each other in mild surprise.*)

> BUDHIYA: Just wrap something around yourselves for a bit, okay? If I don't wash your clothes, bugs will be crawling all over you!

(*Budhiya's pregnancy is showing. She looks anemic. Suddenly, she falls on her back.*)

> GHISU: Ay bahuriya, ay bahuriya.
> MADHAV: Ay Budhiya, ay Budhiya.
> GHISU: Quick. Go fetch your Dhankun Chachi.

Swift fade-out.

(*Madhav and Dhankun talk in the background.*)

> MADHAV: Arey O Dhankun Chachi, Budhiya has fainted. Come fast.
> DHANKUN: Come, let's go.

(*Dhankun and Madhav reenter.*)

GHISU: Arey bitiya, Bahuriya was just fine, she was talking to us and then suddenly fell to the floor. Please take a look, bitiya.

MADHAV: Should I bring some water?

DHANKUN: Yes, get it. Quick.

(*Dhankun checks Budhiya, and with Madhav's help, takes her in the wings.*)

DHANKUN: (*Instructs Madhav.*) Now, you step out!

MADHAV: (*Nervously to Ghisu.*) She is checking her.

GHISU: Yes, you remain outside with me, right here.

(*Dhankun reemerges.*)

DHANKUN: (*To Madhav.*) Listen, your woman is expecting.

(*Madhav smiles beamingly.*)

DHANKUN: Don't show your teeth to me. Your woman is extremely weak. You'd better pay attention to what she eats and drinks—she needs green vegetables, daal, and daliya. Otherwise, if something happens, don't come to me. I'm warning you.

MADHAV: Couldn't you sit by her side for a moment?

DHANKUN: What will happen by me sitting near her? Would that make her okay? You son and father, you should do some work so that you can give her some decent meals. You two don't do any work at all. (*To the audience.*) No one ever ran away from work like these two!

(*Dhankun exits.*)

MADHAV: (*To Ghisu.*) Listen, she's right. We'll have to find some work tomorrow. My wife is expecting. You'd better figure something out fast. We don't have a storeroom full of grain!

GHISU: Don't worry, Son. Tomorrow it'll all happen. All we have to do is cut some wood and sell it in the village market.

MADHAV: I know that. But to get that wood, we'll also have to get out of the home early. We'll also have to reach the bazaar in time.

GHISU: Arey, why're you explaining all this to me? Am I not telling you that you'll get a belly full of food tomorrow? I haven't just fooled around all these years. Haven't I raised you? I am no idiot.

Swift fade-out.

Scene 11

Khilawan, Ghisu, Madhav, mazdoor
Chorus sings:

> Maangan maran saman hai
> Mat koi maango bheekh
> Maangan se marna bhala
> Ye sadguru ki seekh
> To beg is like dying, thus no one should beg.
> Dying is preferable to begging, this is the lesson from the saint.

(*Ghisu goes to a mazdoor in the field. Another mazdoor watches them.*)

KHILAWAN: You are asking me to give you a loan, but I don't have anything myself. From where will I give you?

GHISU: Now, now, Khilawan. Every day you go to work for the thakur or on someone else's field. I'm sure you can find something to put on my palm.

KHILAWAN: I am not lying. Every day I have to dig a well to quench my thirst. You know this.

GHISU: Then why do you say things to me when I refuse to work. At least I don't go and crumble my bones for these thakurs and big kisans. At least I don't follow their orders. Those who make us sweat are the ones who become wealthy. Isn't it? Arey, if you're no better than me, then get out of here and come with me. Why are you burning your body and soul for them!

KHILAWAN: (*Places something on Ghisu's palm.*) Here, keep this half aana.

GHISU: (*Complains to Khilawan.*) What good will this do? (*To the audience.*) So humanity isn't entirely dead yet. I'll live a few more days.

(*Notes of an intense aalaap begin rising, as if everything is going to be drowned in an impenetrable sorrow.*)

MADHAV: Dadda, no damn Dai or Bai is ready to come to see Budhiya. What can we do merely by swinging around this money?

GHISU: None can foretell who will become heartless in which timely or untimely moment.

Scene 12

Ghisu, Madhav, Budhiya
Chorus sings:

> Muthiya risti ret si
> Beetat hain din raat re
> Sau sau baar mare aur jeeve
> Kya aurat ki jaat re
> Days and nights pass, like sand drips from a clenched fist.
> A hundred times she lives and a hundred times she dies: that's the story of the
>   woman caste

(*The whole village is enveloped in a deep darkness. Piercing this darkness are
Budhiya's terrifying screams. Outside the hut, father and son are roasting potatoes
by a fire.*)

GHISU: It doesn't look like she'll live. The whole bloody day has gone running
   around trying to find a way to save her. Go on, go take a look at her.

MADHAV: What will come from my seeing her?

GHISU: What a heartless soul you are, eh. Being so disloyal to the one with
   whom you found so much joy and happiness all year!

MADHAV: I can't bear to watch her thrashing about, writhing and twisting in
   pain.

GHISU: And nothing else is happening besides screaming and crying. (*Takes
   out a potato from the fire, peels it and places it carefully in his mouth.*) Go, go
   and see what state she's in. Maybe it's the witch's wrath. Even the ojha asks
   for a rupee these days. What'll happen with half an aana?

MADHAV: I'm scared to go in.

GHISU: What do you fear? I'm right here.

MADHAV: Yes, and you'll also eat my share of potatoes if I move away for a
   second. Why don't you go in and take a look at her?

GHISU: When your mother left us, I didn't budge from her side for three
   full days. . . . Wouldn't she [Budhiya] feel awkward and shy? The woman
   whose face I haven't seen until today, you're asking me to go see her bare
   body. She wouldn't even have a clue of her own body. She won't even be
   able to thrash about freely.

MADHAV: Dadda, what will happen if a child is born? Ginger, gum, jaggery,
   oil . . . we have nothing.

GHISU: All of that will come. Let God send a child first. The people who
   don't even have a paisa to spare now, the same people will call for us and
   give us rupees tomorrow. I had no less than nine sons, and there was never
   a thing in the home to greet them, but God always carried us through.

(*After a pause.*) Between the time she fell yesterday and this damn potato, I haven't even had a bite to eat.

MADHAV: Eat these potatoes now. That's what is our . . . what do you call it . . . fate!

GHISU: Yes. We had potatoes before, we have potatoes now. This is our kismat!

(*The two are completely focused on eating the potatoes. Both are taking out burning hot potatoes from the fire and swallowing hurriedly. The heat brings tears to their eyes.*)

GHISU: Some twenty years ago, I had attended the thakur's wedding. And what satisfaction I had found in that feast! Even today, I remember every moment as if it just happened yesterday. I can never forget that feast. I have never eaten a meal so fulfilling since then.

MADHAV: Get out of here, Dadda. This kind of feast! (*Skeptically.*) Okay, if you say so.

GHISU: The bride's side made sure that everyone was happily fed, regardless of who it was. Small or big—all! They fed us pooris, that too of pure ghee.

Flashback begins

Chorus sings:

Dulha ji aye hare-hare
Dulha ji aye hare-hare
Dulha ji aye more angana
Raghunandan phoole na samaayen
The beautiful new groom has arrived in my courtyard.
The gods are happy today.

(*In the background, Ghisu's voice narrates the details of the feast and the stage lights up to show a young Ghisu enjoying himself in the scene of the feast.*)

GHISU: (*Voice from backstage.*) Chutney, raita, three kinds of dry sabzi, another juicy tarkari, yogurt, mithai. Now what can I say? The flavors I found in that feast. There was no one to stop me. Whatever you wanted, you could eat as much as you liked. The people ate and ate so much that there wasn't space left in our stomachs even for a sip of water. But the servers were such that even if you refused a thousand times, they poured in fresh hot, round, and fragrant kachoris. I would say, "I am full, I can't eat anymore," I would put my hands above the plate to stop them, but they just wouldn't take "no" for an answer. Then, when everyone had washed their hands . . .

Flashback ends

MADHAV: No one feeds us a feast like that now.

GHISU: How will they? That was a different time. Nowadays all they're worried about is saving. They don't wanna spend money on weddings, they don't wanna spend money on the rituals of the dead. Someone should ask all of them: "Where will you keep all the stuff that you steal from the poor?" There is no end to stealing, but when it comes to spending, everyone's become a miser.

MADHAV: You must've eaten at least twenty pooris?

GHISU: I ate more than twenty.

MADHAV: I would've eaten fifty.

GHISU: I'm pretty sure I ate no less than fifty. I was quite fit and muscular. You're not even half of what I used to be.

MADHAV: (*Mutters to himself.*) Potato in the evening, potato in the night. All there is is potato. (*After a pause.*) If you're still up, maybe I can close my eyes for a bit?

GHISU: Yes, I'm sitting.

(*Both gulp down water, cover themselves in their dhotis, and curl up near the dying fire. Budhiya's screams continue to pierce the darkness.*)

Scene 13

Madhav, Budhiya, Ghisu, Neighbor 1, Neighbor 2, Neighbor 3
(*Birds chirp and the tune of dawn arises along with the morning sun. Madhav opens his eyes and does not hear any sound from Budhiya. Fearfully, he wakes up his father.*)

MADHAV: Dadda, get up. It's morning now.

(*Madhav steps into the hut.*)

MADHAV: Budhiya, O Budhiya. Get up, Budhiya.

Chorus sings:

> Hirdai ma to aag hai
> Nayanan mein barsat
> Sau-sau baar mare aur jeeve
> Kya aurat ki jaat re
> The heart is on fire.
> The eyes are raining tears.
> A hundred times she lives and a hundred times she dies: that's the story of the
> woman's caste.

(*Madhav touches Budhiya's lifeless body like a mad man. He breaks down and cries. Screaming, he runs outside.*)

MADHAV: (*Crying.*) Arey Dadda, Budhiya has gone. I got no place to go now.

GHISU: What are you saying, Madhav? Arey, she was a real saint, such good soul. What calamity has befallen us! My Lord, is this the day you had saved for me to witness?

NEIGHBOR 1: Arey Bhaiyya, don't break apart like this. This is what God must have wished.

NEIGHBOR 2: Who can stop that which must happen! Don't cry, Madhav.

NEIGHBOR 3: Now go and get ready with the kafan and the wood.

(*Madhav pulls his father in one direction.*)

MADHAV: Do you even have a paisa on you?

GHISU: (*Sarcastically.*) Yes, why not! Like there is meat in an eagle's nest!

MADHAV: Let's go to Thakur Sahab.

Fade-out.

Scene 14

Ghisu, Madhav, Thakur, Munshi, Shopkeeper 1, Shopkeeper 2, Man 1, Man 2
(*Ghisu and Madhav arrive at the doorstep of Thakur.*)

THAKUR: What's the matter, Ghisuwa, why do you weep like this? And Madhav, where have you been hiding all these days? Haven't caught a glimpse of you father and son. Doesn't look like you want to live in the village.

GHISU: (*Crying.*) Sir! A huge calamity has befallen us, Sir. Madhav's woman passed away last night. We did everything we could—medicines, herbs, everything, but tricked us! Now, there is not even a soul to give us roti. We are destroyed, maalik. Sahab, the home has been uprooted. We are your slaves, maalik. Who else will give us refuge at this time? Who else will help send that poor woman home. Whatever was in our hands has been spent on her illness. Sarkar, now only with your generosity her corpse will be lifted. I swear by the dead woman that I won't go to anyone else's door than yours. You tell me maalik? How can I go to someone else?

MUNSHI: You're very kind, Sarkar, but you know that these two don't deserve any mercy. To pity them is like dyeing a black blanket. Send them away, maalik. When it's time to work, they don't even come on invitation. When they've been struck by lightning, look how earnestly he's begging! Rascal of the first order. Bloody scoundrel.

THAKUR: (*Gestures to Munshi to be quiet.*) This is not the time for anger and punishment.

(*Thakur throws two rupees at Ghisu and Madhav without looking at them. Munshi also throws some coins at them.*)

Chorus sings:

Manus sohi jaaniye
Jaahi vivek vichar
Jahi vivek vichar nahi
So nar dhor ganwar
The one who has wisdom and thoughtfulness is a human.
Without wisdom and thoughtfulness, a man is an idiot beating his own drum.

(*Outside the thakur's house, father and son talk loudly.*)

GHISU: Thakur Sahab has such a big heart. May all maaliks have a heart like his. If a large-hearted soul helps the poor to have a decent life after death, how can that soul not go to heaven! May God bless those who give, and may he also bless those who don't. Today we are hit by a catastrophe; who knows whose turn it will be tomorrow!

SHOPKEEPER 1: (*Gives some coins.*) Take this, Bhaiyya. I will help in whatever way I can.

SHOPKEEPER 2: (*Gives coins.*) Here, take this, Ghisu.

MAN 1: Bhaiyya, I don't have a paisa to give, but I have some grain and you're welcome to take some. The one who was destined to depart has left, but I'll do whatever I can for her soul.

MAN 2: I will bring some wood to the ghat.

Chorus sings:

Jahi vivek vichar nahi
So nar dhor ganwar

Scene 15

Madhav, Ghisu, shopkeepers, customers, Sahu, his assistant, vendors, drunk men, beggar
(*Madhav and Ghisu arrive in a corner of a bazaar.*)

MADHAV: Dadda, in less than an hour, we have collected five rupees.

GHISU: Here, why don't you give it to me? I'll keep it safely. Otherwise, they might slip.

MADHAV: I can keep it.

(Ignoring Madhav, Ghisu takes the money from him and places it in his kheesa, the long pocket across the front of the hand-woven shirt.)

GHISU: *(Jingles the coins in his kheesa.)* Say, Madhav, we've enough wood to burn her, don't we?

MADHAV: Yes, there's plenty of wood, now we just need to buy the kafan.

GHISU: Okay, let's go and get some cheap kafan then.

MADHAV: That makes sense. By the time we take the body, it will be night. Who will see her kafan in the dark?

GHISU: Ay Madhav, I keep thinking, what kind of evil tradition we follow: she did not get a rag to cover herself while she lived, but now that she is dead, she must be wrapped in a new kafan in order to be cremated!

MADHAV: Kafan simply burns with the body, doesn't it?

GHISU: What else? If we'd gotten the same five rupees in our hands a bit earlier, we could've bought medicine for her, couldn't we? It's hard to get over this world and its strange games!

Chorus sings:

Jahi vivek vichar nahi
So nar dhor ganwar

(Father and son wander in the bazaar, from this shop to that, looking at different kinds of fabrics for Budhiya's shroud.)

SHOPKEEPER 1: *(Opens a roll of fabric.)* Yes, yes, Bhaiyya, take a look.

GHISU: *(To Madhav.)* Why do they have so many different cloths for a kafan? When you live you are constantly teased, tempted, and tormented by all of this; when you die you get the choice of silk, malmal, khaddar, and who knows what! Someone has said it well—None fed him a grain of rice while he lived, but roasted delicacies became available when he died.

MADHAV: I thought dealing with life was hard. But dealing with death is so damn tough. These are quite the mind games, Dadda.

(Shopkeepers talk in the background.)

VOICE 1: Let's go, Bhaiyya. It's evening time. Time to call it a day.

VOICE 2: Let's wrap up the bazaar then, Bhaiyya.

(Shopkeepers fold up their stuff and prepare to leave.)

MADHAV: *(To Ghisu.)* You didn't approve a single kafan. Perhaps we should just get what is available. It's already evening. Who'll see the damn kafan in the evening?

GHISU: Yes, come on, let's take a look. Who'll see it in the evening?

MADHAV: It's evening time, Dadda. Where are you going? The cloth sellers are here, not there . . .

GHISU: Come, come. Come this way. It's a shorter way from here. It's evening now. (*Ghisu leads and Madhav follows.*)

GHISU: Keep coming this way. You see, it's evening now.

(*Father leads the son to the liquor house and the two walk in. They stand for a minute. Some men are drinking, others are in line to get their booze from Sahu. A vendor seated not too far from the Sahu is frying pooris. Another is cooking curried meat. Ghisu walks to the spot before the seller's seat, where a drunkard is standing in line.*)

GHISU: Sahu ji, hand me a bottle, too.

SAHU: (*To his assistant.*) Give him a kulhad. (*Sarcastically.*) He is asking for a bottle! (*To Ghisu.*) And where's the money?

GHISU: Yes, yes, take the money.

SAHU: (*Surprised, hands bottle to Ghisu. Turns to another seller.*) It appears that he has struck it rich today.

GHISU: Sahu ji, these earnings are halal, not haram. It's a game of heart and soul. Not everyone can play by its rules.

(*Father and son sit down to drink. Snacks come. They gulp down several cups in quick succession.*)

GHISU: What would've come out of wrapping her in a kafan? It would've just burned. It isn't like it would've accompanied Bahuriya.

MADHAV: The big people have money to burn. What do we have to burn? But Dadda, what'll we say to people? When they ask where the kafan is?

GHISU: (*Laughs.*) Abey, we'll say that the notes slipped out of the waist—we looked and looked everywhere, but we couldn't find them.

(*Madhav looks disbelievingly.*)

GHISU: They won't believe us, but then they're the ones who will give us the money.

MADHAV: She was such a good soul. Even in death, she made sure that we are well fed.

GHISU: (*Looks at the bottle.*) Only half remains now. Go, get another basket of poori. And don't forget the chutney, pickle, and liver.

(*Madhav dashes out to the vendor in front of the liquor house and brings everything in two leaf plates.*)

MADHAV: That cost a full rupee and a half. Very little money is left now. Eat, Dadda. They're really hot and crispy.

(*Both sit proudly and eat pooris.*)

GHISU: When our souls are getting happiness, wouldn't hers be blessed, too?

MADHAV: Yes, it will. For sure it will. Dear God Almighty, you know all the inner secrets and lies of humans. Nothing is hidden from you. Take her to heaven. We are both blessing her from our hearts. The kind of food we have eaten today, we have never known in our lives.

MADHAV: Say, Dadda. One day you and I will also go there, wouldn't we?

GHISU: (*To the audience.*) Why is he killing the joy of this life by thinking of the next?

MADHAV: If there she asks us why you didn't give me a kafan, then what'll I say?

GHISU: Like hell she'll ask!

MADHAV: Oh, she'll definitely ask.

GHISU: Arey, how do you know that she'll not get a kafan? You think I'm an idiot? I haven't dug grass in this world for sixty years. She'll get a kafan and a very nice one!

MADHAV: And who'll give her a kafan? You ate up all the money! She'll ask me, not you. It was I who wedded her.

GHISU: When I'm telling you that she'll get a kafan, why don't you listen to me?

MADHAV: Fine, so why don't you tell me who'll give it?

GHISU: The same people who gave us money last time will give again. With one difference—this time, the money won't be placed into our hands.

(*The energy of the liquor house is increasing. Someone is singing, another is bragging, yet another is embracing his companion. Someone is attaching a cup of liquor to another's mouth.*)

FIRST DRUNK: After coming here, the whole world seems different.

SECOND DRUNK: The soil of this place is intoxicating.

FIRST: Even the air is intoxicating. All you have to do is inhale.

SECOND: In one palm full this magic sucks all the pains and sorrows. Outside, I am engulfed in a hundred fears, but as soon as I enter this place, I don't even remember whether I'm living or dying. Or merely floating.

FIRST: For some time, everything is forgotten—curses, beatings, debts, starvation . . . all of it!

(*Everyone's eyes are focused on Ghisu and Madhav. Both are still sipping away.*)

THIRD DRUNK: Look, what kismat some people have!

ANOTHER: They are sitting with a whole bottle.

(*A beggar stands and stares at father and son. Madhav gives the leftover pooris to him.*)

GHISU: (*To the beggar.*) Eat to your heart's content, and give all the blessings you can. The one who has earned this is now dead, but your blessings will definitely reach her. Bless her with every breath. This came from extremely hard-earned money.

MADHAV: She will go to heaven, Dadda. My Budhiya will become the queen of heaven.

GHISU: (*Stands up.*) You are right, Son, she will go to heaven. She never mistreated or crushed anyone, never caused anyone pain. Even in death she fulfilled my biggest wish. If she doesn't go to heaven, would these fat people go? These people who steal from the poor with both hands while they live and then go and take a dip in the Ganga and pour water over shrines to wash away their sins?

MADHAV: But Dadda, the poor thing suffered too much in life. She died in so much pain.

(*Madhav lets out tearful screams.*)

GHISU: Why do you cry, Son? Be happy that she became free of this world, got rid of all the chains. She was very fortunate that she could break these worldly bonds so quickly.

A tune emerges, and each actor sings from their own location:

Hansa karo puratan baat
Hansa karo puratan baat
Kaun des se aaya hansa, utare kaun se ghat
Kahan hansa bisram kare hai, kahan lagaye aas
Hansa karo puratan baat
Abahin hansa chet sabera
Abahin hansa chet sabera
Chalo hamare sath
Sansaya sok wahan nahi byape, nahi kaal ke traas
Hansa karo puratan baat
Hansa karo puratan baat
O pure consciousness of the soul, O Hansa, reflect on the ancient truth of your everlasting bonds.
From which land have you emerged? On which bank will you descend as you move beyond this life? Where will you halt and where will you focus your hope?
O Hansa, wake up early so that you can accompany me to that place. The place where there is no sorrow, no suspicion, no fear, nor pain of death.
O Hansa, reflect on your ancient truth.

Fade-out.

Entangled Scripts and Bodies
Theater as Pedagogy

My attempt to translate *Hansa, Karo Puratan Baat* from Awadhi into English is far from perfect. The flavor of its metaphors vanishes in the absence of its own soil. In trying to do justice to the nuances of class, caste, and place that are relayed with emotional and political intensity, what is lost is the passionate playfulness of language with which the group collectively created the play through improvisation over a six-month period. Even as I flow with the poetry and rhythm of the languages I have grown up with, I discover their layered nuances every day through collective journeys with Parakh and SKMS. My saathis make me keenly aware of the ways in which language becomes wrapped up in the meanings of bodies, marked, haunted, and made again and again by caste, gender, status, time, and place. Here, I move from the script to the process of co-learning that created the play, in order to both carry across and retell the embodied and psychological journeys that made the emergence of *Hansa* a transformative journey for each one of us who became a part of its creation.[1]

. . .

> I haven't read much about . . . 'the Dalit question,' but
> I lived Savarna-Dalit politics in my village . . . for more
> than two decades . . . Premchand wrote "Kafan" in 1935
> and here we are in 2014 in Mumbai . . . As an [often]
> unemployed actor from Hardoi [rural Uttar Pradesh],
> I feel that most of us in this room are no different
> than Ghisu or Madhav. We are the chamars of today's
> Bollywood and they are the chamars of rural UP . . .[2]

Twenty actors who come from very different locations in the world, and most of whom are largely unfamiliar with or uninvested in the nuances of academic or political discourses, become actively involved in building situated solidarities through their immersion in the lives of Budhiya, Ghisu, and Madhav, characters that were created by Premchand almost eight decades ago. Their deeply aware engagement with "Kafan" requires from them identification, disidentification, and intense sociopolitical reflection—within and across spatial and temporal borders as well as the borders of their own bodies—individually and collectively. In this process of engaging the story and transforming it into a play, each actor's journey becomes co-constitutively creative, intellectual, and political. Their prolonged embodied immersion in the bodies, contexts, and psyches of Ghisu, Madhav, Budhiya, Thakur, Taka, Khilawan, Dhankun and the rest gives birth to a passionate and dynamic process of creation, reflection, and reinterpretation where ethics, aesthetics, performance, and politics become inseparable. Early on in the journey, the team ceases to articulate its vision as one that is focused on doing justice to what Premchand, the author, may have intended. Instead, all the actors begin imagining their responsibility in terms of whether, how, and to what extent they can ethically come to know and to *be* Ghisu, Madhav, Budhiya, Thakur, and others through their collective creativity.

Of the twenty-six people who participated in the intensive journey that translated "Kafan" into *Hansa* over a course of six months, nineteen—including the workshop facilitator, Tarun—have migrated to Mumbai from rural areas of Uttar Pradesh, Madhya Pradesh, Haryana, Bihar, Jharkhand, Chhattisgarh, Karnataka, and Gujarat.[3] While half of them identify as upper caste or Savarna, the other half identifies as Dalit, Dalit Muslim, Adivasi, or OBCs. Although the majority of these actors aspire to make a successful career in the film industry, five provide domestic help in the homes of film and television artists in the Yari Road area and had never seen a play before participating in the workshop.[4]

In what follows, I entangle the translated script of *Hansa* with more 'scripts' that relive some of the intensity and complexity of the collective process of its making. These scripts emanate from the journals, discussions, rehearsals, and relationships that constituted the workshop. Even without pretending to be systematic or comprehensive, these scripts give an acute sense of the kind of pedagogical moments the workshop offered to each one who participated in the journey, and the ways in which it impacted us emotionally and shaped how we understood ourselves as politically aware artists and beings.

The journals were a relatively small but significant part of the learning process of the group, and actors wrote them as and when they could, with an intention of reflecting through them when possible, and sharing them for advancing the pedagogical and creative labor of Parakh. I encouraged the actors to keep a journal from the outset, and I also did some journaling with them when I co-facilitated the meetings with Tarun in July, August, and December. However, I laid out no specific expectations in terms of requirements, themes, issues, frequency, or length of entries. Each actor decided on their own whether, when, and to what degree they wished to grapple in writing with questions that were arising for them as "Kafan" slowly reemerged as *Hansa*. Sometimes these written and unwritten questions evolved from collective conversations, and sometimes they were part of an actor's inner journey with the story and the workshop. Once or twice, those who had little or no formal literacy dictated their reflections to another coactor, but their engagements with diary writing were limited. For one participant, Sajjan (alias), the journal writing became an incentive to learn how to read and write: his entire journal became a beautiful calligraphy where he learned the Devnagri script by writing and rewriting sentences from the play's emerging dialogue. After the first four shows of the play in December 2014, a handful of actors shared with me photocopied selections from their handwritten journals, while Tarun began a long e-mail dialogue with me to process his reflections. The photocopied fragments ranged from one page each by Anil and Roshan and four pages each by Meena and Mumtaz, to three fat notebooks by Alok. Regardless of the length of what was shared, each page was a precious gift: an actor's contribution toward honing the future journeys of Parakh.

Given the range of what was shared, it can be a worthwhile project to consider how different actors express parts of their journeys with *Hansa* on paper. Here, however, I focus on those written fragments that wrestle with the nuances of the relationships and co-imagination that defined the group's collective journey with *Hansa*. For example, while Tarun's comments provide crucial insights into the vision of alternative aesthetics and politics that guide Parakh's journey with *Hansa*, Alok, a long-time diary writer, is the only actor whose journal offers an ongoing meditation on the process of making *Hansa* from the time of his entry into the group in July until the end of the workshop in December. Most of the shared fragments by actors focus on how the workshop moves them as individuals; the translated excerpts I share from Gaurav's diary give a sense of such turmoil. Alok, by contrast, is the only diary writer who grapples consistently with the conversations unfolding with his coactors, the story's characters, and with Tarun in his role as facilitator. Much is said in academic literature about embodiment and affect in relation to the work of solidarity; however, rarely do we get a palpable sense of how embodiment and affect shape the journeys of co-travelers in a thoroughly entwined process of unlearning and relearning through radical vulnerability. The pieces of diaries I offer in translation give some glimpses of such journeys.

The Challenge Called "Kafan"

The Hunter's Net

When the workshop begins in June 2014, neither Tarun, nor Mumtaz, nor I know where it will go.[5] People hear about it through word of mouth and every day two or three new faces join in for the reading of the stories. On the third day, we take turns reading aloud several stories by Premchand, Ismat Chughtai, and Kamleshwar. "Kafan" is one of these stories. While the group enjoys all of the stories, there is something about the gut reaction several women and men have toward "Kafan" that Tarun and I find both disturbing and challenging. Sanjukta (alias), who often boasts about her literary sophistication, says, "I feel like taking out my sandals and giving it hard on the heads of Ghisu and Madhav." A young man, Rahul (alias), chimes in, "I want to slap the rascals." Two others say how in this day and age you don't see such "heartless rogues even in the villages of Uttar Pradesh and Bihar."

I am struck by how confidently people assume they already know everything about Ghisu and Madhav, and how their assumptions allow them to imagine scenarios beyond what is offered in the story, and to form opinions that foreclose the possibility of the two men being anything other than the most inhuman characters imaginable. Their interpretations of the story disengage with the ethical responsibility of the reader as the receiver of the story. The pain and restlessness I feel at that absence makes me eager to embrace "Kafan" as the focus of the group's creative work through Parakh. A similar turbulence pulls Tarun as a facilitator of the theater workshop. He reflects in his e-journal:

"I found it curious how several people who came to the workshop in the early days responded to the story initially; but then the theatrical games and methodology through which the layers of the story unfolded before us seemed to surprise all of us. A new person joining the group would often begin with, 'I already know this story.' Yet, those who were already there and were reading the same story over and over again for several days were finding that every single day a new fold of the story was unpeeled before them. Then the new readers of the story would also start immersing themselves in this intoxicating process of uncovering new layers beyond their previous readings. My faith in this work was inspired precisely when I witnessed that thirst of the newcomers to continue to journey with the story in order to achieve these new meanings together. Whatever I suggested to my saathi co-artists, they would begin working on it with remarkable intensity. Some of them initially said they could come only for a few days, but once they started swimming in the story and the process, things would change dramatically. It was probably when the visitors started becoming addicted to the nectar that they decided to stay in the workshop and became the co-creators of *Hansa*."

Hunger, Death, and Life

As the workshop evolves, the responsibility of ethically translating "Kafan" into *Hansa* becomes an all-consuming passion for the collective. *Hansa* becomes a play that starts with one kind of hunger, and as it evolves, it embraces more hungers, and becomes a reflection of life itself. In this creative labor, all workshop participants become researchers and thinkers of life. The workshop becomes a process of engaging with all that is alive, with all that infuses us, shapes us, and theorizes us—often without our knowing—so that we may reach a deeper meaning of what it means to exist and be beyond the systems of thought available to us. The process of collective creation demands that all the actors learn to interrogate, suspend, and even erase their inherited positions on all kinds of *isms*, including socialism, feminism, casteism, and elitism. It is only by each one immersing oneself completely into this process that the collective can hope to grasp the meanings of hunger, death, and life that emerge in the story. Significantly, the group begins to see its responsibility not as one that can do justice to Premchand's "Kafan," but as one that can do justice to the story of Budhiya, Ghisu, and Madhav, but without changing their embeddedness in the details of the original story.

The ways in which death is framed and handed down to us forces us to respond to it through modes that are consistent with the demands of the systems we live in. We learn from our society how to mourn and ritualize the end of a life, as well as when and how to make peace with death. Those journeying with "Kafan" must confront through an embodied and shared process of action and reflection that it is not in fact 'natural' for all of us to stay within that framework, and how crucial it is to push ourselves to breathe beyond its regulations.

Tarun asks the actors, "How many of us can claim to actually understand the warlike social conditions in which Ghisu and Madhav were living?" As the actors grapple with this question day after day, they learn to disentangle themselves from the pregiven social meanings and deployments of such concepts as baikunthh and narak, heaven and hell. Along with Tarun, they struggle with the last scene of the story that Premchand ends with the song, 'Thagini kyon nayana matkave' (Temptress don't seduce me with your playful eyes). Even as they decide on an alternative song in *Hansa*, Tarun continues to feel like it is an ending that the "literate" world of literature and theater has imposed on Ghisu, Madhav, and Budhiya. Tarun comments, "I do not know what Ghisu would have really done at the end of the story. I can't say whether the ending that Premchand gave, or the one that we gave in the play, would work for Ghisu as a conclusion to this story. My journey with this question will always continue."

Each one of us begins to delve deeper into the moments when we have accompanied the process of dying in intimate settings, and our sleep vanishes for days. We think of those moments when someone near and dear to us was lying close by, as when Budhiya was lying close to Madhav and Ghisu, and what we were able or unable to do for them. As we bring back our own churnings into the workshop, each participant steps in bravely to create a space of radical vulnerability and to reflect on the complex meanings of death, dying, and living. Tarun articulates this for his co-travelers:

"In all of our lives, there come moments of great challenge and we all accept the truth of those moments; we take them in stride without sitting down to contemplate them rigorously. We often recognize full well the reality of the social or political situations that we are thrown into and accordingly we do whatever we can for our nearest and dearest. No matter whose life we are fighting and praying for, there comes a time when even the most accomplished doctor gives up and says, 'You can only ask for the duas of the gods now.' At that point even if we are the richest person on earth, we understand and, eventually, accept that even if the person whose life we are praying for is in the intensive care unit, the best we can do is hover near them. In that situation, much like Ghisu's and Madhav's in 'Kafan,' the teemardar who is looking after their loved one also has to take care of their own belly. None of us can compromise our stomach's hunger for too long, and how long one can confront starvation would depend on the physical state of our body. It would be quite silly, wouldn't it, to question Ghisu's and Madhav's sensitivity toward Budhiya simply on the basis of the fact that they were extremely hungry and those stolen potatoes were their lifeline in that same moment of starvation when Budhiya was also dying?

"Have you ever gone to a cremation ground or a burial? If you have, you will have witnessed something like this: not too long after a funeral pyre is lit, people begin to joke around. Sometimes they even invoke the dead person and say if the dead person would look at them she would laugh at their sad faces and ask them to take a break! I don't state this lightly: this is what people do. It's only when a writer or filmmaker tries too hard to narrate or dramatize these normal realities that we tend to put all of our intelligence and critical faculties into excessively evaluating and questioning such representations. It is important to see everything in gray. There is simultaneously a great villain and a great hero in each one of us and the duty of the actor or artist is to live that gray honestly in our performance. Premchand's 'Kafan' is an invitation to his readers to confront this truth of our human psyche and existence."

What does it mean, then, to revisit the meanings of life through death? The opening scene of the play is one of a hungry father and son who have not eaten anything for two days but are not defeated. When Madhav says to Ghisu that he is dying of starvation, Ghisu immediately reminds him that he is not dead yet. Ghisu is signaling a key fact of the lives of two men, whose battle with the stomach's hunger must continue until they breathe their last: if we are not yet dead, there is a lot that still exists in our share. The play depicts Madhav as a young man who is trying to learn a few tricks to survive with dignity in a world where he and his father are humiliated and mistreated every day. He wants to absorb the rich wisdom that his father offers about life. As he learns the tricks of survival through what the mainstream calls 'deceit,' Ghisu tries to cover for the errors his son makes in that process of learning.

Living is complicated by the web of relationships in which each of us is entangled, and doing justice to Ghisu, Madhav, Budhiya, Thakur, and others involves factoring this into the creative process of transforming "Kafan" into *Hansa*. Accordingly, in the scene where Ghisu confronts the thakur's man, Taka, for paying him only half of his wage, he and Madhav are beaten up by their own saathis, but when they cross their limit, Ghisu screams at them to ensure his own and his son's safety, and the saathis step back. Then, on a different night, father and son sing and dance with the same people, including Taka, and the same Taka invites them again for work, and the scene of them being chased away by the thakur with the help of the same saathis repeats itself. In developing these layers of the story, the play tries to go beyond a superficial engagement with exploitation, and even beyond personal animosities or grudges. It points to an overtly stabilized system of co-living, one where the socially powerful and resourceful class is exploiting the mazdoors and also using the same mazdoors to register its opposition to Ghisu's and Madhav's way of living and surviving. The mazdoors also function within this shared sphere of understanding and co-living. There is not a simple enmity between the thakur and Ghisu; as the one wielding the power, Thakur must refuse to accept Ghisu's and Madhav's way of life, which provides a terrifying critique of the power that Thakur represents. Yet all of this happens in the course of life serendipitously, and our acts of translation as writer, actor, facilitator, and reader must embrace this challenge as well. Without embracing this challenge, we can never fathom why it is so hard to untangle the suffocating webs of the Hindu brahmanical patriarchal order.

At the same time, when Budhiya dies, the same thakur who has repeatedly mistreated Ghisu and Madhav tells Taka, "This is not the time for anger and punishment." Premchand has not wasted any words in this seven-page story. In these words, taken directly from the story, the writer opens a possibility for a relationship between human beings at a level that rises above that of the system that governs the relationship between Thakur as the landlord and Ghisu as a Dalit mazdoor who is dependent on him. If we see the labor of ethical translation as one where the possibilities of what the text can do for justice are in fact created in and through responsible receiving and interpretation, then this line offers a rich opportunity for carrying out that work. The distance between belief and disbelief, between what might be believable and what is absurd or unbelievable always tends to be a tiny one. It is the creative and political obligation of the artist to learn to travel that distance in search of justice.

If we expect Ghisu and Madhav to behave toward the dying Budhiya in neat and clean ways prescribed by a previously inherited idea of 'wrong' or 'right,' we are likely to only focus on a fixed definition of ethics defined in terms of the two men's individual goodness or lack thereof. We miss out on an alternative ethic in the form of a powerful structural critique that father and son enact against all sorts of systemic power in "Kafan" and that Budhiya, too, brings to life in *Hansa*. This systemic critique encompasses casteism, classism, patriarchy, as well as prevailing logics of the social and religious order. The process of creating *Hansa* and the openings offered by the story push the actors to confront the double-sidedness of all humans, and the ways that every human being has an implicit or explicit desire to control. The actors also begin to interrogate their own eagerness to be seen as socially or politically correct. Becoming a good actor in and through *Hansa*, then, becomes contingent on internalizing and embodying the truth of the shared humanity and inhumanity that define Ghisu, Thakur, and each one of us. As the group grapples with these layers that erase the differences between their own psyches and that of *Hansa*'s characters, Tarun notes: "Even as a very ordinary human, Ghisu is extraordinary in the ways that he is able to rule his own life despite his very debilitating circumstances. He wants to make sure that his son learns that skill, too. Ghisu's approach to life cannot be reduced simply to his material poverty or his caste. He is much more than that—he is a betaj baadshah, a crownless king, of his own life. For his son, Madhav, he is the ultimate hero, and this is not insignificant."

Collapsing Distances

In Mumbai, where 'struggler' is a common term for actors who seek work in the film and media industry, artists do not have any time to waste. Although the practice of giving honoraria for theater workshops is almost unknown in Mumbai, Mumtaz, Tarun, and I conclude early on that in the absence of a monthly stipend it would be impossible to build a collective space for actors to work together over several months. It is determined that I should use my research funds to pay a monthly honorarium of 5,000 rupees to each participant who commits their labor to making *Hansa* with Parakh, but that the provision of honoraria should not compromise in any way the group's control over its own creative process. The fact that fourteen of the twenty-four weeks of the workshop coincide with my fall semester teaching in Minnesota proves infinitely helpful in minimizing my direct interference in the everyday process. At the same time, the group asks me to remain connected with what is evolving through daily contact by Skype and phone. Interestingly, professional actors such as Alok, Bhagwan Das, and Gaurav, who face major economic hardships in the film industry, continue with the workshop for five to six months, but not because of these stipends. Instead, they are hooked on *Hansa* because of the process of discovery that is pushing them in unanticipated ways, even if this creative intoxication jeopardizes their chances of obtaining an acting assignment in a film. Tarun notes: "Despite the grave economic circumstances that each professional actor in the workshop faced, I don't think economic reasons were sufficient motivation for people to walk together during the long course of the workshop. Even those who joined the workshop quite late and without any promise of a stipend remained with the group's demanding process until the end, simply out of their passion. Whatever they did receive in the form of stipends in the end was not expected in advance."

At the heart of the process is the actors' collective intellectual and emotional commitment to collapse the distance between their own locations and those of the characters they are playing. During the course of reading "Kafan," Tarun's pedagogical labor centers on facilitating the actors' reading about the worlds of Ghisu, Madhav, and Budhiya with a generosity and openness. Rather than fixing the story in the lenses of a named class or caste, or time or place, the group reflects on how similar stories unfold in each of their own everyday lives—whether it is in the life of a Bai who has immigrated from Karnataka and who works as a cleaner and cook, or in the life of an actor who has left behind his family and village in Uttar Pradesh to come find work and, hopefully, stardom in Mumbai.

Actors quickly see parallels between their own lives and those of Madhav's and Ghisu's: "Don't we hear from the producers year after year the same things that Ghisu and Madhav heard from the thakur and Taka? That there is work for sure, but there's very little budget to pay for that work! And we actors work year after year for little or no money." Tarun asks them to linger further on this point: the relatively recent establishment of the Film Actors' Association ensures some payment but even so, the payment is made only after ninety days, which allows film producers to continue to take advantage of the huge desperation of the laboring actors. How do those actors pay the rents of their tiny overpriced rooms? How do they "decorate themselves on empty pockets" and pretend to look happy and bright as they desperately look for new work every day? How do casting directors become Taka Bhaiyyas and take advantage of their circumstances? This is what so many actors, writers, and technicians live in the film industry moment after moment, year after year.

Such intensive discussions feed into a six-month process of improvisation and allow the actors to delve into the meanings of being human in a complex social, economic, and psychological world they share with the characters of *Hansa*. During this exploration, Tarun introduces the scenes where we see Taka Bhaiyya in seemingly contradictory positions. In one scene, he serves in his capacity as the thakur's man, showering sticks on the bodies of Ghisu and Madhav—and, ironically, they are expecting and accepting those thrashes. In another scene, Taka joins the mazdoors he disciplines, and all of them, including Ghisu and Madhav, entertain themselves by bantering and dancing together at night. "After all, the father and son won't go to another village to find entertainment, right?" remarks Tarun. "There are parallels here between Taka and the casting director to whom the exploited actors give their 'cut,' *and* who is also the person whom they invite to join them for evening dinners in the hopes of finding another acting assignment!"

Meena, Mumtaz, Anil, and Sajjan point out the limitations of a discussion that merely draws parallels with the acting industry. They remind the group of the thakurs and Takas who are present in the space of the workshop, and who employ Bais to work in their homes and expect them to cook and clean for them without fail seven days a week. When that same Bai misses a day, there is no shortage of people who will deduct that day's wage from her meager monthly payment. So many actors and artists engage in the big talk of helping society through their visionary artistry or charitable work, but when it comes to paying their domestic worker, they count every paisa before handing over their monthly payment. Even the thought of asking these people to pay for a domestic worker's health or their children's schooling is considered ludicrous. If this is how our contradictory system defined by casteism, communalism, and patriarchy works, then how can one honestly label as "deceit" or "laziness" the little bit of lying one must do in order to steal some hours to breathe or be with one's children or lover or family or friends?

As participants dwell on these questions, they also reflect together on how migrating from a small village or town to a giant city such as Mumbai changes attitudes and insights about caste and the gendered practices of labor. A pundit from the village becomes a watchman in Mumbai. The wife of a rural migrant goes to someone's home to cook, and if a need arises, she also learns to do all the washing and cleaning because she will earn something for that labor that she cannot earn elsewhere. She may not have done the same work in her own village because, in the context of the social values determined for her there, her only choice might have been to die hungry with her social status intact.

Her movement away from her village, however, changes the system of labor, shaped by the system of caste. This is what the journey was like for Mumtaz and Meena, who migrated from rural areas of Karnataka and Gujarat and now work in the homes of actors and producers here in Mumbai. In Sajjan's village, who would have thought that he would one day go thousands of kilometers away to Mumbai to take care of someone's three dogs? Did he ever imagine himself in this situation, or prepare himself for it?

As the participants revisit every sentence of the story collectively, over and over again, each finds the circumstances of mazdoors, of Thakur, of Taka Bhaiyya, and even of Budhiya, very close to their own. The intense connections they feel with the characters who breathe in "Kafan" help them determine what it might mean to do justice to their story.

Unlearning Caste

Ghisu is a sharp critic of his society. Doing justice to "Kafan" means grappling consistently with his character. The actor must immerse oneself in imagining everything that may account for the knotty layers of sociopolitical analysis as well as everyday wisdom of living and surviving that Ghisu offers.

"Who knows," Tarun once asks the participants, "if Ghisu, on the strength of his own revolutionary spirit and his nuanced analysis of the intricate relationships between the upper caste landlord and the Dalit mazdoor, could have stepped out of his village today?" Intimately aware of every pulse of the Savarnas—who are almost always in the position to give work and living wages to mazdoors but who almost never do it—it is entirely possible that Ghisu may have become an important political leader of this country today, eighty years after Premchand created the character. Then how would his caste or community figure in our thinking? What would it mean to do justice to that Ghisu who we may encounter not as a hungry Dalit mazdoor but a cosmopolitan revolutionary? Premchand persistently emphasizes Ghisu's sharp foresight and uncompromising social analysis, but if the reader or actor receives Ghisu merely as 'a cruel chamar,' that problem cannot be laid at the door of the writer. It is the receiver of the story who has failed to read and embody Ghisu with the generosity and imagination that his circumstances and statements demand.

The group works extremely hard to begin to feel the characters without becoming caged in the dominant terminologies and paradigms that flatten the complexities of the caste system. If jatiwaad, casteism, is a social poison, several members agree in the discussions, then we all pay a huge price for living and supporting this toxic system—how do we recognize that price? If we want to dismantle a society that is nourished by the caste poison, what might it mean to eject that poison entirely from our thinking systems? As the saying goes, "Grab your enemy by the neck—otherwise, if you place your arms in your foe's arms, then it doesn't take much for the enemy to take over." What might the work of grabbing caste by the neck mean in the context of doing justice to Budhiya, Ghisu, and Madhav?

Just Aesthetics

The collective labor of twenty bodies who make *Hansa* is at once analytical, emotional, physical, and psychological. In evolving this all-consuming translation of hungers, life, and death, the group also searches to articulate its shared aesthetics and ethics. Tarun's words give a sense of what this labor looks like:

"My saathis in this work were women and men who came from many different regions, languages, and social backgrounds. Yet, [in the beginning one could see] the tendency of associating with someone in accordance with their pregiven social status. For example, in order for all of us to work intensively together, it was necessary for us to have each other's numbers, so we exchanged numbers. However, no one took Mumtaz's phone number for four or five days after the workshop began. I first observed quietly and then said openly—'If instead of Mumtaz a model had come to join us, then everyone would be competing aggressively to get her number . . . and she would have acted all arrogant and pricey . . . but because we have Mumtaz instead of a model, no one cared to ask her for her number?' That was probably the first time when people registered that there was some other 'play' going on in the workshop that was bigger than the play they had assumed they had come to create: in addition to the dramatic performance, there were profoundly linked sociopolitical issues and attitudes at stake."

Gaurav sketches out some of the contours of this other 'play' that made the actors rethink their prior assumptions about who each of them was and what was at stake in the relationships that were forming in and around the rehearsals. He notes, "[Sajjan] does not know how to read, but he learned the play by heart just by absorbing everything that was unfolding. One day, after we were done improvising the whole story, we did a full run through in the group. On the next day, however, none of us could remember those nuances or transitions. That is, none except for [Sajjan]. [Sajjan] remembered one scene after another with startling precision. I realized then that [Sajjan] had been more deeply involved in the process than any one else." Gaurav slowly sheds his previously held beliefs about Sajjan as a nonactor. He recalls: "One day Sumit just couldn't say his lines, so [Sajjan] stepped in and recited all of Sumit's lines without pause, and with perfect texture and tone. Then one day [during the opening scene], I teased [Sajjan in Awadhi, a language he is only beginning to learn with us], 'O Maikuwa, look your bride has taken off!' [I had replaced the water buffalo with bride]. At that time, the spontaneous expression that he gave in response was miraculous! [Sajjan] is changing—in his clothes, in his manner, in his poise. He's becoming more and more a city person, [a Mumbaiwala]. . . . One day, he was rehearsing with me and Anil began to correct him. [Sajjan] reacted sharply and said [in perfect Hindi], his eyes gleaming with confidence, 'You work on you. I will manage me.'"

The process of unlearning and relearning for Gaurav did not entail simply coming to appreciate what Sajjan, Anil, Mumtaz, and Meena had to offer. Even as he came to admire each of them, Gaurav felt challenged by them in unantici- pated ways, and this rattled him. Gaurav's journey as Madhav with Mumtaz as Budhiya, proved particularly difficult for him; Mumtaz's presence intimidated Gaurav, but he persisted:

"For me, working with Mumtaz ji is the biggest challenge. . . . After doing demanding physical work all day when she gives herself fully to the rehearsal and when after the rehearsal she says that she is headed to two more places to cook, I begin to sweat. . . . One day Mumtaz ji started scolding me, 'Why do you get stuck while doing the scene with me? Why do you stop in the middle of your sentences?' I stammered that it was important for me to take the pauses, but she was not listening. I was slowly able to explain myself to her, and she agreed to let me have my pauses. One day I suggested to Mumtaz ji that [in Budhiya's role] she might like to try speaking with an Awadhi flavor. She asked curiously, 'you mean, the Bhaiyya tongue?' I smiled at her, 'yes,' and she started working on her 'Bhaiyya' tongue in earnest. To tell the truth, I am scared of Mumtaz ji. She gets sharp and angry with me. Yet, I am full of admiration. I see her becoming more and more a Budhiya now. The scene when she reenacts her labor pains is really powerful. What a great sense of timing she has."

Meena, too, pushes Gaurav by becoming a close friend and critic, something he never expected: "Meena ji walks back with me after rehearsals at night, and she is always humming songs as we talk. I was out of form for several days, so Meena ji chided me, 'What happened to you, eh? Why do you get stuck so much while acting. Where is your head these days?' I was at a loss for words. I could not tell her openly about the phase I was going through [with respect to my health] and what it took for me to just maintain my continuity [in this workshop]."

The workshop stirs Gaurav. One night he returns from the rehearsal and writes on the pages of his notebook a letter to me, trying to communicate that which the workshop is making him rethink about his own past and people:

"I'd only read the story 'Kafan' before; I had not felt 'Kafan' before. . . . I am from a baniya family in the Hardoi district of Uttar Pradesh, where a boundary is always kept intact between the dominant and subordinated castes. I am talking about the kind of space where the [Dalit] woman who washes the dirty utensils of my family takes off her slippers before she enters the door. I am talking about a place where when she is given something to eat, it is offered on piece of newspaper or in a 'retired' vessel.

. . . Since I am looking for work in films, my grandmother tells me that I can marry any girl I want as long as she is not a chamar or paasi. This kind of casteism against Dalits has been created by my own [Savarna] ancestors. . . . I have loved a Muslim girl. Once I took her with me to a family event. There was such an uproar. My folks beat me up while [her] relatives also tried to hunt me down. This went on with both of us for six months. [I remember this when I see] . . . how Yasmin ji and Patel Saheb have become so attached to us. . . . At first, Yasmin ji used to only come and watch our rehearsal for a short time, hand over the chai, and leave. [On the day when all of us enacted the scene of labor pains], however, she became hooked to the rehearsals. Something about Budhiya's labor pains grabbed Yasmin ji's heart, and now she is there for the entire duration of rehearsals. I feel that one reason Yasmin ji connects so intimately to us now is because of the anomalous story that 'Kafan' is. It shakes everyone because it tells about the brutal doublefacedness of the world we are socialized into."

As someone who accompanied each participant in significant moments and phases of their journey with "Kafan," Tarun remarked in his post-workshop reflections, "To expect that the social knots accumulated from years of life would vanish in a period of six months would be immature; still, our collective undertaking took the work of loosening those knots seriously. Some rules were also established and underlined—for example, we agreed that the collective will work to not turn every disagreement or error into a moralistic competition trapped in the vocabulary of 'right' and 'wrong.' We also considered our choices in our everyday spoken language: is it possible to frame what we are saying in slightly richer terms? Is the word or phrase we are using the most appropriate word or phrase available to us to convey the nuances we are discovering, or is there an alternative expression that might work better? When we act, then all this sociopolitical and aesthetic labor becomes absorbed in the challenging responsibility of acting. When our search for something new and creative is not confined merely to our own narrowly and individualistically defined work, then that search permeates everything we do in life. Only then does it become possible for us to make our life's vision more open and multi-dimensional. This vision, in turn, is what makes our aesthetics and our politics, as well as our ability to transform that which is not just or ethical into something that is.

Swimming with *Hansa*

Arriving

Alok Panday, Bhagwan Das, who is affectionately called BD, and Tarun meet in May 2014 on the set of *Prem Ratan Dhan Paayo* when the three land acting assignments in that film.[6] Despite Alok and BD's distance in age from Tarun, there is a magical spark of connectivity among them—maybe it's their shared language, maybe it's their passion for acting, or maybe it's their origins in rural North India that link many migrants from the 'Hindi belt' in Bollywood, regardless of when they join the community of 'strugglers.' While chatting during the shoot one day, Alok and BD find out that Tarun is co-organizing a theater workshop in the Yari Road area where BD and Alok also happen to live. After the shoot wraps up, the three return to Mumbai and lose touch with one another, but several weeks later, on 12 July, BD calls Alok excitedly, "Hey, come along. Tarun ji is about to start his workshop."

Alok stalls for two or three days. He can't put his heart into the idea. Six days later, though, he hesitatingly shows up at the gate of Tefla's Studio at 129 Aram Nagar. Little does he know that the space in which he is about to enter would consume him completely and six months will pass by in a flash. Alok notes in his journal: "On the first day . . . I hadn't imagined that I would go there regularly. But once I entered, I was so absorbed in the intensity of that environment. The workshop was intoxicating. . . . Sitting at home, one can think all one wants to about acting, but you can never truly prepare yourself rigorously. This is something I realized after coming here. Body control, breath, relaxation—I was losing the deeper meanings of all of these words [until I found them again here]."

Observing

From the beginning, Alok is keenly aware of his co-participants. There is BD, whom Alok already admires for his dedication to acting, but in the workshop Alok comes to appreciate BD's thoughtfulness as a profound observer of life. Then, there is Anil, the young man who is about four and a half feet tall, who always seems to be in some kind of hurry, and who, with his continuous bursts of rare energy, comes into the workshop space with an unusual eagerness to learn something. Alok notes that everyone is in a rush to speak and share their insights after each reading of the story, and questions are often thrown at Anil, who does not quite comprehend where they are coming from. One day, Sanjay Tripathi shreds Anil to pieces with his sharp and pointed arrows, and Anil, entirely unsure of how to respond, only smiles back.

The interaction between Anil and Sanjay allows Alok to understand some of the goals of the workshop he did not reflect on earlier. Those who are full of arrogance about their own knowledge often cannot check themselves; they quickly attack the other person they think knows less than them. As an actor, Sanjay's attitude toward Anil made Alok reflect critically on his own—"Somehow [those who are supposedly more learned] find it imperative to make the other recognize that 'look, you've got this wrong' . . . I really felt like saying something [to the others who were attacking Anil], but I decided that this would be my lesson for today: learn from another's mistake without raising a finger at their errors."

Embodying

Alok becomes entangled in acting in a way he has not known before. He feels himself responding to the workshop in unanticipated ways. Three days after joining the workshop, he writes: "Today . . . there was more energy than ever. . . . There were several new people today. After [reading the story and] much discussion, we started improvising the scene of Thakur's wedding procession and I sat in the pangat with others to eat. . . . Then I threw up. It was rather spontaneous and took me by complete surprise. During the scene of eating at the feast, I remembered a drunkard in my village: Rajaram Chamar. In my village, too, people are fed in pangats, and I have seen how there are people who drink so much that they puke right there, and then they are chased away from the feast. I was remembering the faces of many men, characters from my village whose faces come alive for me, as do their actions. So during that scene, I remembered a feast in my village with all of these people present. [Something stirred in me then.] That's how the vomiting incident occurred."

Later, Tarun's comments in the workshop lead Alok to dwell on the encounter between Madhav and Pundit. Here, Madhav must both realize and satirize: "Pundit ji, if it gets touched by me, it will become impure for you, wouldn't it?" In this situation, someone from Madhav's location would himself maintain the gap, even as he resents it. The distance, then, cannot merely come from the language. The simultaneity of the social response he has inherited and his satirical questioning of it must both be reflected in his body and his language. Working on this scene stirs Alok's memory: once a man bought a samosa in a shop in Shahjahanpur, and the owner of the dhaba said, "Come inside and sit." So that man said, "Arey, nahin, nahin. This is fine." Yet, everyone knew what he was saying; the man was communicating through his words and gestures that he should not sit inside because he is untouchable. The tragic irony of this exchange is what must come to life in the interaction between Madhav and the pundit while also keeping in mind the specificities of Madhav's situation. Can I do justice to this, Alok asks himself?

The methodology of the workshop pushes Alok to mobilize his memories and feelings through his body, while also alerting him that he should not impose them in unjust ways on the characters of the story. Once when BD and Sanjay Yadav are improvising the scene where Ghisu and Madhav are roasting the potatoes they have stolen, Alok feels that the rhythm between the two has quickly taken the scene off track. Ghisu starts reflecting sympathy for Madhav. He also shows great concern for Budhiya. Alok sees that the actor, Sanjay, has decided how he wants to enact the scene. This is the problem of the actor. Sanjay has decided how 'I' as Sanjay should interpret and enact Ghisu's actions. This is the actor's I, then, not the character's I. Then Suleiman enacts the same scene with a newcomer and Tarun reminds them that Ghisu is a man with a profound awareness and wisdom about everything that is happening around him. Each action of the actors must reflect the internalizing of this basic element about Ghisu's character as well as his social location. When the third pair, Bhole and Binod, improvises the same scene, Binod as Madhav kicks Bhole as Ghisu when the latter eats the potato they are supposed to share. The group discusses where this interpretation came from and whether this does justice to the characters. Each person in the workshop brings their own histories and heartaches to their interpretations of the story and tries to transmit it faithfully in their acting. Bhole has his own pain. Mumtaz has hers. Even so, Alok feels that the key challenge for each actor is to work through these pains, without ever forgetting the truth of the character they are living.

Rehearsing

It is after 1:30 a.m. on a drizzly night in the middle of August. Almost a month has passed since Alok joined the workshop. Sleep is nowhere near him. The story seems to have taken over his life already. Even when no rehearsal is scheduled because of a public holiday, the workshop is becoming a habit. Every day at 5:30 p.m. something inside him tells him that it is time to rehearse. Never has Alok worked on any story or character like this. He has taken out everything he had been carrying in his bag of acting tools, and he is filling that bag with new lessons as an artist and as a human. At this hour, too, the story pulls him in again and whispers something in his ear, and he drifts into another world. Alok exits his body and soul; Madhav takes over.

> My name is Madhav. My wife's name is Budhiya. My father's name is Ghisuram Jatav. I am a very lazy human being. Laboring with my body, doing chores, none of this interests me. There are some real brutes in my village who have mistreated me, so I just don't bother doing anything anymore.

[My father and I], we are very poor men. In our home, all we have are a couple of old broken vessels. We have two pairs of rags to wear on our bodies and we wear those in turns. Right now we are roasting some potatoes that we have dug out from the field of Chaitu Mahatiya. My Dadda has aged. He can't see so well at night, so it's me who has to do the work of stealthily digging out the potatoes. During the day, Dadda can sometimes do this work.

Tonight, Budhiya is screaming crazily. She is having our baby. What can I do? I can't even comprehend what's going on. Here, [sitting outside in the blistery cold], my insides have been screaming with hunger for two days. Inside, she's screaming nonstop as if she'll die in there. I am telling her over and over again, 'Arey, be a bit strong now. As soon as morning comes, I'll go to beg and borrow. I can't hang someone to death if they refuse to loan me anything, can I?'

Next, Alok struggles with hunger:
"In the story, hunger has been mentioned about five times, each time in a different way. The places that a human being's hunger can take them to, the things their hunger can make them do. That's what 'Kafan' is."

Alok dwells on the hunger of Ghisu and Madhav who are eating potatoes while Budhiya is suffering inside. Then, he wonders about his hunger for sex: is it true that when a man's hunger for a woman's jism, her body, is quenched, that woman's body gets reduced to the status of a toy that has served its purpose? Is it possible that all the affection and lust that gush in one moment, vanish as soon as the hunger of the body finds peace? Is it fair for him to pose these questions in relation to Madhav's relationship with Budhiya or are these questions emerging from prior assumptions he has inherited from a dominant framework?

If Madhav is not a mean rascal, then how does he think of sex? Is it only for pleasure? If a man gets formed by his circumstances, and if Madhav's circumstances have taught him to steal potatoes and sugarcane to take care of his stomach's hunger, to work a bit and smoke a lot, and then go to sleep and forget for a few hours about the world in which he is only ridiculed, mistreated, and ignored, then how would that approach to life shape Madhav's attitude to women, to society, to sex, to the screaming Budhiya?

The group's discussion earlier this week triggers a whole host of questions about what Budhiya would be thinking as she was dying. If Madhav actually stepped inside the room where she was dying, would she challenge him bitterly and ask: if the little body inside me is a girl, and I choose to kill her in my womb and die myself, what would be wrong with that? If she were to live, wouldn't she become yet another victim of the hunger of some men who want to consume her body, her dignity, her life. Just as they did with Jyoti Singh during the Delhi rape

Bhagwan Das and Alok Panday as Ghisu and Madhav. (Photo by Tarun Kumar)

of 2012. Just as Savarna men do with so many Dalit women whose names we never find out. If this body in my womb emerges with the body of a boy, would not he leave another Budhiya screaming, alone, and in pain—just like you and your father are doing today?

When Alok shares these reflections in the rehearsal space, I am struck by how he is collapsing the distances of time, place, and embodied locations. We also discuss the ways in which our preconceived notions lead us to expect what a woman in Budhiya's place should be thinking as she is dying. How much can we try to know Budhiya's thinking at the time of her death when in the play of life, our responses to a situation can never be predicted? When regardless of how accurate our analyses of social systems or pressures may be, as translators we must always juggle and weigh the contradictory and endless 'what-ifs' that make life? All these questions grab Alok and inform his continued outpourings as he journeys nonstop with the characters of the story.

Entangling

Whatever each participant achieves in the rehearsals has become inseparable from what they sense and learn from their own interactions and conversations in the workshop. This is true not only for those who are enacting the roles of specific characters, but also for those who are active as supporters in the journey.

Roshan is one such person, perhaps, because he comes from a more economically prosperous family. Perhaps not. Unbeknownst to most participants, all of Roshan's interactions with the group are shaped significantly by his autism and acute depression. Because his condition is not publicly known, he tends to grate on everyone's nerves. There is something about Roshan's attitude toward Sajjan that constantly bothers Alok, and yet, in keeping with his new principle of not correcting anyone else's errors, Alok opens himself up to learning from their conversations. They teach him about the society in which we all live.

One day Sajjan shares his experiences as a dog nanny and then asks Roshan about those who work for his family. Roshan replies that he does not even know the name of his driver. He also reports that the woman who cleans his house tends to run away from work, and this justifies his mother's anger toward the worker. Roshan's elitism is made worse by his excessive reliance on terms such as 'this society' and 'that society,' 'that class' and 'this class' during group discussions. At one point when he states that there is a strange comedy in the first scene of the play, Alok almost loses it. Alok expresses that Roshan does not seem to fit with the goals of the workshop. Tarun wishes he could talk more openly about Roshan's situation and somehow explain to everyone how the workshop is giving him a reason to smile and talk with people again. Instead, Tarun simply communicates to the group that Roshan belongs to the workshop because he, too, is honestly struggling with significant questions in his journey with the story.

Then there is Yasmin, the caretaker of the studio who spends considerable amount of time with members of the Parakh team along with her husband, who everyone calls Patel Saheb, and their eight-year-old son, Aijaz. The family is so immersed in the workshop that when the owner talks about increasing the daily charge for the group's rehearsals, Patel Saheb, whom many people only see as the "drunkard husband who beats his wife," says openly to all the workshop participants, "No, you'll do rehearsals right here. . . . If there're difficulties, I'll deal with those consequences." Every day, when Yasmin comes into the rehearsal hall with a tray of chai cups and smiles teasingly at Anil saying, "Ay, Rajpal Yadav, here's your chai," her gentle smile melts Alok. He wants Yasmin to know that she commands enormous respect from every workshop participant.

One day, Patel Saheb becomes emotional after some tension with the owner about the studio space. With a shaky voice and tearful eyes, he places his right hand on Tarun's head and pulls his son, Aijaz, close to himself. Then, making a gesture as if he is entrusting Aijaz to the workshop participants, he says, "He is all that I have. You all take care of him if something bad happens to me."

Patel Saheb is a bit drunk, but Alok still finds the scene heart wrenching. It reminds him of the affection flowing among all who are part of the rehearsal space: Yasmin ji, Patel Saheb, and Aijaz—even though they are not part of the rehearsals as actors—register their presence in that space fully and passionately. For Alok, this is the collective space the workshop has created for everyone who has stepped into it—a space where all speak freely, and receive respect and love; a space where everyone works hard to listen deeply to one another.

Co-Acting

In the roles of Madhav and Ghisu, Alok and BD have become completely consumed by the drinking scene at the end of the story and the play. Despite all efforts, they feel they are overdramatizing the drunkenness, causing the soul of the scene to disappear. Both decide to keep working on this scene in their homes. Tarun warns that in their zeal to get it right they should not over-rehearse, but Alok and BD are already addicted. Some days, he goes to BD's home, some days BD comes to his, but their shared frustration with not being able to do justice to that scene grows. Then the two start rehearsing by themselves in Tefla's Studio every morning. Then, about a month before the shows, they begin to live together. Together they read the story, over and over again, and with every reading, they find something new in it. The two become Madhav and Ghisu round the clock:

"I woke up at 7:30 this morning and then went to the park [with BD]. There, Dadda [Ghisu] and I strolled for a long time, and we talked. We maintained the same tone and style of speaking as in the play. Dehati. Grameen. This helps a lot. Now when I walk on the streets [after spending my morning that way], I feel the world differently. Our lives have become like those of ascetics. All day, all night, it's Ghisu and Madhav, Ghisu and Madhav, now these dynamics, now these dimensions, here it's this logic, what logic must be there? This is what goes on all day."

A few days later, Alok writes:

"Today, my Dadda and I went to the park again. We continued our conversations and came a bit closer to Ghisu and Madhav. After spending two to three hours together, we walked back home on foot. We found something new in relation to the last scene. That festivity, acting, singing, and dancing, which

Ghisu and Madhav engage in in a drunken state, somehow that had been missing so far . . ."

As the two rehearse, they hear Tarun's voice in their heads: If the rope is not tied thoroughly and carefully to the handle of the bucket, and then someone fills the bucket with the water from the well, it is always possible the knot will come loose by the time the bucket has been pulled to the surface. The rope will untie and the bucket will drop straight back into the well. Similarly, the knot that ties one actor to another should be strong; there should be a deep understanding, a continuous conversation—only then can a scene take us to a new place where we never expected to go.

BD and Alok continue to wrestle with the scene until the end. Sometimes it comes to the top; at others it slips back into the well.

Relearning

To fully open oneself to something that involves unlearning almost everything we have inherited—not simply in our heads so that we can regurgitate it, but to internalize it in our spirit so that it can be transmitted through our bodies—is no simple undertaking. However, this is what the workshop demands of the participants who translate "Kafan" into *Hansa*. Like Gaurav, Alok's biggest hurdle is his discomfort with working with those who have no formal training in acting. He reflects: "when we first started out, my uneasiness was so intense that my mind would go blank." The workshop required him to "free himself from this hang-up," and as he did so, a new world unfolded before him:

"[Meena ji, Mumtaz ji, Sajjan, and Anil] were there from the beginning. But at that time, I used to see them differently—'Arey yaar, how will these people do [real] acting? How will there be any tuning between them and us [the real actors]?' My head was burdened with previously learned ideas about theater, dialogue, et cetera. Then I slowly found out that each one of them is a far more alive, passionate, and truthful actor than the rest of us [trained actors] because they did not go to a school to get trained; they have learned acting from life. . . . I tried blending myself with the simplicity and ease with which they approached acting. I found that a natural innocence [toward characters and scenes] was automatically present in their work—something that's so essential for a [good] actor.

"[Sajjan] did not speak much in the beginning. He didn't have words [it seemed], but now he sits us down to retell 'Kafan.' He tells us about the deeper expressions that Premchand has tried to weave into the story, [he helps develop understandings that others of us are unable to grasp at times]. Now, when I finish a scene, [Sajjan] comes and gives me suggestions about how I can make it better. This is also the miracle of this collective space."

This ability to recognize the "true" meanings of acting also brings for Alok "a feeling, a recognition of some kind of change from within that is giving me sukoon, contentment." For instance, he notes, when "Budhiya [Mumtaz] tells me that she feels more relaxed with me [in the role of Madhav than she does with Gaurav], . . . I feel profoundly happy." Then the transformation permeates Alok's whole life: he feels a change inside himself when he interacts with the man who comes to pick up his trash every morning. He feels a change in how he thinks of his work in this world. He feels a change in what he defines as "that space of another," which for an actor captures the most precious ingredient on the stage of life: who is where? What is whose place? What becomes of life when our struggle focuses on dismantling the authority of the people and systems that pre-decide our places and spaces in this world? In what ways can I learn to critique and undo that authority?

At times this process of relearning hurts Alok's ego "deep inside," but "Alok's ego was not bigger than Alok," he writes. "So the ego was defeated and something creative was achieved." One of the achievements that results from this defeat is a courage to disagree: "Today, . . . I think very hard before consenting easily to a view, regardless of who is present before me. It's not that I've decided to only critique and to refuse another's position. If it feels correct, then it's correct. If it feels wrong to me, then I must disagree. . . . My ability to grasp, to be in the world . . . have been transforming along with the making of the play. . . . Like inhaling fresh air . . . I've become attentive to those things that were always there but that I had not felt before . . . my village, my farm, my people, their language, their manner, their attitude, what matters to them, what troubles them.

"Before the workshop I had gone back to my village many times and I did think about these aspects, but not with so much care. This time when I returned for Deepawali, my trip took me on paths I hadn't known. I focused on the farms and fields in ways that I had never done before. When I spotted a young man or a woman, I'd say to myself, 'Look, maybe Madhav is a bit like him' or 'maybe Budhiya is a bit like her,' or 'Ghisu might be a bit like this.' The characters of the story traveled with me, and their images continuously stayed in the forefront of my consciousness. . . . I did not even come to know how the story's characters, seasons, and geographical conditions became one with my being. Anil's naughty acts, [Sajjan's] innocence, Mumtaz ji's diligence, Meena ji's commitment—I have learned so much from each one of them."

Calculating

Alok notes that his journey with the workshop was at times marked by "calculativeness": "At times it felt like, 'Yaar, I can't even cover my expenses and here I'm killing myself in this workshop.' . . . From July through November now, . . . , all I have had [in the name of work assignments] is a couple of insignificant shoots. Although Richa ji did make sure that we got a respectable amount for our labor in this workshop, but how much could that do to save me from my overall condition of hardship? One morning, I woke up and saw my landlord. My mind made an immediate 'cut' to 'Today, I have to pay my rent.' Everyday turmoil of this sort shook me, and I'd say to myself, "Ditch this workshop! Let me . . . do an audition or two, I need to get some real work otherwise, how in the world will I take care of my expenses? 25,000 rupees fly from the hand in a month. . . . This . . . is the story of every second, third, fourth actor or artist, but somehow or another ooparwala [god] helps us carry through."

Initially, Alok's concerns do not lead him to reflect on the lives of Mumtaz, Meena, Anil, and Sajjan, although he does assume that their position is somehow more stable than that of 'strugglers' like himself. However, as the workshop advances, Alok sees things differently: "Rehearsals are continuing. The play is building, blossoming, becoming vibrant with new colors every day. Mumtaz ji's acting has become very powerful. The musical scene with the men's dance went very well yesterday. Mumtaz ji and I walked together from the rehearsal to my place. [Handing her cell phone to me,] she said, 'Bhaiyya, why don't you record my dialogues in Awadhi here. This way, I can listen and practice as I do my work [in homes].'

"I was so happy [and also a bit stunned] to hear that she works so hard day and night, such back-breaking labor and even then she gives so much space to acting, and so passionately. Her dedication challenges professional actors like me. This so-called 'struggle' that so many of us do in my profession—we talk about . . . how much we kill ourselves, all this rona-dhona, this whining and complaining. . . . But look at her: she is always there with a twenty-four-hour Close-Up smile, with her eyes bright, and with so much energy. Waah! kamaal hai. Mumtaz ji, you really are a source of continuous inspiration for us all."

Just over a month before the shows of *Hansa* in Mumbai, Alok travels to Shahjahanpur in Uttar Pradesh to see his parents and other family members during Diwali. He is also eager to meet Aarti, his fiancée, who he will wed in a few months. However, he cannot get away from the spaces and sounds of Tefla's Studio in Mumbai. Everywhere he turns, he finds himself looking for his Dadda. Every other person he greets reminds him of various shades of Thakur, Taka, Munshi, shopkeepers, Dhankun, and of all those mazdoors who sit and drink with Ghisu and Madhav in the liquor house. No matter where he finds himself, he is haunted by the sorrows, greed, and short-lived pleasures that mark his life as Madhav.

Even meeting Aarti is hard. Extremely hard, in fact. For, he cannot stop thinking about his Budhiya. *Hansa* seems to have possessed his body and spirit. He can no longer discern between Madhav and Alok, between living and performing. He wants to translate these feelings to Aarti, but he doesn't know where to begin. He is afraid she might misunderstand him when he begins to tell her about Budhiya.

He does not have any money to spare, but he feels compelled to call Mumtaz ji; he knows she must be finding it difficult to play Budhiya without him. He sorely misses his whole team, his Dadda, and Tarun, but most of all he misses Budhiya. This recognition baffles him, but he does not try to overanalyze it. He accepts it as one of lessons of the journey that cannot be captured in the pages of a journal.

As Alok prepares to return to Mumbai, he asks his Amma for her green sari, the one in which she does all her chores and the one he always imagines her in when he misses his home from his tiny little shared room on Yari Road. Amma is happy to give him the sari. She thinks she is sending the sari for Mumtaz, the domestic worker. Alok corrects his mother. He tells her that Mumtaz, his Budhiya, does not own or wear a sari. She only wears salwaar qameez. He tells his mother that her sari will become an essential prop for Budhiya and for *Hansa*. It will make Budhiya come alive—from her first appearance on stage, until her death.

Swimming

As the dates of the show approach in December, Alok realizes that "Time has flown by without a whisper. Half a year! . . . In the two years of my journey in Mumbai, the six months of participating in this workshop will prove invaluable for my future as an actor and as a person."

As the momentum builds, everyone swims in waves of excitement. On Tarun's invitation, several well-respected actors, writers, and intellectuals associated with the world of film and theater watch the rehearsals and give their feedback: Sanjay Mishra, Vineet Kumar, Dileep Shukla, Munira Surati, Purnima Kharga, Deepraj Rana, and Devendra Nath Misra. Purnima and Munira also become centrally involved in the creative process during the last stretch. These supporters join Yasmin, Patel Saheb, their families and visitors, and Kaajal Singh, the owner of the studio, in motivating the group. The enthusiasm of the actors goes up several notches when Dileep Shukla, the dialogue writer of several mega hit films, remarks, "This is great work that's quite different from anything we've seen before. The media should cover this so that people know this kind of deep work is happening in this day and age."

With the support of friends at the Central Institute of Fisheries Education, I secure a free auditorium for the purposes of the show in the heart of the Yari Road area, where most of the workshop participants and their intended audiences live. Although the space of the auditorium and the stage are far from ideal, especially from the perspective of the professional actors in the group, finalizing the space for the shows instills a new energy. Alok comments:

"Arriving on the stage immediately circulates a unique vigor and inspiration. . . . All the aspects of this play are being worked out and refined by all of us—the set, costumes, music, and makeup. Everything is evolving from our own creativity and imagination . . . whether it is Mumtaz ji bringing in the coconut gunny sacks, or whether it is [Sajjan] contributing a stack of old newspapers, or Meena ji painting a picture [to express her feelings about the workshop], or Anil bringing biscuits for all of us. . . . No one's share is any less than another's. The characters [of the play] may be small or big, but each workshop participant is carrying out the responsibilities at their own levels in equal measure."

To become comfortable with the space, Tarun invites the actors to attend events in the Fisheries auditorium; several times, the group walks from Tefla's Studio to the auditorium to watch programs together. As they watch a program of ghazals, Alok agonizes: "All the while, my mind kept churning. Is the stage too small? People on the stage were not visible from the back row of the hall . . . but now it is not possible to have the show anywhere else."

The weeks leading up to the shows are saturated with madness. The rehearsals stretch for hours. When Yasmin can no longer cope with serving multiple rounds of chai for rehearsal after rehearsal, the actors order the chai from Thakkar's dhaba. Sometimes people forgo dinner and just order vada-paav from Thakkar's as well. Alok's friends begin to comment, "Bhai, what kind of strange work are you doing, after all?" Lost in Madhav's world, Alok responds with a few "hmms" followed by one line or another from the play that perfectly suits the situation, "Halal ki hai, haram ki nahin. . . . Ee sab hai bhavna ka khel, tumhri samajh ka naahin. These earnings are halal, not haram. It's a game of heart and soul; you may not be able to understand it." The words from the play have melded with his life; the distance between Mumbai and Madhav's village has vanished.

The overwhelming intensity of 'living in character' leaves no time for Alok to speak to his parents or to his fiancée, Aarti: "Usually, I speak to my Pitaji and Mataji in the village every day by phone, no matter what happens and no matter how busy my schedule. But nowadays two–three days go by without my speaking to them. Then, my Madam [fiancée] also stays upset with me these days. . . . She does not know that I can't find the time for her because I am too busy meeting up with Budhiya in the fields here. Ha, ha, ha."

However, the story is continuously making Alok rethink his relationships with his parents and with his fiancée: "Many a time I have proceeded to talk to the Budhiya of my real life, only to find myself a Madhav each time." He reflects on the ways in which he might be unthinkingly dominating Aarti, how he might not be giving her enough space to be angry with him, how he goes on and on with her about the workshop and about his own needs as an artist. Alok also recalls one of the scenes when Madhav screams at his dadda in anger. In that scene, Ghisu is shaken by his son's outburst. He suffers. As Alok improvises and rehearses that dialogue with BD, he remembers a time when he screamed at his father: "Working with Dadda has enabled me to think hard about my relationship with Pitaji . . . to thicken my understanding of that relationship."

Living

On the night of 8 December, Alok can't sleep. Sitting in a corner of the tight spaces of his shared room, he pulls out his notebook again: "Now I try . . . talking in the language of the character as much as possible. At home I rehearse the same body language. I try to come closer in my body to the people who have enabled me to reach Madhav: Rajaram Chamar of my village, whose facial expressions and moods I dissolve into the character of Madhav. . . . Ramnath Teli, also of my village, whose walk I try to blend in Madhav's character—for example, the way he stands or walks while holding his hands behind him. . . . My niece Sheetal—her tone from her early childhood, especially her innocence. . . . My chacha Munnalal Panday—I use his style of standing. . . . Harishchandra Chamar, also of my village, the way he locks both of his hands with one another, and makes an impressive gesture. . . . My nephew Vikas—his way of watching others.

"And then in the scene where Budhiya has died and I am watching her, Mumtaz ji wears my mother's green sari. In that scene I see the corpse of my mother. Sometimes it is hard for me to control myself. Because of that sari, I come close to my mother and through that proximity I come close to the trauma of that scene. [Madhav's] pain in that scene from the cruel untimely death of his wife is no less than the pain of a mother's loss. [But that connection with my mother's body does not interfere with the connection I feel with Budhiya's body]."

Dancing

When Tarun invites Purnima Kharga into the workshop space in the final weeks of making *Hansa*, she brings with herself not only the dedicated vision and vigor of a dancer, but also a generous imagination and nurturing of a cocreator. At times, Tarun removes himself entirely from the workshop space so that it can be molded by Purnima. Alok describes the effects of this cocreativity:

"Today we warmed up with music and also did a 'follow the leader' exercise. We had so much fun. We were all sweating profusely. Dance moves were also invented today in Parakh; [Sajjan], Deep, and Aijaz were the ones who shone

Gaurav playing Madhav, with Mumtaz as Budhiya. (Photo by Tarun Kumar)

in that process. There was so much joy. Then me and my bappa [BD] did . . . a full rehearsal. I really missed [Satish's dholak]. Then Bhole Dada and Gaurav played Ghisu and Madhav."

Everyone leaves at 9:30 p.m., except Madhav and his dadda. Energized by all the singing and dancing tonight, the two are inspired to rework their most challenging and adventurous scene—the last scene of drinking. Yasmin is worried about the two going hungry again, and brings some of the food she has cooked for her family's dinner tonight. As the two rehearse late into the night, Madhav and Ghisu become hungry again, and Madhav steps out to get some sevpuri from a street vendor:

"Outside, I chatted some with the sevpuri wala. That Bhai Sahab was from Azamgarh. He has been here [in Mumbai] for the last thirteen or fourteen years. His mother, father, wife, and two children are in the village. I feel I got an opportunity to know a family. When I stepped out of [the studio] everything was still. . . . I was hungry. [The sevpuri wala] was about to pack up. . . . I just chit-chatted with him, and he could not tell who I was. My whole state was that of Madhav—dusty hair, torn dhoti, a dirty gamchha . . . when I started speaking to him in my own dehati, he became very relaxed and switched from his khadi boli to dehati. He asked, "How much are you able to earn in a day, Bhaiyya?" I was quiet for an instant and then taking a deep breath, I said: "Oh, maybe about 150–200 rupees."

After six hours of formally rehearsing every day and spending at least ten hours per day living with his dadda and thinking of himself only as Madhav, Alok writes, "I do not know where all of this is going, but at this time all my waking hours are 'Kafan,' 'Kafan,' 'Kafan.'"

Revisiting

Less than two weeks before the workshop, Tarun suggests that the group try to distance themselves from the scripted lines and to revisit, once again, the story, history, and context of each character. Alok notes everything about Madhav that is now on the tips of his fingers:

> Madhav—age 22 years. Height—5' 8" . . . dark hair, dusty like a mazdoor's.

> Rags on the body. Gharib-maha gharib. Chamar by caste. Oppressed by untouchability . . .

> Father's name—Ghisu. Mother does not exist. She is dead. Her name was Bitoli Devi. Ghisu and Bitoli, they had nine children. But only Madhav survived. Eight of them died. The same situation persists in Ghisu's home today. All the children died of hunger or malnourishment. The manner in which Madhav's wife is dying—of weakness, of hunger—Madhav's mother, Bitoli Devi, died in exactly the same way.

> Ghisu and Madhav belonged to a village located in a small district called Shahjahanpur in Uttar Pradesh. In this village, thakurs, pundits, and big kisans ruled. In this same village, there was a thakur by the name of Balister Singh. His family was very prosperous. The chamars had a separate kunba. There was also a sizable community of kisans. Yet it was Ghisu and Madhav who were the focus of an impressive amount of gossip throughout the village.
>
> The two were lazy, always avoiding work, and always eager to tactlessly blurt out whatever right or wrong came first to their tongues, without heeding whether they were speaking to a thakur, kisan, or pundit. Both had the habit of muttering and grumbling about everything. That was the reason cited by Savarna men who hit or scolded or cursed them every other day. Sukhdev Pundit beat them a few times, as did Munnalal Panday. Several times, Balister Singh physically abused them. Sukhdev, Munnalal, and Balister only hired Madhav and Ghisu out of desperation—that is, when no other mazdoor was available. If the two were hired to peel sugarcanes, together they could suck on fifty sugarcanes while they peeled them.

Other chamars in the village were in a better position than these two. For instance, Ramesh Jatav, Bechelal, Bhoopram, Rajesh Jatav, Maiku, Gangaram. These people were better off because they didn't mind sycophancy and obeying orders. However, Ghisu and Madhav did not engage in these practices; their approach was 'Well, if you are a thakur, that's good for you. If you own twenty acres of land, it's great that's there for you. Why should we lick your feet?'

Although Ghisu frequently hung out with Ramesh Jatav, Bechelal, Bhoopram, and Maiku, he did not run around and serve the thakurs like these other men from his caste did. That's why the whole village pointed fingers at him. It's not that the whole village was against him. There were some people in the village who treated him with high regard—for example, Shivram Pundit and Shyamlal Pundit, who enjoyed good reputations in their own ways and who also felt a kind of intimacy with people such as Ghisu and Madhav. Sometimes Ghisu and Madhav were found merrily eating and drinking away at the homes [of Shivram and Shyamlal], which also caused agony among those who could not stand them.

That's exactly how Rajaram was. Lazybones, he worked on everything so slowly. Even if someone called his name standing right behind him, he pretended he didn't hear it. . . . [Ghisu and Madhav] are present in every village. Rajaram of my village. Sualal of Pasiyani village. Kanthua, Mohan, and so many others. . . . As soon as you reach between the layers, you can probably find Ghisu and Madhav [everywhere].

Very early on in the workshop, Alok learns the difference between "reading a story only in the head versus learning the layers of the story through acting." The contrast between the two practices gives birth to a new understanding: "If you give the measurements to the tailor over the phone or through someone else, he won't be able to sew the outfit as well as when he measures you himself. That's when the outfit will fit you perfectly and enhance your grace." Alok recognizes that, as an actor, he is a tailor: "My job is to measure a story with the best of my ability. The better I measure, the better the result will be. [This involves] being normal, being natural with the language of the [context], with that expression, that dialogue, that delivery. At times, I am so consumed by it all that I feel my mind has turned into yogurt."

Alok immerses himself completely in everything he can tap into through his intimate memories from his village. He feels that people from those fields and streets are walking with him all the time. However, the demanding process that turns Alok's mind into yogurt is not related merely to learning how to be 'normal and natural' with respect to the worlds of Ghisu and Madhav. The process also demands that he resist any pregiven or packaged understandings of caste politics in order to *feel* Bhudhiya, Madhav, and Ghisu as much larger than just their material poverty or their hunger or their status as Dalit mazdoors.

This means struggling honestly with all that makes him cringe and gives him nightmares. It means being able to process memories and events that he is too scared to touch:

"Once upon a time, I remember this well, when I was little—around eight or ten years old, I think, when in my village, Mahendra Singh, the son-in-law of Thakur Balister Singh, got drunk and publicly beat up a poor farmer from our village. The poor man was tied to a plow to till the field. The whole village just watched this as if it were a tamasha, a spectacle.

"Similarly, there was another incident in 1995 or 1996 when there was polling for the election of a sarpanch in our village and Thakur Balister Singh lost. He was so embarrassed and piqued at his own defeat that he latched on to a poor Muslim man by the name of Zaheer and beat him crazily. Once again, everyone else watched this tamasha.

"Even today, in my village of Shahjahanpur the mazdoors sit out early in the morning on the pukka bridge, and there is something akin to a human auction. People come on motorbikes and take away the most muscular men from the lot on their backseats after settling on a price. The physically weaker ones just stand and watch. How many Ghisus and Madhavs must be hidden in those clusters? We can never imagine the extent to which unemployment, lack of formal education, grinding poverty, and everyday humiliation can break a person. These issues have come alive within me throughout my waking hours as a result of this workshop."

Daring to go to places he had not dared to recall, Alok takes on multiple journeys into his past. Each journey leaves him restless, in pain, and without resolutions, but Alok understands that this is the part of the difficult and unending process of learning by living in character. Such learning has taught him to grapple honestly with the truths he may have "seen" but not lived; truths which he must struggle with so that he can come closer to feeling them in and through his body. If the task of seeking justice through hungry translations comes with a responsibility of resisting closures, then, the journey of an actor who has hungrily begun to rethink his life in relation to caste politics must continue without arriving.

Hungry for *Hansa*

One hunger burns the stomach, the other burns the heart. Stomach's hunger can be extinguished by eating from another's plate, but the hunger for theater can only be satisfied by one's own creativity. . . . In political theater, this creativity must be collectively owned.[1]

Poetic justice and social justice are polar opposites. While the former provides consolation and courage in an imaginary realm, the latter seeks tangible gains in the immediate political and historical context. Normally, one would expect these to be non-intersecting discourses, operating as they do on entirely different planes. However, as the Dalit cultural upsurge of the last few decades shows, there is an aesthetic corollary of the claim of social justice. And it is at that level that one may see some infection by the notion of poetic justice, that is, in the demand for representations in which that which is yet to become actual in the material-historical world is represented as already-achieved.[2]

Playing Budhiya, and singing the songs of Hansa *make me come alive. . . . [Alok] makes me free and light. Unburdened. . . . My daughters and granddaughters . . . can't recognize me anymore. . . . I wrap up all my work quickly because I can't wait to get to the rehearsals. . . . I used to think that my responsibility was to try to earn as much money as possible so that I could feed my children and take care of their needs, but somehow, this work [of acting in* Hansa*] feels more zaroori [essential] for my soul now. . . . Now I just work in six [instead of seven] homes because I need more time for myself in order to feel like Budhiya.*[3]

The common senses handed down to us by dominant frameworks often require us to separate hunger of the belly from hunger of the soul, unemployment from resistance, activism from spirituality, social justice from poetic justice, law from poetry. They also isolate Premchand from Kabir, Sufi and Bhakti poetry from wedding songs, political theater from romantic tragedy. However, these are precisely the common senses whose premises are refused by those who come together to imbibe and rethink "Kafan" through an all-consuming process that 'rescripts' it into the fluid poetical play called *Hansa, Karo Puratan Baat*.

In his essay on the Premchand-Dalit controversy, Alok Rai addresses the entanglement between social and poetic justice through a focus on "Kafan." He defines poetic justice as "the idea, broadly speaking, that the poet or artist has not only the freedom but even a duty to invent his imaginary worlds in such a fashion that, in it, the wrongs of the everyday world are redressed."[4] At the same time, he disaggregates social justice into two distinct dimensions: those aspects of justice that can be legislated, and dignity and recognition, which cannot be legislated but can only be realized through a necessarily consensual process. For Rai, it is this impossibility of legislating dignity and recognition that unavoidably embeds social justice in the cultural aesthetic realm through which poetic justice emerges. In Ajay Skaria's helpful distillation of this argument, "law is never adequate by itself; law also needs an order, and the lack of this order is what poetic justice calls attention to."[5] In other words, it is the impossibility of arriving fully at social justice—through rights, rules, and responsibilities, for example—that provides fresh openings for continuing to reimagine poetic justice, and that makes one justice perpetually hungry for the other. An ethical retelling—a hungry translation—of the journey of Parakh Theatre with *Hansa* can happen within such a frame of poetic justice. Indeed, it is precisely this longing for poetic justice that is echoed in the quotes that accompany Alok Rai's at the outset of this section: Tarun expresses it in the form of a collectively owned creative hunger for political theater; Mumtaz experiences it as her soul's hunger for *Hansa*.

Reimagining Poetics of Justice

> To me, "Kafan" . . . will always be . . . a story of two merciless brutes who merrily eat roasted potatoes while Budhiya is dying from labor pains . . . This is what is imprinted on my mind. I came to your rehearsal fully prepared to hate Madhav and Ghisu. Instead, I am sitting here crying and empathizing with these two . . . You are making me fall in love with two men I was supposed to hate. This can't be "Kafan" . . . [Yet,] it is "Kafan"![6]

The hungers for food and theater are neither equivalent nor sequential. Rather, a hunger for theater—as Dia Da Costa argues—resists captivity to existing configurations of power as well as to current imaginings of how transformation will come; it yearns "for all that makes life serendipitous" and that bears witness to the "ambivalent, unsettling, . . . potential that makes life a moving, unforeseeable becoming, still worthy of being called life."[8] In taking the form of a creative journey as well as a destination, the making of *Hansa* refuses the commonly invoked separation between process and product, between being and becoming. Rather, it is in and through theater that all the travelers on this creative journey become hungry for new embodied understandings of the interbraided politics of caste, class, gender, location, and language. These new understandings are constituted by a commitment to what Viet Thanh Nguyen refers to as "just memory"—a memory that demands not only just remembering, but also just forgetting. Recalling the words and sentiments of workshop participants from previous sections, this commitment implies rejecting the idea that the actors can absorb the story by simply "reading [it] in the head"; unlearning and relearning through the workshop means "reading the story through acting."[9] This acting, moreover, is not about 'getting it right' in terms of technique, language, motions, or dialogue. Rather, acting becomes a radically vulnerable mode in which bodies that are previously trained *or* untrained in acting surrender together to the serendipitous creativity of an unfolding process. The actors tirelessly work through the structures and relationships that have formed them, as well as with respect to their connections and responses to "Kafan." Significantly, this endless grappling with just memory and ethical retelling cannot happen in isolation. It requires each actor to have intense embodied and psychic conversations with what they are recalling and learning about the pasts and presents, dreams and desires, traumas and tragedies of all the other participants who step into and out of the workshop over a course of six months. The ethics, aesthetics, and poetics of what becomes *Hansa* emerge from these demanding collective journeys. They push the actors to reconnect and disconnect with inherited and internalized narratives, to name and let go of sorrows and abuses, and to feel and acknowledge hitherto unrecognized pleasures, pains, humiliations, and sacrifices. It is the affective and political labor of this theater that gives the actors the courage to engage some of the most difficult questions that arise in relation to "Kafan."

The men dance to the tune of "Gagri Sambharo." (Photo by Tarun Kumar)

The question of whether someone who is not born Dalit can represent or do justice to Dalitness in the Indian context has acquired enormous salience, especially after the 2001 World Conference against Racism in Durban.[10] While this concern has generated important conversations about representation, consumption, and manipulation of Dalit lives and struggles in all forms of knowledge making, it is the ethics and politics of narrating the self that have dominated the debates in the literary realm. Dalit thought often regards *atma-katha* or *story of the self* as a chiefly Savarna or privileged mode of self-narration, and distinguishes it from narratives of *swaanubhuti* or *experience of the self* that establish "Dalit personhood as a figure of suffering" and that regard "the Dalit protagonist as the representative of the Dalit community and Dalit identity" in order to goad the moral imagination of the reader and to demand ameliorative action.[11] Such deployment of swaanubhuti is considered necessary to resist the violent consumption of Dalitness by the Savarna in and through dominant modes of narration and analysis.[12] At the same time, notes Sajid, the tendency to delimit Dalit literature and representations of Dalit selfhood vis-à-vis caste politics has negated this literature's potential to reinvent itself in ways that can allow for border crossings. Sajid draws on the work of the novelist Mohandas Naimishraya to provide examples of Dalit writing that look beyond experiences of a single caste in order to create a literature that deploys empathy or connectedness of feeling (samaanubhuti) to create a politically and aesthetically rich poetics of alliance (samanvaya) and equality (samata), and to reflect critically on all of Indian society.[13] The Premchand-Dalit controversy that Rai intervenes in through his aforementioned meditation on social and poetic justice is rooted in this political and intellectual landscape, and this is the terrain the workshop participants step into by choosing to journey with "Kafan." This happens unintentionally and serendipitously, and only after *Hansa* is ready to be shared on stage. Even without having read or debated the controversy surrounding "Kafan," the participants feel that their journey has made them search many truths about hunger—Budhiya's, Madhav's, Ghisu's, and their own.

> *Ghisu turns Budhiya's death into an utsav, a festival, not because he is heartless but because he has a penetrating critique of the world in which he and Madhav are treated like crap. . . . I keep returning to this seven-page story . . . sometimes in the middle of the night . . . even after memorizing its text by heart. . . . Ghisu's wisdom is like that of a saint. That doesn't mean he is not witty and smart and cunning. His . . . wisdom includes all of this. I've been trying to internalize these facts so that I can transmit them through my body. . . . . I can't think of myself as Bhagwan Das anymore. I have become Ghisu. Grappling with "Kafan" has changed how I approach life.*[14]

> *Somehow, this work [of acting in* Hansa*] feels more zaroori [essential] for my soul now. . . . I need more time for myself in order to feel like Budhiya.*[15]

> *I never imagined that Mumtaz ji [a mother and grandmother], who goes from one house to another to cook nice meals, would become my Budhiya. . . . But . . . today when Mumtaz ji enters the stage in her green sari and bright red bindi on her forehead, she looks no less than any Budhiya that I might have imagined for myself. Her commitment and devotion to this work forces me to think: "Yaar, even after running around between seven houses and completing a hundred chores in each place, when Mumtaz ji enters [the rehearsal space] in the evening, her innocent face glows with a rare energizing smile. . . . Meena ji, Mumtaz ji, [Sajjan], and Anil. . . . I used to see them differently—"Arey yaar, how will these people do [real] acting? . . ." My head was burdened with previously learned ideas about theater, dialogue, et cetera. Then I slowly learned that each one of them is a far more alive and truthful actor than the rest of us [trained actors] because they did not go to school to learn acting; they have learned acting from life.*[16]

The sentences I quote here locate several actors of *Hansa* in relation to their own personal and political journeys while providing glimpses of the ways in which the collective making of *Hansa* opened up spaces for us to reengage the concepts of swaanubhuti, samaanubhuti, and samanvaya. For example, Gaurav arrives at samaanubhuti through a self-reflexive comparison between the treatment suffered by Ghisu and Madhav and the ways Hindi-speaking migrant actors from rural areas are treated in Bollywood. Mumtaz comes to see herself—and be regarded by other participants—as "much more than a poor Dalit Muslim who cooks and cleans"; she becomes an "artist" who not only grapples profoundly with Budhiya's pain because of her own experience (samaanubhuti), but whose involvement inspires other actors to feel and enact "Kafan" differently.

Mumtaz's presence makes *Hansa* as much a story about Budhiya as it is about Ghisu and Madhav in the dominant imagination. Alok and Bhagwan Das (BD) work relentlessly for months to love, respect, and embrace Madhav, Ghisu, and Budhiya as parts of themselves, and the process is marked by deep psychological transitions for them, one during which they find themselves unable to undertake any other acting assignments.

It would be inaccurate, even unfair, to read the diaries of Gaurav, BD, Alok, and Mumtaz as products of 'participatory research' or even as 'testimonies' of the 'actors behind the masks.' They are the actors' own scripting and analysis of, as well as their struggles with, the emotional and psychic transitions through which their so-called masks start breathing through their skins as each of them struggles through soul-wrenching questions about the hierarchies and paradigms they have previously taken for granted. Alok's journal, for instance, reflects how the all-consuming labor of acting is not simply about staging a scene of the story. Rather, improvisation becomes one with social reflection and political analysis, and performance comes to be constituted through rehearsals, re-visions, and re-embodiments of socially ascribed positions defined by caste, gender, and occupation. In the making of *Hansa*, these rehearsals and revisions evolve in and through performances of labor.

Mumtaz's transformative labor of performing Budhiya is a key example of this powerful creativity. Mumtaz's performance of Budhiya's labor pains—preceded by all the other scenes in which she injects life into Madhav's and Ghisu's world and into *Hansa*—reworks and revolutionizes how audiences come to read Premchand's Budhiya. This labor is further enhanced and enriched by the lyrics of Kabir and the music cocreated by Neeraj, Satish, Tarun, and others. In this way Mumtaz, Premchand, Kabir, the musicians and actors on and off stage, all become coauthors of a new character that turns the apparently speechless Budhiya of "Kafan" into a pivotal character of *Hansa*.

Mumtaz writes her reflections with Neeraj's help. (Photo by Tarun Kumar)

Discussions become intense as the *Hansa* show draws near. (Photo by Tarun Kumar)

Mumtaz's complete immersion in Budhiya allows us to rethink radically the many meanings and manifestations of multiply intertwined hungers. These do not merely encompass the hunger of the belly that kills Budhiya from malnourishment, or the hunger that dissuades Madhav from leaving his father's side in the fear that he will eat more than his share of stolen potatoes, or the hunger that makes Ghisu remember the thakur's wedding feast as Budhiya is dying, or even the hunger that takes Ghisu and Madhav to the liquor house, where they turn Budhiya's death into a festival of life and death. Mumtaz's deep involvement in *Hansa* and her identification with Budhiya instill in the play the hunger to embrace life—in the form of youth, love, lust, intoxication, greed, charity, musicality, and a desire for spiritual freedom. At the same time, these enmeshed hungers articulated through *Hansa* refuse to become concepts, categories, or analyses that can be fully known. Instead, these enmeshings become part of a politically and aesthetically aware pedagogical praxis that collectively searches for ethics, desires, and dreams in affective and relational ways. Such embodied praxis allows for theoretical, spiritual, and lived reinterpretations of the 'self' as well as for imagining futures that may otherwise seem difficult or impossible.

Extinguishing and Sustaining Hungers

Let me return to a point where I began: Whereas the hunger that burns one's stomach must be extinguished, the creative and collective hunger for political theater seeks not to be extinguished, but only to be fueled and refueled. The challenge posed by these entangled hungers is inseparable from the ongoing possibility of creativity and critique through political theater. This complexity of the hungers of the belly and the soul also makes it necessary to recognize political theater as a process that comprises at least three forms of mutually co-constitutive production: First, the creation (e.g., a play) through which political messages are articulated. Second, the building and sustaining of a collectivity that must find ways to converse and coexist productively with the individualized hungers for creativity and creative egos in the collective. Third, the building of political theater must wrestle with the making of an audience that can sustain that theater without reducing it to a series of commodities. This last aspect connects the question of political theater's survival to the risks and sociopolitical contradictions of funding, professionalization, and NGOization.

The making of *Hansa* in Mumbai involves an intense exploration of the systemic and psychic dimensions of exploitation, desire, greed, attachment, and indifference. The collective emotional and creative labor of the workshop participants—which includes difficult dialogues rooted in each actor's encounters with multiple hungers—complicates the dominant reading of "Kafan" as a story of hunger (for food), untouchability, and inhumanity in the context of the prevailing structures of caste, class, and gender. It entangles Ghisu's, Madhav's, and Budhiya's hunger for food with their hunger for emotional and sexual intimacy; for aesthetic, sensuous, spiritual, and intellectual comforts, and for their desire to feel "charitable." Moreover, by infusing the radical spiritualism of Bhakti poetry into "Kafan," *Hansa* provocatively—and for some, disturbingly—reinterprets Budhiya's death as liberation from the exploitative materiality of class, religion, and the body itself.

The intense process of making *Hansa*, and the manner in which it moves its audience in each show, produces a hunger—among both actors and spectators—for continuing theater that allows domestic workers in the Yari Road area to continue to read, reflect, and perform with professional actors. However, while all of those participants who earn their living as domestic help (Mumtaz, Meena, Sajjan, Yasmin) are willing to surrender some of their paid work in order to continue to build a political and creative platform through theater, several young men who aspire for success in Bollywood (Alok, Bhagwan Das, Gaurav, Neeraj) fear that their continued participation in such theater would injure their future prospects. As much as this theater continues to pull them, they fear that its all-consuming nature—in terms of time, energy, and emotional and political labor—threatens their chances of earning recognition and sustained livelihood in the long run. While the transgressive energy from the collective creation of *Hansa* sparks new relationships and analyses, it is not easy to translate those transgressions into continuous creative labor for social transformation because of these very real fears. Yet, the group members also yearn to realize again the creative and political energy *and* community they built through *Hansa*.

For example, Sajjan, a sixteen-year-old Adivasi from Bihar, comes to Mumbai in May 2014 when his two brothers, already employed as domestic help in Mumbai, find him a job that involves taking care of three dogs in the home of a Bollywood actor. Sajjan's employers, Narendra and Uma (aliases), encourage him to participate in the theater workshop between June and December, in part because they feel he "cannot utter even a sound from his throat" and the theater workshop would help him become "smarter" and better adjusted to his new social atmosphere. Two of Uma and Narendra's nephews—who have recently arrived in Mumbai from Haryana and UP—also participate in the workshop.[17] Although Narendra and Uma are out of town during the shows, they hear rave reviews from their family about Sajjan's incredible performance, especially as someone who never learned "proper Hindi," and they are proud of "his new personality and confidence."

Five months later, however, Uma and Narendra report to Tarun and me that the theater workshop has spoiled Sajjan: Sajjan has opened a Facebook account where he logs in with their internet password to entertain himself with pornographic material. When they scold him for his "ill manners," he talks back while looking them straight in the eye, something he had never done when he first arrived. Uma and Narendra can no longer love Sajjan like a "family member" because, rather than being grateful for what he is getting, he assumes he deserves "equality and space" all the time. Sajjan is stepping out of what is defined by them to be his auqat, his proper place, and both Sajjan and his employers attribute its credit or blame to the theater workshop. In a way, Sajjan transforms the original text ascribed to him by Narendra and Uma and performs a translation that is relationally produced by his experiences in the workshop; this translation, moreover, is in flux and cannot be grasped by his employers. At the same time, the inability of the workshop participants to continue as a collective means that Sajjan no longer has access to the creative and aesthetic space and community of theater to process his new struggles, experiences, and understandings. His ability to build on the political sensibilities gained from theater is currently foreclosed because of that theater's inability to sustain itself.

The process of awakening a hunger for theater occurs in Mumbai just as it has occurred in other places, including Sitapur, Lucknow, and Minneapolis, where Tarun and I have worked with similar processes of collective learning. It allows participants to articulate and internalize new political interpretations of their pasts and presents, in profoundly relational terms, through an embodied immersion in stories, texts, and languages whose previously inherited meanings they had often taken for granted. This hunger has also allowed for creation of innovative 'texts' that were only possible to imagine collectively with the specific (hi)stories, memories, and commitments each participant brought to the process. In so doing, each exploration in political theater has created spaces for situated solidarities that inspire fresh engagements with life and its possibilities and limitations. Since these theatrical exercises are unburdened by a need to seek resources that can sustain the activity and provide livelihoods to the actors, the plays do not become commodities to be sold for profit.

Yet, Sajjan's example points to the structural limits of such work to sustain the creative and political hunger it generates. Unless backed by an ongoing movement, such as the SKMS, as a key resource for its sustenance, theatrical productions do not readily translate into projects that can continue in the absence of a registered organization or individual donors. Building registered organizations to continue theater is often accompanied by needs such as infrastructure and staff that threaten to turn theatrical production into a process of manufacturing commodities through NGOs. This also raises a key contradiction in the dance of hungers: how to continue living, and performing, the hunger for transformative politics relationally through theater? How to learn by enacting situated solidarities with those whose varied locations in the theater of the 'margins' resist dominant imagination associated with poverty politics? How to grapple with these challenges in ways that can ensure that the burden of reproducing the actors' own bodies does not threaten to take away the collective's transformative creativity, and vice versa?

· · ·

In the face of divisive caste-based and communal violence against communities that face the most acute hunger of the belly, the embodied pedagogies of *Hansa* articulate a politics of belonging through samanvaya, which can be loosely conceptualized as situated solidarity.[18] Far from replaying inherited lessons or interpretations about differences of caste, class, or geographical location, the creative process enables unanticipated articulations of swaanubhuti, albeit in ways that one's own histories and geographies become interwoven with those of other coactors, even as the collective searches for new analytical resonances and epiphanies through empathy or samaanubhuti. For example, Mumtaz identifies closely as Budhiya *and* as an artist who feels her responsibility as a coeducator in a collective process. We also get a glimpse in an earlier section of how Gaurav acquires humility as an actor as he begins to embed the story in the caste and communal violence that his own Savarna family members have perpetrated.

Such collaboration generates the potential to build solidarities through a radical rethinking of marginality. Thus, Alok and Gaurav realign their notions about who is who in the world based on their appreciation of the lives, labor, and talents of Sajjan, Meena, Anil, and Mumtaz ji, with whom Alok also enters into a special bond as Madhav. BD tries to internalize Ghisu's wisdom as a penetrating sociopolitical critique in the face of cruel forces that seem overpowering. In each instance, theater becomes an aesthetically rich mode through which the individual actors become one with the characters—undertaking intense journeys across time, place, and immediate embodied contexts—in order to collectively grapple with the political limitations of both sahaanubhuti (sympathy) and swaanubhuti (one's own experience), and to work through the ethical nuances of samaanubhuti (connectedness of experience), samata (equity), and samanvaya (alliance).[19]

At the same time, Sajjan's experience suggests that samanvaya requires continued relational groundedness of theater so that political awakening can evolve into articulations of new social futures. In a politics that simultaneously challenges the violence of commodification, professionalization, and NGOization, such groundedness is hard to sustain. However, once a creative collective hunger is implanted, it keeps the actors restless for the next opportunity for creation through theater. The hope of transformation through political theater lies in this continued embodied yearning that can only be produced collectively and that must demand radical shifts in the ways we come to know, feel, or translate those who are reductively named 'poor' or 'hungry.'[20]

Just Retelling, Just Reading: Planting New Hungers

The creation of *Hansa* is a slow process of embodiment through which participants translate the characters into their own lives while breathing their own lives into the characters. Their rereading and rescripting of Premchand's seven-page story through acting inspires a radical vulnerability that can enable shared aesthetics and ethics for an active remaking of oneself in relation to the collective.[21] If doing justice to the nuances of a hungry belly is only possible through the hunger of the soul, then this learning must be communicated through the movements of the body itself. Acting, then, becomes a nonstop interrogation of internalized frameworks and embodied practices around caste, gender, labor, and language, not only in relation to the interactions among characters, but also in the actors' day-to-day lives as they begin to 'live in character.'

How, then, can Sajjan return to being a servant-as-usual after becoming part of an artistry that longs for new interpretations? How can Mumtaz not distinguish between the ways Alok and Gaurav approach the character of Madhav with different sensitivities toward Budhiya, and how can she as Budhiya not let those sensitivities shape her own responses to the two Madhavs? The poetics enabled in the political space of theater are never not in dialogue with the tense or tender moments outside of that space, as participants continue to pay what Tarun calls the "psychological price" of casteism. Surrendering to artistry, which demands a non-separation between creativity and embodied thought, means continuously paying this psychological price.

Ghisu and Madhav are willfully unemployed not because they cannot or do not want to work, but because they do not find the compensation worth the toil and humiliation they must suffer. They prefer to withstand the uncertainty of the next meal in a context where even those with steady work do not always have what it takes to be 'full.' Their attitude does not simply challenge the norms of labor and capital; they refuse to participate any more than absolutely necessary in an interbraided socioeconomic, cultural, spiritual, political, and psychological system that does them no good: as Tarun puts it, "If this is how this contradictory system of ours works, then how can one honestly label the little bit of lying one has to do in order to steal some hours to breathe or be with one's children or lover or family or friends as deceit? As laziness?" While some fellow villagers look on Ghisu and Madhav with disdain, others envy their perplexing ability to withstand hunger and beatings; one notes: "Such mysterious souls trick the world. My brain stops working when I see them."

As readers and retellers of the story, each participant's journey with "Kafan" begins with cultivating a new common sense that refuses to reduce Ghisu and Madhav to selfish, lazy, and cruel villains. The participants step out of all kinds of prepackaged ideas, not only about poverty, hunger, chamar, Dalit, and mazdoor, but also about acting, laboring, being, and transforming. Doing justice to Ghisu, Madhav, Budhiya, and their worlds means surrendering to their characters and reassessing the world through their lenses, without assuming we can fully know them. Such identification requires keeping in perpetual tension one's own feelings of distance, disgust, or pity toward them. The sheer magnitude of this emotional, psychic, and physical labor makes the journey impossible to replicate even as it transforms each of us forever. By multiply retelling *Hansa* and its making, then, I do not claim to capture all the complexities of this complex and dynamic play or process. Rather, my tellings are hungry translations of the committed vision and artistry that birthed this creative journey of becoming, one where acting became synonymous with living, learning, and longing in a radically vulnerable mode.

The making of *Hansa* defies the binary between 'good' and 'bad' that often underwrites conversations about social justice. It muddies the distinctions between villain and protagonist, between victim and victimizer, by demanding what Inayatullah calls "full generosity to the antagonist."[22] This principle involves "appreciating in the other's point of view a core grain of truth that must not be ignored, transformed, or assimilated." It asks, "Why do we work so hard to forget our overlap with others, so that what appears is our innocence and their guilt, and sometimes our guilt and their innocence, but never their overlap? Why do we strain to forget our simultaneous overlap but different embedding in violence, war, and even genocide? Why do we ignore our complicity?"[23] A generosity toward our antagonists also asks us to embrace the unexpected: if each rereading of a text must resist what has already been scripted and rehearsed, then each new round of enacting that text should continue to surprise us through an ongoing embodied, affective, and political translation of the characters, the plot, and the meanings of the words and actions that are being staged. Only then can we move beyond encaging Ghisu's and Madhav's resistance within our familiar frameworks of just and unjust, and revisit, with them, the meanings of life through death.

"If we are not dead yet," says Ghisu early on in the play, "there is a lot that still exists in our share." Hunger, death, and life become the essential meditative points around which the collective search for new poetics, politics, and artistry evolves. Budhiya's death connects various hungers and longings: in addition to her own malnourishment, Ghisu and Madhav's sharing of stolen potatoes after two days of starvation, and Ghisu's reminiscing of the thakur's unforgettable feast, there is Madhav's longing for marriage and a lineage, and Ghisu's wise warning that such yearning would only make them more vulnerable to the brutal system in which they are already outcasts. Toward the end, however, the same father and son turn Budhiya's death into a festival of life. As the two unknowingly move, by a divine plan, toward the liquor shop, we hear the words, "To beg is like dying, thus no one should beg. Dying is preferable to begging, this is the lesson from the saint." "What else?," asks Ghisu. "If we had gotten the same five rupees in our hands a bit earlier, we could have bought medicine for her, couldn't we? Hard to get over this world and its strange games!" And then later, "Why do you cry, Son? Be happy that she became free of this world, got rid of all the chains. She was very fortunate that she could break these worldly bonds so quickly."

Hansa jars and disturbs. It does not ask the spectator to move with Madhav and Ghisu. Nor does it expect its audience to fully understand its script or idioms. It plants a new longing, however: to radically rewrite the scripts of caste, gender, and poverty politics by relearning the meanings of death, and of that which is worth laboring for and hungering for in life.

• • •

The embodied pedagogies explored and revealed through my co-participation in Parakh's journey with "Kafan" and *Hansa* coincided, not entirely accidentally, with a period of trauma and mourning in my familial and work lives. These pains, however, merged with those of the entire Parakh team as we all immersed ourselves in a deeply enriching journey with one another. Each of us gave pieces of our souls to the work even when honest sharing made things hard with respect to interpretations and processes. We brought our pasts and presents, our emotions and languages, our sorrows and joys, making *Hansa* a continuous convening of unforeseen spirits. The workshop became an ongoing meditation on life and death as well as on the definitions of family and foes, a poetic tribute to those we had lost or gained. Ironically, the magic of *Hansa*—as a production on stage as well as in the form of bonds and moments it created—was wrapped up with the painful truth that what had been created could not be replicated. The profound lessons absorbed throughout the period of six months could only be sustained by learning to let go of an attachment to the product called *Hansa*.

At the same time, the making of *Hansa* gives me courage to embrace translational journeys that previously seemed too difficult to undertake in a US-based classroom. It underlines the necessity to ethically translate the entanglement of social and poetic justice into an ever-evolving pedagogical labor that requires crossing borders with stories—of not only Budhiya, Ghisu, and Madhav, but also of Rambeti, Sunita, SKMS, and CGIAR—as a facilitator and co-learner in the formal classrooms of a research 1 university. Far from erasing the distances of places, times, contexts, and struggles, this necessity for hungry translations of the confluences of poetic and social justice in the classroom is about collectively grappling with the politics of borders and boundaries in intimate and embodied ways. It is about unlearning and relearning with humility the definitions of antagonists and protagonists, of victims and perpetrators, of the good and the distasteful that have been handed down to us through expertly defined frameworks, methodologies, and pedagogies. It sets me on a new path in the classroom—to wrestle relationally with telling and receiving stories as an ever-incomplete exercise in ethically responsible and responsive mediation: as a hungry translation that collectively seeks justice for violated lives and subordinated truths without searching for permanent resolutions or closures.

• • •

Frances W. Pritchett's translation of Premchand's "Kafan" as the "The Shroud" is an assigned reading in the humanistic commons Stories, Bodies, and Bordercrossings freshman seminar that I am teaching with Professor Diyah Larasati at the University of Minnesota, at the same time as the group in Mumbai is evolving the story into *Hansa*. The students are all eighteen to nineteen years old from varied social locations, most of them raised in Minnesota, Wisconsin, or California, and three of them are of Indian or Thai background. Members of the class have generatively grappled for several weeks with such issues as the violence and contradictions of uneven development and exoticization in representation of rural lives, as well as activist and artistic resistance to these. Still, the context and content of "Kafan" seem to baffle them. I realize that it is going to take more than a classroom discussion to gradually turn "Kafan" into a generatively haunting story for the students. I am reminded of my eleventh grade Hindi teacher in Lucknow, Chandra Cornelius, who first taught me in 1983 how to appreciate Ghisu as an intelligent rebel hero rather than a villain, without undermining the profound tragedy of Budhiya's death. If Ms. Cornelius could teach the story ethically to me as a young teenager, could I not try to do justice to it as a teacher, too? What tools would I need to explore to come up with a translational process that might work for my students in Minnesota?

To initiate a discussion about the story, I ask the class, "What do you think this story is about?"

"It's about acute poverty and desperation," remarks A.

"It's about two very lazy men," says B.

So far, the responses are similar to what we heard in Mumbai when we first began to read the story. I ask: "What makes you think that Madhav and Ghisu are lazy? And if they are lazy, what makes them so?"

C responds first: "They are lazy because they don't have any hope. It is their low caste status that makes them hopeless."

D picks up the thread where C leaves it: "Their hopelessness makes them selfish, and they can think only of themselves and their hunger. I would never treat someone I love in the way that Ghisu and Madhav treat Budhiya. To me, their selfishness and greed are no different than the greed and selfishness of the most evil capitalists. The only difference is that their violence is happening in the intimacy of a hut, and the other violence happens in the global market."

The first part of D's remarks reminds me of S, who was present in Mumbai during the first reading of "Kafan" and who commented that Ghisu and Madhav were scoundrels of the first order. She had said that reading about them made her want to hit both of them hard; thank god the world is different now, or at least one doesn't see these things in the middle-class homes in big cities. I remember Mumtaz agreeing wholeheartedly with S's passionate hatred for the two "villains" at that time.

During the beginning of the workshop in Mumbai, as well as in our classroom in Minnesota, most participants tend to read the story as something of a distant past and place when it came to caste and untouchability: it was then, not now; it was there, not here. However, the second part of D's comment is more complex—she equates the selfish and greedy heartlessness of Ghisu and Madhav with the evil of capitalist individualism. Yet, even in this more complex reading, D herself remains far from Madhav, Ghisu, and Budhiya on the one hand, and from the evil capitalists on the other. In both Mumbai and Minneapolis, the initial readings of "Kafan" suggest a zeroing in on the cruelty of Ghisu and Madhav through a refusal to engage with the bodily hunger that persists so saliently in the story, along with the politics of knowledge and truth claims that are subtly interbraided with that hunger.

In Mumbai, however, this refusal dies out naturally as participants go through an all-consuming process of learning the hungers, longings, and hopelessness of Ghisu, Madhav, and Budhiya. Participants dive deep into the story to feel every character and their contexts and psyches in their bones through their own memories, stories, and accents; as they do so, each ripple and curve, each phrase and punctuation of the story, unfold into nuanced interpretations. Each actor becomes a hungry translator—as well as a continuously translated text—that gives a vibrant life to the story. Perhaps the most powerful example of this can be found in Budhiya's labor pains, which go neglected by Ghisu and Madhav and result in her death in "Kafan." Yet, Mumtaz's labor as an actor performing those labor pains in *Hansa* breathes into Budhiya a new life, even in the scene of her death. Producing a different version of the same text, the Parakh team articulates a new ethic to engage the question of hungry translation as an intensely embodied, affective, spiritual, and poetic process that is simultaneously political as well. In part, this labor hinges on unlearning 'laziness' as a negative trait, and relearning it as a mode of expressing systemic critique through which Ghisu and Madhav declare their nonparticipation in the intertwined socioreligious and political and economic order that insists on degrading and killing them. This reading of Ghisu and Madhav sees them as creative resistors to casteist and capitalist powers that construct the 'lazy' mazdoor; it also suggests that their refusal to cooperate with the ways of their cruel world and their ways of thinking and acting in the face of grave crises cannot be fully accessed by their readers, or even their fellow village people who do not inhabit the same epistemic mold or political-spiritual-intellectual domain as they do.

The process unfolding in Mumbai's theater workshop enables me to bring to Diyah's and my classroom in Minnesota the insights from the restless negotiations and unlearning that are emerging in the rehearsal space and in the relationships among the actors. As students work on their written reflections, I ask them to revisit their initial impressions and to unlearn their gut feelings about the story. I provide examples from the conversations that are emerging through the intense labor the workshop participants are placing into the making of *Hansa* in Mumbai. While the story baffles the class at first, by the end of the semester almost half the class voluntarily embraces the challenge of "The Shroud" in at least one of the reflection papers. Below, I share some edited fragments from six of these papers:

> *Ghisu and Madhav work very little and . . . appear lazy, but in actuality these men have realized that no matter how much work they do, they will never be able to rise above the status they are in. When they receive money from the richer people in their community, they believe it is owed to them and they decide to spend it on food and drinks for themselves. After they are fulfilled, they give the last of their food to a beggar. Ghisu tells the beggar that he should thank Budhiya because her death allowed them to eat like prosperous people and although she is dead, the beggar's "blessing will certainly reach her" in heaven. In that moment, the two men are more generous than the entire system that oppresses them, despite lacking the material means to achieve this generosity.*

> *Class, caste and gender shape the experiences of Ghisu and Madhav who are trying to make space for themselves in a society that humiliates and starves them. They do this by ignoring the rules created by those who oppress them. What appears to us as laziness seems to be the only kind of empowerment available to them. Their radical acceptance of their life's condi-*

tions leads them to accept Budhiya's death. If I can merely recognize this as heartlessness, that suggests that I do not have the tools to understand or appreciate their critique.

Ghisu and his son, Madhav, lack almost any sort of influence over their lives. In "[a] society in which those who labored night and day were not in much better shape than these two," father and son find themselves mostly alone. They resist the societal structure that places them at the bottom by, ironically enough, doing almost nothing. "[If Ghisu] was in bad shape, at least he wasn't forced to do the back-breaking labor of the peasants, and others didn't take improper advantage of his simplicity and voicelessness."[24] In the face of their almost complete powerlessness, this simple resistance by way of unconformity is almost all that is feasible for them.

Unlike some other stories [we read about collective resistance of those in the margins], Ghisu and Madhav are as powerless at the end of the story as they were in the beginning, except for a brief time of blissful plentifulness purchased from the same money that they were given to shroud Budhiya's dead body. Although the functioning of power hierarchies in this story is difficult to comprehend, the duo is very much alone in their resistance. It is said that, "compared to the peasants, Ghisu was more insightful,"[25] implying that even if others were capable of similar resistance, they wouldn't even consider it because they did not have the courage that Ghisu could gather from his insights.

Noticing that those around them who work much harder are not much better off, Madhav and Ghisu rebel against their societal standards and take on a life that derives meaning and where they find strength from their intentional solidarity. By completely neglecting society's constraints, they set themselves off from everyone else, including from Budhiya. . . . Although they set themselves apart from Budhiya, their simultaneous dependence on her introduces us to the idea of sexual intimacy and gendered interdependence in a feudal and casteist patriarchy. In this complex intersectionality Ghisu and Madhav, as poor men of a very low caste, not only face oppression from those who are 'higher' in their society, but they cannot help oppressing Budhiya either . . . [which] coincides with their resistance of all the rules that demand conformity.

Madhav and Ghisu undertake an unreal journey across the levels of the same society that starves them. After attaining the money for the shroud, they momentarily live like the rich. There is great irony in this moment. Although it is the wealthier people's supposed generosity that allows them to become rich, in the brief moment when they do occupy the stage of life as people of means, the two give even more generously than the wealthy who allowed them to experience fulfillment in the first place. When they fulfill their hunger, they refuse to put away anything for later convenience, and share their feast with a poor person who is more mistreated than they are. Grappling with . . . their rebellion toward societal rules and hierarchies requires imagination that may be possible only through suffering and displacement.

Each of the students whose writing I summarize above undergoes an emotional and intellectual journey with respect to "The Shroud." The relatively brief duration and disembodied and distant nature of their journeys do not allow them to linger in the worlds of Budhiya, Madhav, and Ghisu in the ways the actors in Mumbai do. However, the journey pushes them to come closer to a story they initially felt alienated from; this makes it necessary for them to radically question some of their fundamental beliefs about goodness, laziness, systemic critique, and critical agency.

Mumtaz's longer-term embodied immersion in the process of making *Hansa* gives birth to her conviction that there can be no "Kafan" without Budhiya. The students in Stories, Bodies, and Bordercrossings do not get a chance to inject life into the dying Budhiya of "The Shroud" in the absence of a similarly embodied process. However, they do travel a significant distance with Madhav and Ghisu. It would have been impossible for me to help them undertake even this part of their journey without the creative courage and inspiration of Mumtaz, Tarun, Alok, BD, Sajjan, Gaurav, Meena, Neeraj, and all the others in Parakh, who threw themselves fully into a collective hungry translation of "Kafan" that eventually birthed *Hansa* in Mumbai.

PART FOUR

Stories, Bodies, Movements

A Syllabus in Fifteen Acts

Prologue

Working together for a more equitable and just world often requires unlearning and relearning the stories that make global politics. This six-part syllabus for Stories, Bodies, Movements, a combined graduate and undergraduate class, invites us to embrace such collective labor by grappling with the meanings of building situated solidarities through radical vulnerability as a collectively honed praxis. Taking as its inspiration the methodologies of building and sustaining long-term situated solidarities with social movements, the course uses storytelling and theater as modes of embodied unlearning and relearning. It searches for an intense intimacy with sites that are claimed by academics of the global north as sites of their research or activism, but that are often simultaneously othered in the classroom as places far removed from the researcher, teacher, and student. In so doing, the course seeks to unsettle the modes of learning that dominate many neoliberal research 1 universities in the United States by exploring the possibility and impossibility of translating through the classroom: a 'methodology' of building and sustaining deep relationships with ongoing struggles in the global south. It asks: How do we bring 'our' stories into serious conversations with the histories and geographies we have inherited? How do we learn to see these stories as simultaneously global and intimate; as marked by both love and violence; and as constituted of protagonists who may also be antagonists, and of victims who may also be victimizers?

The course asks that all the course participants become co-travelers and co-authors as they grapple with these questions through reading, writing, remembering, telling, sculpting, scripting, and performing together in an unfolding journey over the semester. In striving to learn from writings, films, songs, plays, and visions of writers, artists, activists, and thinkers from a range of historical and contemporary locations, we must suspend our usual expectations about a semester-long course. Instead of approaching this syllabus as an account of what I am offering or expecting from the class, then, I invite you to soak in its spirit and swim in it. One way to do this is by meditating weekly on the first four sections of the syllabus, and reflecting on where the previous weeks of the course have brought us and where we might go next.

One More Time

One more time
you ask me to tell you
another one of those stories
piercing eyes   on fire
chase the dark
      turmeric saris bleed
large callused hands
      pound against eardrums
umbilical cords entwine
      bamboo pens
stab guts   unverified
ancestors
out of time
turn away words
poison dictionaries footnotes glossaries
without permission
a million needles sigh
      wounds desires destinies
received out of line
snatched blessings
      girls don't inherit
and you ask me one more time
to tell you a story oozing secrets—

sun soaked green mangoes in heeng kalaunji
young feet salted in ocean's chest don't return to shore
bonded server parent unbound
—not so you may heave a sob hounded
nor honor it by
communing with the
haunted   haunting—
collisions
but to frame
another Intervention
pronounce meaning
          accentless
strip flesh   muscle   sensation
          plastic petals
          incapable of twisting
          exploring, moving, collaborating
lips don't come together
to echo
sounds rebound unregistered.

but Tongues,
lips,
throats,
guts
          stripped of sensations
will beat stories flat
like a drenched old rag
beaten repeatedly with a heavy washing bat
on stone by a
body squatting
bent over it   beating
          breathing
                              beating
surrounded by a mountain
          bedsheets, bras, salwaars, shirts, skirts, saris,
rags, pants, petticoats, underwear, and heavy blue jeans
                    blood-stained and
waiting to be washed before the
trickle in the tap disappears, before the

legs become overwhelmed by that full
heavy feeling making it
        impossible to stand
on your feet after you are
        done
washing that mountain.

If my metaphors do not
make sense it's
because
your body does not know
what I know
from learning what it is like
to beat clothes
on stones under trickles of water for
years   decades
        generations
yet you demand another story
as if my tongue was not my own hot
        flesh
you retell
without shiver or stammer without
feeling in a piece of your bones
for a second my
wounded everyday sort   of
        joy,   pain,   of
that overwhelming fullness
that piercing, deadening Heaviness
in my thighs
moving upwards and spreading in to
arms shoulders
up my neck
connects with veins
of my Soul.
        you will never
realize, you cannot
know:
in your eagerness to retell another
one of these
stories you've gone

without learning
how to squat
for hours
washing
        breathing
        beating
cloth after cloth
on the stone
before that trickle vanishes.

*"One More Time" first flowed as I envisioned this
syllabus, and I share it here as a gesture of radical
vulnerability. In expressing a desire for common goals
in this journey where I am asking each of us to offer
intimate pieces of ourselves, this is an initial offering.
I invite you to respond to this poem in whatever ways
make the most sense to you. Explore what it might
mean for you to grapple with what Édouard Glissant[1]
calls the "right to opacity" of one's stories, movements,
and locations, and to guard against an engagement
with an other that slips into appropriation, or into a
desire to fully know or translate.*

Synopsis and Backdrop

All politics are politics of storytelling. Stories shape our sense of self: who we believe we are, our sense of our own inherited privileges and misfortunes, our affinities, identifications, and allegiances. Stories also shape what we wish or hope to do in order to give our existence meaning: whom we want to stand or fight with, whom or what we want to help or rescue in order to uphold what we think is ethical or just. This is a basic truth when thinking about the ethical and the political in relation to global politics. It allows us to see 'global politics' as deriving its meanings, affects, and effects from the circulation and retellings of stories across borders.

If we agree broadly on this starting point, then a praxis of ethical engagement with politics can be imagined as a praxis of *retelling* stories. Such praxis translates stories of *being in struggle* in ways that are grounded in the embodied experience of knowing, even as those very translations must migrate out to other sites of struggle in order to find resonances and to build situated solidarities. This recognition pushes us to theorize across forms of oppression and axes of difference[1] while remaining grounded in the specificities of each context. For it is the resonances between, across, and within struggles that generate a collective stake in justice. In fact, it is the ongoing hungering and laboring to build resonances that teaches us about the many depths and contradictions of each struggle and the nuances of place-specific configurations of power, difference, and desire.

This course interrupts the widely upheld assumption that we do research or community engagement in sites that are separated from the university, while education happens in formal classroom spaces where students are secluded, sheltered, or disembedded from the spaces where politics are actively made and remade. It conceptualizes the *stage* as a site and moment of performance that also involves *staging* as a deliberate, yet relational, fluid, and forever-evolving act. Pedagogy, then, becomes a praxis of embodied performance where teaching, unlearning, and relearning happen in and through strategic and staged retellings. Far from exploring texts merely as stories of what happens 'out there' in 'the community,' in 'the struggle,' or in 'the world,' such praxis requires us to feel and grapple with ourselves and our pasts, presents, and futures in intimate entanglement with what we have been taught to see as the other. In such an approach, there can be no ideal set of texts or cannons; I offer as a point of departure some of the texts that are embedded in my own safars—or journeys—with collective pedagogies, movements, and translations. By exploring the convergences, affinities, tensions, and disjunctures between these assigned texts and the texts that each of you will offer and create through your own journeys, Stories, Bodies, Movements seeks to stitch together spaces of learning, performance, and activism as dynamic shared spaces in deep conversation, where one does not wait to see the impact of one's labor in terms of a product after the teaching and learning have happened. Rather, the product, politics, process, and poetics of sharing, embodied theory, and living resistance all become a thoroughly entangled journey of theater, movement, and translation. This fluid relational articulation—that is rough and bumpy and marked with both joys and pains— pushes back against many standardized pedagogies and replaces them with a deep relational process that may continue to evolve as critical learning long after the fifteen weeks within which this formal course is circumscribed.

Receiving, Retelling, Responsibility

For most of us, stories simply happen. Many a time, they happen as naturally and easily as breathing does: We listen to stories, we tell stories, we are moved by stories, and we retell stories. However, while we are not often conscious of our breathing, stories are another matter. Telling stories involves making decisions or moves, and each retelling of a familiar story may either give birth to new meanings, nuances, and affects, or erase their possibility. Thus, each storyteller can be seen as a translator of stories with a responsibility to retell stories in ways that can do justice to them. Sometimes our stories center on us and sometimes they focus on another, but no matter what or who a story is about, its teller and receiver are almost always implicated in representing or translating a self that is entangled and co-constitutive with an other. It is precisely through these translational acts that all politics become politics of storytelling.

Stories, Bodies, Movements considers the ways in which the politics of the global and the intimate derive their meanings, effects, and affects from the circulation and retellings of stories within and across borders. It asks: What kind of responsibility comes with the acts of telling and receiving stories? What is at stake, and for whom, when a story is narrated? The course imagines ethical engagement with politics as a continuous search for justice through a praxis of receiving *and* retelling stories. Such praxis requires us to keep moving in relation to stories, and it urges us to grapple with the accents, tones, intentions, and meanderings of an other's stories through a conscious remembering and retelling of our own stories. By immersing ourselves in the process of recalling, telling, listening, trimming, interweaving, distilling, and performing stories, we will consider how just receiving and just retelling of stories involves endless editing, repositioning, and retheorizing of such vexed and entangled terrains and terminologies as identity, community, rights, and belonging, as well as the contingent meanings of knowledge, truth, ethics, and justice.

This course seeks to create a world of stories through a mode of active learning in which we will read and reflect, listen and discuss, tell and retell, watch and play, move and perform collectively. It asks that we become aware of the ways in which our bodies—as inseparable from our beings—process and express the conjunctures of histories, geographies, and sociopolitical and spiritual contexts that make each story unique. It asks us to recognize how we are inserted in the reception and translation of each story and to grapple with what it might mean to embrace a mode of radical vulnerability in order to receive a story ethically.

Stories, Bodies, Movements emerges from more than fifteen years of working with saathis of SKMS and Parakh Theatre (see parts 1–3 of *Hungry Translations*), where theater has appeared as a critical genre *and* a mode of co-learning and co-evolving pedagogies of collective political analyses and action. It emerges, too, from concurrent critical conversations with students, colleagues, and interlocutors of related topics in many academic locations. It explores the creative continuities and connections between the intellectual and pedagogical labors of political theater and political struggle. It emphasizes the serendipitous ways in which movements of the body *and* bodies form the movement of the social, and how these movements blend, shift, and flow in and through the labors of cocreating affective and political energies—inside and outside the spaces we know as classrooms, and inside and outside what we have learned to recognize as social movement. Here, moving and movement embrace all that moves within us and that inspires us to move in hitherto unforeseen ways. This movement, in turn, holds the potential to give birth to a collectively owned political theater that is hungry to receive and perform stories by opening itself to continuous revision and improvisation. In such embodied journeys—where the actors become restless translators who yearn to find new meanings in a continuously unfolding relationship with the pasts, presents, and futures of themselves, their coactors, and the characters and lives they are internalizing—theater *becomes* transformative unlearning and relearning.

The structure, content, and processes of Stories, Bodies, Movements are molded by long-term relationships in and through which I have learned some whys and hows of building and sustaining long-term situated solidarities across multiple sites of engagement. The ongoing and unfolding long-term temporality and trajectories of these relationships disengage from the instrumentalist or project-specific affiliations that academics are often expected to make with their 'research subjects.' In translating some of these lessons into this syllabus, I do not wish to offer an authoritative blueprint or template that is stamped by my so-called expertise or that contains the perfect texts and activities that can be replicated in other contexts. Rather, in grounding this document in my own embodied journeys, I embrace radical vulnerability as a mode of co-learning. I invite each one of you, the reader and the co-learner, to also retell your own locations, journeys, encounters, and struggles and to bring them into conversation with texts, moments, and movements that have inspired you. Then, we can together learn how to meet, cross, counter, and respect the borders between self and other as an essential part of grappling with politics that are simultaneously intimate and global.[2]

Politics, Pedagogy, Performance

Each week of this class will unfold as an act of a play over the course of a semester. We will reflect together on the kinds of sociopolitical-psychological-spiritual work that retellings of a story do, and on the ways that storytelling becomes a performative practice as well as an ethical responsibility that cannot be shirked. We will seriously attend to the labor and responsibility of receiving a story through a mode of active learning where we read and reflect, listen and discuss, tell and retell, rehearse and revise, watch and perform collectively. Recognizing that each of our social locations impose *and* enable certain kinds of embodiment on us, Stories, Bodies, Movements pushes us to begin feeling the story of an other. It asks: what kind of labor might it take on the part of those who inhabit the classroom to co-develop and co-own a pedagogy through which our reception of a story can simultaneously trouble, displace, or extend the disciplined 'I' and the inherited eye? What does such disruption, revision, or extension imply for our understanding of the social and the political?

The course creates the soil for evolving a collectively owned political pedagogical sensibility that continuously strives to *feel* another's story by learning and playing that is at once grounded, dynamic, and antihierarchical. It eschews modes of studying or theorizing the complexity of an other from a distance. At the same time, it asks that we remain attuned to the risks and contradictions that accompany this process, especially when the displaced words of those inhabiting the socioeconomic margins may be spoken and enacted by those who represent the mainstream. Rather than letting these contradictions slip into a narcissistic or reductive politics of identity and guilt, we will strive to shape an antiessentialist politics that strives to ethically remember, forget, and retell in order to do justice to the stories, histories, and struggles of bodies who occupy marginal spaces in dominant institutionalized memories, imaginations, languages, and modes of narrations.

i/I, You, They, We, Us

Unlearning and relearning how to receive, retell, and perform stories requires a complex ongoing dance among the i/I, we, you, they, and us while refusing such reductive compartments as mind-body-soul-being. In hungering for justice through ethical engagement with lives and struggles, memories and wars, hauntings and hopes, such critical creativity opens up fresh ontological and epistemological possibilities by interweaving questions of translation, storytelling, and embodiment. By bringing your own journeys into conversation with the assigned texts, you will work through the evolving processes of narration and grapple with the theoretical and political challenges of negotiating multiple i/Is in relation to multiple wes: both in the collective that is, or is not, emerging through the retelling of stories in the classroom and in the contexts and struggles you are learning about through the course materials, and from one another. This grappling will nourish our ongoing discussion about the ethos of telling and receiving stories, the contingencies and responsibilities that define such telling and receiving, as well as the possibilities and impossibilities that accompany this terrain. We will keep returning to the gaps, risks, and uncertainties of narration and translation by confronting and processing our own vulnerabilities as individuals as well as the ways in which our vulnerability can become radical *through* collective cocreation. We will become alive to the complex entanglements between the universal and the particular; and to the ways in which theorizing must happen through the processes of reading, reflection, and improvisation in conversation with all the bodies and (hi)stories that inhabit the classroom.

Stories, Bodies, Movements will continue to evolve in conversation with our stories and learning processes throughout the semester. This may require moving away from what is articulated in the syllabus, and it may also necessitate that we share and create in spaces beyond the classroom and the university. If you are interested, some of our class activities may be filmed so that we can document, reflect on, and refine our processes of co-learning through an audiovisual medium.

Contradictions

Stories, Bodies, Movements reflects dreams, questions, and labors that have been close to my heart for a long time. Yet, I am offering this course in the traditionally structured spaces of an institution where I am a designated instructor, who is not only articulating the expectations and criteria for assessment and grading, but who must also do so in advance of a shared process of embodied learning that is intended to unfold serendipitously. Moreover, radical vulnerability as an ethical mode of forming collectivity and solidarity cannot be demanded; it can only emerge organically from the very movement of co-travelers. *Its absence, too, provides opportunities to reflect in embodied ways on why radical vulnerability cannot become a formula for cultivating collectivity or solidarity.*

Thus, the inherent contradictions of grappling, in the institutional context, with a mode of learning that resists institutionalization remain. In reminding us about the impossibility of achieving an entirely nonhierarchical space the course ironically mirrors a common condition of life where movements and collectives who oppose hierarchy have to simultaneously confront the realities of social and structural locations that its members differentially occupy. It also is a bitter reminder of the difficulties of achieving radical political aspirations through institutionalized research and pedagogical projects. Nevertheless, Stories, Bodies, Movements refuses to compromise its fundamental search: for methodologies of creating politically-informed pedagogical spaces and practices that foster a different kind of modality in which co-learning can be imagined as an "uncoercive rearrangement of desires."[3] An arrangement that fiercely embraces the responsibility of retelling and receiving stories ethically in a continuous search for justice, without assuming the meanings of justice outside of the specificities of the journey, and without looking for permanent closures.

Initial Keywords, Props, Premises

Let us revisit and build on the following keywords, props, and premises throughout the semester. Let us explore their multiple definitions and possibilities for the work that they can or cannot do.

Keywords and Working Definitions

Radical	That which goes to the roots, in order to reroot or uproot[1]
Praxis	The inseparability of thought and action where doing and theorizing can only be realized in and through each other
Embodied	Thinking, feeling, recognizing, and doing in and through the body, as opposed to disembodied or detached ways of knowing and doing
Aesthetics	A set of principles concerned with the nature and appreciation of beauty and artistic taste
Ethics	Morals, beliefs, integrity, conscience, principles
Move (noun)	Shift, attempt
Move (verb)	Progress, cause, go, reposition

To build on this list, we will together create in class the working definitions of three more terms: 'politics,' 'responsibility,' and 'stories.' We will keep adding more terms as our conversations evolve.

Props

- *Radical Vulnerability.* When we do not think of ourselves as autonomous, sovereign, or independent social beings or actors. Rather, we see our self as intensely relational and co-constitutive with the other. Thus, i and I can only evolve through an openness to and an intimacy with the other. This implies dissolving our singular individualized egos: whatever we learn, whatever we come to be, becomes deeply contingent on what each one of us is prepared to give to the collective journey that brings the i/I and we together with the *you* and *they.*
- *Empathetic Reflection.* Strives to empathize and connect generously with the viewpoint, experience, or argument of an other. Even if we are critical of that other's viewpoint or argument, we must locate that position or story in the conditions, contexts, and structures from which it is emerging. This is necessary to develop what Inayatullah calls "generosity to antagonist."
- *Ethical Listening.* Deep listening that pays close attention to words, gestures, and affects of what is being communicated, when, and how. Such listening strives to not misrepresent, oversimplify, caricature, or violate the spirit of what is being communicated even if we cannot understand or grasp or agree with its meanings.
- *Ethical (Re)Telling.* Careful and caring narration that pays close attention to words, gestures, and affects of what is being communicated, when, and how. Such retelling strives to not misrepresent, oversimplify, caricature, or violate the spirit of what is being communicated even if we cannot understand or grasp or agree with its meanings.
- *Animated and Respectful Discussion.* Engaging one another in a mode of radical vulnerability, empathetic reflection, ethical listening, and ethical retelling births trust that allows us to agree and disagree freely, in a nonaggressive and noncompetitive mode in which all of the participants or co-travelers in the intellectual and creative journey are able to speak their hearts and minds without fear and in a dignified manner. This makes possible animated discussion where ideas, analyses, moves, and strategies are generated in passionate and creative ways that are generous toward and respectful of one another but that do not romanticize collectivity by stifling disagreement.
- *Embodied Writing.* Writing—as a yatra, a safar, a journey of our minds, souls, and bodies—that strives to remember, engage, and represent in ways that do not compartmentalize the mind, body, and spirit. Such writing is alive to what our body is feeling and doing as we write.
- *Collective Movement.* The ability of being moved emotionally, politically, intellectually, and physically not as an isolated individual but as a member

of this class; being aware of how this collective movement is unfolding in a space where each one of us enables the learning and growth of not only ourselves but also of one another. Such moving requires provisional agreements that shift as the collective grapples with how to ethically address and express the disagreements and fractures.

- *Coauthorship.* Creating and learning by sharing authority with one another. Each member of this class is a coauthor of what is being understood, created, translated, and performed here. As such, we are accountable to one another so that all of us can continue to grow as coauthors.
- *Polyvocal Script.* Strives to do justice to the journeys and commitments of each voice that has contributed to the making of the larger moving whole, without seeking permanent closures. This is one of the many potential outcomes of a process in which multiple bodies labor together to remember, listen, trust, explore, retell, write, move, and perform.
- *Hungry Translations.* The dominant landscape of knowledge and policy rests on a fundamental inequality: bodies who are seen as hungry are assumed to be available for the interventions of experts, but those experts often obliterate the ways that hungry people actively create politics and knowledge by living a dynamic vision of what is ethical and what makes the good life. The idea of 'hungry translation' approaches this entanglement of deep sociopolitical and epistemic injustice by calling for, and by working to embody, a mode of unlearning and relearning that interweaves critical epistemology with critical pedagogy. An imperfect metaphor for an ever-present hunger to ethically mediate across the unevenness of our social locations, hungry translation argues for just knowledges in the form of an ever-evolving quest. In sharp contrast to modes of engagement that consume and annihilate an other, a hungry engagement actively refuses imposed frameworks and yearns for all that is serendipitous and untranslatable in the relation between self and other. Learning and evolving through such hunger on an unjust social terrain require open and flowing translations, or retellings, that cannot be demanded and that can only emerge from solidarities situated in place, time, and struggle. These dynamic situated solidarities, moreover, require a collectively honed praxis of radical vulnerability, which can enable ever-unfolding relationships across incommensurable landscapes of struggles and meanings. Such relationships can birth translations that co-agitate against universalized languages, which erase the vocabularies and visions of those who are reduced to hungry bodies. In reconceptualizing politics as a shared and unending labour on an uneven terrain and in approaching hunger as a vision and an episteme, hungry translation becomes a collective commitment to troubling inherited meanings of the social, and to making our knowledges more alive to the creativity, unpre-

dictability, and untranslatability of life and of sociopolitical struggle. Such commitment must fearlessly move between worlds in search of poetic justice *and* social justice without defining an origin or destination and without compromising the singularities that constitute each community of struggle.[2]

We will discuss two videos to begin enhancing this list of shared props:

- *Brené Brown on Empathy*: https://www.youtube.com/watch?v=1Evwgu369Jw
- *Lost Voices*, by Darius Simpson and Scout Bostley: https://www.youtube .com/watch?v=lpPASWlnZIA&sns=em

Premises

- Stories, Bodies, Movements is a collectively owned fluid text that seeks to critically explore and constructively reinvent its own genre and processes as it evolves. It proposes a map for a journey that I believe can be generative, creative, and empowering. We will keep revisiting this proposed map as a class so we can make necessary modifications in our approach: where to linger, where to flow, and what to alter in the interests of the issues, events, and commitments that we are learning collectively to care about.
- This class is a learning space where all of us will grapple with the work of responsibly telling and receiving stories as an essential part of social justice work. The success of this exploration depends on our collective labor. The Acts we will perform will require grappling with our own our histories, geographies, desires, and dreams, as a way to continuously rethink ourselves and our own stories in relation to what we are reading, hearing, viewing, and discussing. This requires each one to share fragments from one's own life while engaging ethically with the fragments offered by others.
- We must recognize and address the structural violence and constraints of the spaces we occupy even as we strive for an antihierarchical learning.
- Rather than make you a master of a set of topics, this course seeks to generate a series of turbulences that inspire all of us to think and feel what it means to become a responsible receiver, teller, and reteller of a story as part of a collective creative process.

Formal Outcomes, Expectations, Grades, and Assignments

This class requires a sustained cycle of focused reading, empathetic reflection, animated discussion, embodied writing, and collective movement. We will assess from time to time how well we are moving together toward our goals as co-travelers, as well as the questions, discomforts, critiques, or refusals that should inform our future Acts.

Basic Expectations

Regular attendance, active participation, and timely completion of assigned work are basic requirements for this course, which depends on full presence and generous collaboration among all of us. Please come well prepared to participate in class activities. This includes completing all the readings, reflections, and assigned tasks specified under 'Preparation' for each Act. Schedule at least ten hours before each weekly meeting to complete this work. As you read, write notes in a notepad, journal, or your electronic device, and use these as a basis for crafting your reflections and writing for your weekly posts.

We must create a noncompetitive space that inspires honest reflection and fosters the creativity of all. We should mobilize our energy and ideas to give momentum and flow to the class activities. These commitments also involve becoming aware of how much space we ourselves are taking, and of how we can encourage others to more fully contribute their energies and ideas to the collective flow. To facilitate such collaboration, I invite you to revisit the key words, props, and premises and propose modifications in them as needed.

Grades and Assignments

Your final grade will be based on: the effort you have put into completing assignments in a timely way, your regular attendance, and the quality of your presence and participation in class. The grade breakdown is as follows:

Participation and reflection: weekly posts, journal, and class activities   44%
Retelling, moving, and playing together: building a polyvocal script   40%
Final performance and the continuation of the journey   16%

Participation and Reflection: Weekly Posts, Journal, and Class Activities

Participation in the class includes:

- Completing the work specified under 'Preparation' for each Act before coming to class each week. This includes completing your own reflections and writing, and reading the work of your peers;
- contributing thoughtfully and generously to class activities; and
- asking questions if you do not understand a concept, argument, rule, principle, or expectation, or if you feel stifled, hurt, or overwhelmed by something that is unfolding in the class. No question or concern is out of place, and posing or revisiting issues and questions often allows for new openings and engagements.

Each of you will post your weekly reading reflections on the course's online forum. In this writing, I invite you to:

- Briefly share your thoughts, arguments, and questions about the week's readings, linking these to the questions posed for the week in the syllabus. You may also identify a specific quote from assigned texts, making sure to provide a complete citation (author, title of the text, publication year, and page number) and say why the quote you identified is significant for the claims of the author or for the discussions we are having in class.
- Share a story you can dwell in and can expand and deepen in order to engage the questions we are addressing in this class.
- Feel free to add any thoughts or observations in relation to our class activities, including the collective processes of sharing and scripting our stories.
- Submit the post at least 24 hours before our class meeting so everyone has time to read each other's reflections prior to our next meeting.

The reflections will feed centrally into the group work of discussion, writing, and performing during the next Act. At the end of each Act, I will assign you a score based on your preparation, reflection, and participation.

Retelling, Moving, and Playing Together: Building a Polyvocal Script

Throughout the course, we will explore the ways in which the writing, narration, performance, and revision of stories constitute conscious and continuous creative labor that is at once embodied, poetic, intellectual, and political. You will share, revisit, and revise stories, and co-perform them in conversation with other stories you are learning about. The last four weeks of the course are devoted exclusively to group work in which you will be creating, revising, refining, and performing a polyvocal script with your classmates. This work will require working in close partnership with other members of the team on assigned tasks that will coevolve with the course itself.

Final Performance and the Continuation of the Journey

The final performance will take place before an invited audience determined collectively by the members of this class, followed by a post-performance discussion. Subsequently, we will gather over a meal to reflect together on questions listed under **Act Fifteen**.

The Fifteen Acts

Act One. Letting Go of Our Story

Synopsis: Understanding the goals and vision of this class. What does it mean to let go of our stories?[1]

Scene 1

In my role as a facilitator of this class, I ask you to listen attentively as I share with you my vision for this course and invite you to become part of this journey. I see this course as a collective journey whose path can be outlined by me, but whose meanings and outcomes cannot be predicted because, by its very definition, the journey has to be co-owned by, and co-evolve with, all the travelers. In other words, how the vision unfolds and acquires its resonances and depths depends on how much of ourselves each of us is prepared to give and take in this journey; how much of ourselves we are prepared to risk in this journey of learning and internalizing critical lessons about the aesthetics, ethics, and responsibility of telling and receiving stories.

   This journey of collectively honing and realizing a vision or dream—at once personal and political, as well as individual and collective—begins with a few key understandings. As I sketch out these understandings, I invite you to give them flesh and meaning with your own thoughts and concerns. Remember, from beginning to end, this syllabus remains a fluid text, a flowing river into which each of us brings some of the many streams and rivulets that make us. The text is meant to remain a work in progress, one that would hopefully continue to find meanings in our future lives, long after the end of this semester.

STORIES, BODIES, AND BORDERS Let us all focus on our bodies for a moment. Let us think of the body not as a container that is compartmentalized from our mind or heart, but the body as a series of flows and confluences in which the physical body that is flesh, muscles, blood, and bones is inseparable from what we call the mind, the soul, and the heart. All these parts blur and blend into and out of one another in a series of never-ending movements that is our body.

Now, let us think of a story from our childhoods that we are attached to. Let us try to feel what this body—as an ever-flowing confluence of mind, soul, heart, and all that makes us—*does* when we remember, tell, or perform, or what it does when we see, hear, or read that story. How does an awareness of the ways in which our bodies are inserted in the telling and receiving of stories affect how we recall, narrate, and absorb stories? How do we experience our stories or memories through the language of our senses, such as smell, taste, touch, hearing, or sight? How might we connect with the stories that make each one of us by working consciously to move beyond words? How might our efforts to connect with another through hearing, seeing, or touching allow us to embrace and retell stories in hitherto unfamiliar ways while appreciating the plurality of practices through which translations or retellings happen? These questions urge us to grapple with the ways in which our bodies help to *relationally* shape not only our own performances but also our responses to the performances of other living and moving bodies around us. They invite us collectively to remember and deconstruct the ways in which histories of past violence, traumas, and oppressions continue to inhabit our bodies and inform our responses and our movements.

Reimagine the space of the classroom as dynamically co-constituted with everything that exists outside of this space, a space where a disembodied or isolated self, or *I*, cannot exist independently of the other selves or *they* who cohabit this space. Rethink this relationally defined body as a primary site of knowledge that allows multiple streams of stories to crisscross, overlap, erupt, flow and permeate—through our consciousness, our skins, and our movements—as they navigate the borders of not only place and time, but also of flesh, muscles, memories, and desires. Let us reflect on our own bodily responses to specific stories and passages while simultaneously grappling with how to share, and how not to share, those responses with one another. Such efforts, at once individual and collective, are essential pieces of learning how to read and reread ethically in order to form radically collaborative practices of storytelling.

TELLING IN TURN / DANCING WITH STORIES Stories have the capacity to cross borders, but when and how do they cross borders? When do they refuse to cross borders? What are the implications of these border crossings and refusals to cross? What happens to a familiar story when we tell it to a new audience in a new setting?

We often think about these questions in terms of 'carrying across' a story—an act where the storyteller is expected to faithfully relay a story (in singular form) from one context to another. But what if we rethink story as an inherently plural text where the story is not a property to be owned or exchanged but a dynamic text that lives in and through a series of tellings in which it is passed along from one person to the next? In this sense, a storyteller becomes someone who tells in turn, and in so doing, becomes a small part of the ocean of the streams of story, contributing to the life of the story while also redirecting its flow.[2] Yet another way to reimagine retellings of a story is in terms of a never ending dance where the story has no pure origin or destination, but where the praxis of engagement and transformation places the origin and the destination in a continuous state of productive tension and overlap so that the storytelling becomes a continuous process of revision and translation.[3]

STORYTELLING AS RESPONSIBILITY What responsibilities come with being entrusted with the task of telling in turn, when our commitments between and across worlds require us to dance with stories? What is the difference between being entrusted with the responsibility to retell and move with stories on the one hand, and feeling entitled to narrate a story on the other? What kind of responsibility comes when we receive a story from the 'other' side? What does it take to retell stories of another without making that other into an *Other*?

Can we begin to think together about what constitute the ethics and politics of storytelling based on this preliminary conversation: a set of tentative collective understandings that we can revisit and refine over the course of the semester? Some evolving rules and principles, perhaps, that help us articulate a politically aware methodology attuned to the power structures and dynamics that shape how every story is performed or retold? Even in its tentativeness and continuously evolving form, how might such methodology critically approach the narrations and theorizations that have been handed down to us by 'authorized' (hi)story tellers in multiple locations?

STORYTELLING AS GLOBAL POLITICS What do we think constitutes 'the global' and how do we understand 'politics'? What happens if we regard struggles for justice in relation to global politics as centrally constituted by telling and receiving stories about an other? Viewed this way, storytelling becomes a space in which the intimate and the global are continuously invoked and constituted in relation to each other in ways that the global is always present in the intimate, and vice versa.[4]

I invite you to explore these questions while also adding one more requirement to this collective journey: what might it mean for you to become radically vulnerable with one another in the collective context of this class, and to accept such vulnerability as the first step in building the trust that is essential in order to swim together in an ocean of ever flowing stories?[5] In this ocean, the labor of encountering, immersing, meandering, resisting, and reflowing alongside and within each stream must struggle continuously with what it means to do justice to a story as its receiver and teller in any given context.

If such radical vulnerability feels forced or uncomfortable in the context of this class, what kinds of questions must this discomfort raise about stories that researchers, educators, activists, and other experts retell about those who are absent or excluded from the spaces where their stories are retold? What are the implications of this discussion for questions of social justice, and for the ways in which knowledges are made, claimed, and consumed?

Scene 2

Introduce yourself with a wordless gesture to the whole group.

Then find a partner and share the intended meaning of your gesture with them, followed by a story that tells something about you that is often not apparent to most people in this university.

After 10 minutes of sharing by both partners, the whole class reassembles as a large group. Each person shares what they learned about their partner.

Scene 3

Now, each person finds a different partner. Each pair has approximately 8 minutes in which both members share with each other a story from their childhoods that carries meaning for them. Listen attentively, as each person will soon be asked to retell the story. Do not take written notes. Just listen.

Scene 4

Return to the large group and, in no more than 2 minutes, share your partner's story as if it is your own story. This recalling and retelling in an edited form will require you to restructure the story. You cannot make eye contact to check in with your partner while you are retelling their story as your own. After everyone has had a chance to retell the stories, the class collectively considers the following questions:

- What did it feel like to 'own' the story of your partner?
- What did it feel like to let go of your own story? What was it like to not be able to make eye contact with your partner while telling their story and again while listening to your own story being told?
- How did you *feel* another's story? Was there any pain, regret, or satisfaction derived from the process?
- How did you make decisions about editing the story, about what should be said and what should remain unsaid?
- What happened to the story when it was carried across?
- What did we collectively learn about the ethical responsibility of storytelling from this exercise?

End of Act One

Preparation for Act Two

Read:

- Revisit Parts I–V of this syllabus.
- Beaudelaine Pierre and Nataša Ďurovičová, eds., *How to Write an Earthquake* (selections)
- Marie Lily Cerat, "Maloulou."
- Omise'eke Natasha Tinsley et al., "So Much to Remind Us We Are Dancing on Other People's Blood."

Watch:

- Saredo Mohamed, "The Process of De-Colonization."

As you prepare to write your post, reflect on:

- The manner in which each author or creator lets go of their story.
- Note the specific ways in which the bodies of those who inhabit these stories come alive in the words and gestures, and try to become aware of your own embodied response to such writing.
- What can you glean about the context in which each piece was created, and about the intentionality of the creator? In what ways do context and intention matter in the pieces you read? Are there times when the context and intentions cease to matter? When and why?
- Choose a passage of any length from the assigned readings that resonated with you, that you found challenging or particularly generative, or that raised questions, discomforts or restlessness for you. Make a note of this passage as well as of your questions or response to it in a way that you can refer to it in class.
- Try to match the spirit of the readings by offering a story, or a fragment of a

story, in your online post. While writing this post, ask yourself: What must I give of myself as a reader to become an ethical receiver of the stories I am receiving? Try to explore modes and styles of writing you have been drawn to but may not have tried previously.

Act Two. Seeking Resonances through Radical Vulnerability

Synopsis: What does it mean to write relationally and to become vulnerable in one's writing? Why is vulnerability required to create in, and grow with, a collective? What makes vulnerability radical?

Scene 1

Together we discuss the context and vision that drove each piece of writing and the concepts of relationality and radical vulnerability as they come into play in these works. Using your selections and notations, we meditate on how such vulnerability allows us to search for resonances across the borders of our own individual bodies.

Scene 2

In small groups of three, each person shares the story you wrote in your online journal. Then each small group works together to distill their shared stories in a collective form that tries to captures the resonances and the divergences in the group's reflections. This distilled expression can take the form of prose, poetry, skit, mime, picture, symbol, or a blend of these and any other form of expression. As you participate in this process, reflect on the following: *How does this collective revision serve as a translation between mediums of expression? What is happening in this translational process where three individually articulated fragments of memories, thoughts, and feelings are consciously merged with one another and then—via negotiated reading, telling, and retelling—re-created or re-presented as a jointly owned or coauthored piece of prose, poetry, skit, symbol, picture, or mixed genre? How, if at all, is this creative process reminiscent of migratory translations and the hunger for resonances discussed previously?*

This exercise explores when and how a search for resonances between and across individual articulations becomes a social and political act—an act that is undergirded by the responsibility to *revise* each individual story ethically while also recognizing that every such attempt may require a revisiting of what 'ethical' or 'just' might mean in a given context. An ethical search for resonances requires modes of listening, retelling, and performing that can allow individual stories to flourish and evolve into collective visions and articulations. Such a mode of being pushes us to recognize and complicate the individual egos that have been so central to many writing forms, including diary, memoir, and autobiography. It asks that we seek embodied alliances and *feel* the joys and risks that come from making ourselves radically vulnerable across differential locations and positions of power and privilege. As an ongoing process of negotiation between narrators and listeners, instructors and students, writers and editors, such praxis introduces us to the work of building situated solidarities that strive for justice and radical transformation, without settling for a singular translation. If critical pedagogy is an uncoercive rearrangement of desires, then embodied alliances grounded in this ever-evolving translational praxis can allow us to appreciate radical vulnerability as a methodology of being and becoming through collectivity. This methodology transforms an individually claimed notion of the self through an intimate dance of subjectivity where the *i/I* and *you* cannot emerge without a *we* that grapples with the responsibility of ethically receiving and retelling a *they*. Furthermore, this responsibility requires us to insert the *i/I* and *we* in the *you* and *they* as an active commitment to wrestle against narrow politics of authenticity and identity that often shape dominant discursive practices of philanthropy, development, and human rights.

Scene 3

Small groups return to the large group to share their collective articulation, and to reflect on the following:

- Why did it make sense for your group to articulate your collective response in the way you did? What was consciously edited and why? What did you retain and why? What was unintentionally erased?
- What went into your process of negotiation? What seemed just or fair about the process? What seemed unjust?
- If you were to participate in the same process again, what would you change to try to ensure that the things that seemed unjust in the process might work differently?
- What, if any, are the questions you might not have thought of without the collective labor of remembering, sharing, merging, and resharing?

End of Act Two

Preparation for Act Three

Read:

- NYC Stands with Standing Rock Collective, "Timeline of United States Settler Colonialism."
- J. Kēhaulani Kauanui, "'A Structure, Not an Event': Settler Colonialism and Enduring Indigeneity."

- Leanne Betasamosake Simpson, *As We Have Always Done: Indigenous Freedom through Radical Resistance*, 145–73.
- Middle East Research and Information Project. "Primer on Palestine, Israel and the Arab-Israeli Conflict."
- Suheir Hammad, *Born Palestinian, Born Black: And The Gaza Suite*, 7–39, 87–95.

Reflect:

- How does each reading educate us differently about settler colonialism?
- How are the political and theoretical insights from each piece embedded in specific locations and contexts? How do these insights resonate across and beyond the specificity of their locations?
- Bring to class a story that connects your own familial or community histories with the then and now of settler colonialism. Please come prepared to share this story in some form—verbal or nonverbal, written or unwritten.

Act Three. Settler Colonialism, Refusals, Pedagogy

Synopsis: From radical vulnerability to radical refusals. What makes a refusal radical?

Scene 1

Together we discuss your reflections from online journals. Then we delve into the idea of refusals, with the following words from the writings of Audra Simpson and of Eve Tuck and K. Wayne Yang as our entry points:

> . . . the labor of principle and sovereignty, labor that begins with refusal. That refusal is simply to disappear, a refusal to be on the other end of Patrick Wolfe's critical, comparative history—to be "eliminated."[6] In refusing to go away, to cease to be, in asserting something beyond difference, lies the position that re-quires one to "co-exist" with others, with settlers, with "arrivants," . . . meaning the formerly enslaved or the indentured who did not voluntarily come to North America—and to live tacitly and taciturnly in a "settled state." In this there is acceptance of the dispossession of your lands, of internalizing and believing the things that you have been taught about you to you: that you are a savage, that your language is incoherent, that you are less than white people . . .[7]

> . . . the refusal stance pushes us to *limit* settler territorialization of Indigenous/Na-tive/community knowledge, and *expand* the space for other forms of knowledge, thought-worlds to live. Refusal makes space for recognition, and for reciprocity. Refusal turns the gaze back upon power. . . . It makes transparent the metanarra-tive of knowledge production—its spectatorship for pain and its preoccupation for documenting and ruling over racial difference. Refusal generates, expands,

champions representational territories that colonial knowledge endeavors to settle, enclose, domesticate. We again insist that refusal is not just a no, but is a generative, analytic practice.[8]

Scene 2

View:

- Sterlin Harjo, *Barking Waters*

Scene 3

Take a 15-minute break to process the film. During this time jot down: (a) two sentences describing what the film was about and (b) two sentences on the kinds of refusals the film performs.

Scene 4

Come together to consider the following:

- What kinds of emotions did the readings and the film stir?
- How does the film inspire us to ask new questions of the stories where we connected our own familial or community histories with the then and now of settler colonialism? What kinds of shared understandings about settler colonialism and its violence do these stories allow us to develop across locales and times?
- In what ways are the stories that we read and saw a refusal to disappear? When and how do they refuse the terms of settler colonialism?
- The ways in which the power of a refusal emanates from the time, place, context, and audience in which that refusal is performed. What responsibility accompanies this understanding?
- Let us try to represent our discussion in some form (e.g., words, pictures, gestures, movements).

End of Act Three

Preparation for Act Four

Read:

- W. E. B. Du Bois, *The Souls of Black Folk* (read the following chapters and anything else that moves you and that you can make the time to read):
    The Forethought
    I. Of Our Spiritual Strivings
    XIV. Of the Sorrow Songs
    The Afterthought

- Saidiya Hartman, *Lose Your Mother: A Journey along the Atlantic Slave Route*, parts 1–4.
- Audre Lorde, Poems.
- A. Loudermilk, "Nina Simone and the Civil Rights Movement: Protest at Her Piano, Audience at Her Feet."
- June Jordan, "Poem about My Rights."

Reflect: In "The Forethought" to *The Souls of Black Folk*, W. E. B. Du Bois writes— "Herein lie buried many things which if read with patience may show the strange meaning of being black here at the dawning of the Twentieth Century. This meaning is not without interest to you, Gentle Reader; for the problem of the Twentieth Century is the problem of the color line. I pray you, then, receive my little book in all charity, studying my words with me, forgiving mistake and foible for sake of the faith and passion that is in me, and seeking the grain of truth hidden there."

- Take a minute to feel these words. Reflect on the ways in which they invite a full-bodied engagement from you as a reader.
- Reflect on the ways in which all the writers and artists that you are reading for Act 4 confront the problem of the twentieth century as the problem of the color line. What kinds of truths emerge from each of their churnings?
- Do these truths allow you to feel politics, theory, and art differently than how you have felt them previously in your work or in your life's journey? If so, how?
- Bring two passages to class that you found particularly significant or moving in our reading this week and come prepared to discuss why these carried special meaning or resonance for you.

Act Four. Color Line, Consciousness, Poetry

Synopsis: How can artistic expression enable engagement through affect by refusing a separation among the political, the social, the poetic, the psychic, and the intellectual? How does such expression mobilize or inspire embodied engagement, while allowing us to feel previously muffled truths and thereby to live, to love, and to do politics differently?

Scene 1

View and discuss excerpt from Liz Garbus's film, *What Happened, Ms. Simone?*

Scene 2

Write a fragment of your own life in conversation with the thoughts evoked by the film and the readings. In writing the fragment, be aware of the crossings of time, place, and struggle, and of the political and intellectual work you want that crossing to do.

Scene 3

Share, interbraid, and perform the fragments you wrote. We will continue to build our embodied writing in conversation with the stories and songs we have learned from this week.

End of Act Four

Preparation for Act Five

Read:

- Eve Tuck and K. Wayne Yang, "Decolonization Is Not a Metaphor."
- Suheir Hammad, *Born Palestinian, Born Black: And The Gaza Suite*, 40–84.
- Suheir Hammad, *Breaking Poems*. Linger with a selection of poems that you want to reflect on in relation to the previous book.
- Stefano Harney and Fred Moten, *The Undercommons: Fugitive Planning and Black Study*, 5–68.

Reflect:

- Why, according to Tuck and Yang, is decolonization not a metaphor?
- How do Hammad's poems approach the vexed question of decolonization and metaphor in the context of settler colonialism? Do you note any continuities or divergences in the tone embraced by Hammad in her two collections?
- Harney and Moten write: "Justice is only possible where debt never obliges, never demands, never equals credit, payment, payback. Justice is possible only where it is never asked, in the refuge of bad debt, in the fugitive public of strangers not communities, of undercommons not neighborhoods, among those who have been there all along from somewhere. To seek justice through restoration is to return debt to the balance sheet and the balance sheet never balances" (63). In what ways do the authors for this week approach justice—where are the convergences and divergences among them?
- What would you like to offer to the authors in the form of your own creative expression?

Act Five. Decolonization, Metaphors, Justice

Synopsis: Rescripting the Undercommons: Stitching New Wor(l)ds.

Scene 1

Word harvest: On the board, we will make a spread of words and phrases that capture the thoughts and feelings that the readings inspired in you.

Scene 2

Everyone stands in a circle. One person steps inside the circle and shares a fragment from their life that connects in some way with the word harvest. The next one gains inspiration from the first and starting with "this reminds me . . ." offers another fragment. The process of sharing and building on fragments goes on until the group is ready to move on to the next scene.

Scene 3

Everyone takes 10 minutes to do free writing and then shares it in the large group.

Scene 4

The group transitions into sculpting with our bodies. One person acquires a shape or embraces a gesture and another adds a different layer to it, until everyone has had a chance to become part of the sculpture. Then the group reflects on what has emerged and revises the sculpture collectively.

Scene 5

Open discussion.

End of Act Five

Preparation for Act Six

Read:

- Naeem Inayatullah, "Pulling Threads: Intimate Systematicity in 'The Politics of Exile.'"
- Viet Thanh Nguyen, *Nothing Ever Dies: Vietnam and the Memory of War*, 1–189.

Reflect:

- Why does Inayatullah ask us to have generosity toward the antagonist?
- What is just memory according to Nguyen? Do you see overlaps in Inayatullah's and Nguyen's arguments? If so, what are they and why should they matter for ethical telling and receiving of stories?

Act Six. Just Memory

Synopsis: Entangling bodies and overlaying memories.

Scene 1

Zip-zap-zop. Overlay names and colors as we stand in a circle, then transition into statements, arguments, and stories we have been thinking about in relation to this week's readings.

Scene 2

"This reminds me . . ."

Scene 3

Scripting, sculpting, and revising collectively.

Scene 4

Open discussion.

End of Act Six

Preparation for Act Seven

Read:

- Viet Thanh Nguyen, *Nothing Ever Dies: Vietnam and the Memory of War*, 191–end.

Reflect:

- How does Nguyen work with the idea of justice by entangling it with re-membering, forgetting, and writing? What kind of labor is he asking us to undertake? How does he make us aware of the politics and poetics of writing?
- Revisit some of the stories you have shared over the course of the class thus far and rewrite a fragment in ways that converse seriously with Nguyen's arguments. Come prepared to talk about how your retelling of your stories shifted as you became attentive to the arguments made by Nguyen.

Act Seven. Just Forgetting

Synopsis: rescripting stories for justice.

Scene 1

Discuss our reflections.

Scene 2

Share rescripted stories.

Scene 3

Revise rescripted stories through performance.

End of Act Seven

Preparation for Act Eight

Read:

- June Jordan, *Soldier: A Poet's Childhood*

Reflect:

- What gives you pleasure in Jordan's writing? What is difficult about reading Jordan?
- Why was what you found difficult, difficult? Why was what you found pleasurable, pleasurable?
- What kinds of connections did you make with your past and present, with the news and images you have received, with the ways in which you have learned to think of adulthood and childhood, love and violence, parenting and friendships, whiteness and blackness, immigration and citizenship, home and homelessness?
- What might it mean to show generosity to the antagonist in the case of this story—for the author? For you?
- Do you see Jordan's storytelling as an example of just memory, just forgetting, or both? How?

Act Eight. Just Storytelling

Synopsis: What does it mean to become generous toward the antagonist? What is the political significance of this generosity? What are its creative implications?

Scene 1

In two paragraphs, write a story from your childhood where you first represent yourself as a protagonist and then as an antagonist. Now write another story in a third paragraph, making sure to bring forth an antagonist (other than you) while trying to represent that person generously.

As you write, reflect on the following questions:

- What inspired you to choose the stories that you did? What parts of the stories are easy to share and why? What parts are difficult to share and why? What did you choose to include and exclude? Why?
- What kinds of connections and disconnections do you feel between your own stories and the ones we have read, viewed or learned about? Can you give examples?
- Did you feel a sense of responsibility toward any specific people, places, or issues as you narrated your stories? Can you tell us about what you felt and why?
- Did you feel vulnerable as you wrote the story? Can you tell us about that vulnerability?

Scene 2

Based on your brief experience of writing a childhood story, reflect on the following: In what ways is Jordan as a writer becoming vulnerable before the reader in this story? What kind of trust is she placing in us as readers? What do we owe her as her readers? What would make us responsible receivers of her story?

Scene 3

Let us try to enact two of the stories we wrote today, with different people in the group taking on different characters and being mindful of the responsibility of being generous toward the antagonist. Feel free to interrupt each other, to disagree with a representation, and to share ideas about how to participate in a just representation of the story.

End of Act Eight

Preparation for Act Nine

Read:

- K. Satyanarayana and Susie Tharu, eds., *The Exercise of Freedom: An Introduction to Dalit Writing*. Begin reading this week and continue until done.
- Karin Kapadia, "Introduction: We Ask You to Rethink: Different Dalit Women and Their Subaltern Politics."
- Sujatha Gidla, *Ants among Elephants: An Untouchable Family and the Making of Modern India*. Begin reading this week and continue until done.
- Nida Sajid, "Resisting Together Separately: Representations of the Dalit-Muslim Question in Literature."

Reflect: In their introduction to *The Exercise of Freedom*, Satyanarayana and Tharu underline the complex relationship of Dalits and modernity. Citing the example of Devanoora Mahadeva's masterpiece, "Tar Comes," they write: "modernity in the form of official 'development'—here a tarred road leading to the village—means little to the dalits who walk everywhere. In this case it also turns out that the tar brings death. But there is another modernity in the story . . . which the young educated dalits embrace and make use of—much to the discomfiture of the upper caste contractor. This is the modernity of the press, of a government that formally at least is accessible to everyone, and not least, the empowering modernity of education."[9]

Satyanarayana's and Tharu's second point, which is also echoed in Sajid's chapter, relates to how Dalit autobiographies "are not, at root, about the individual"; rather, they acquire significance as important social and historical documents that have the ability to turn terrible experiences into what Gopal Guru calls "subversive chemicals." The authors point out that far from being simply 'narratives of suffering,' autobiographies "illuminate the social world, provide new material for dalit politics and raise new questions for aesthetics."[10]

What questions and reflections does a consideration of these points spark for you as you absorb the readings for this week? How do these readings advance or complicate our previous discussions on questions of ethics, justice, and aesthetics of storytelling, and about the entanglements of the singular and the plural, the individual and collective, and the i/I, we, they, and you.

Act Nine. Storytelling, Aesthetics, Justice

Synopsis: Developing a shared politics and aesthetics of storytelling for justice.

Scene 1

- In groups of three, share your reflections on the questions provided for this week's preparation.
- Now revisit your stories from last week. How might this week's readings and discussion inspire you to revise your story and introduce themes, issues, complexities, and contradictions that you may not have thought of before? As you reflect on each story, ask difficult questions of each other, identify the strands that you consider critical, and reflect on points of connections and disjunctures between various stories shared in the group.
- Then, using pseudonyms, rewrite the story so that your individual stories are interwoven. The characters in this story can be as few and as many as you wish, but the critical strands that you noted should all come through. Be deliberate about the political questions and themes you would like to foreground in your collective articulation.

Scene 2

In the large group, each small group shares the collectively created piece while reflecting on the following:

- What did you keep in the interbraided story? What did you edit out of the story?
- What parts were easier or more difficult to speak about in the merged story than in the individual articulation?
- Was the form of the interbraided story shaped by the issues or concerns we discussed in relation to the readings today? How?
- How did you negotiate power, voice, and authority in creating your narrative?
- In what ways did you feel responsible for each story? How did you approach that responsibility?

Scene 3

Open discussion: What have we learned from our work today about the politics and aesthetics of storytelling for justice?

End of Act Nine

Preparation for Act Ten

Read:

- Sangtin Writers and Richa Nagar, *Playing with Fire: Feminist Thought and Activism through Seven Lives in India*. Read the chapters in the same sequence in which the authors wrote them: first chapters 1–6 in ascending order, then the Introduction and postscript, and then the foreword by Chandra Talpade Mohanty.

Reflect: After reading each chapter, reflect on: (a) the stories of each character; (b) the form and process of storytelling; and (c) the ways that the form and process were shaped by the writers' context.

- Did the nature and form of storytelling remind you of anything from your own storytelling exercise? Where were the points of connection? Where did the connections stop? Why?
- Did reading chapters 1–3 feel any different from reading chapters 4–6? If so, how? What work do the introduction, postscript, and foreword do in the book? What do they add or take away? How does each chapter grapple with questions of power, trust, authority, and vulnerability?

- Do you see a radical vulnerability emerging from the collectivity of the writers?
- How do the Sangtin Writers approach ethics and responsibility? Is their approach shaped by the shifting sociopolitical context of their storytelling? How?
- What forms do embodied knowledges take in the work of Sangtin Writers? How do how these allow for polyvocality?

Act Ten. Blended but Fractured *We*

Synopsis: Blending fractured *we*s and approaching collectivity as continuous revision of understandings.

Scene 1

In large group, discuss:

- How is the purpose, form, affect, and effect of *Playing with Fire* similar to, or different from, that of Jordan's *Solider*?
- In what ways are Sangtin Writers being vulnerable before one another and before the reader? How are they becoming *radically* vulnerable? What does that radical vulnerability enable for the writers and for the reader?
- What does it mean to read these stories in a language other than the one in which they were originally written?
- Why did Sangtin Writers choose pseudonyms to tell their stories?
- What do we owe the storytellers as readers? What would make us responsible receivers of the sangtins' stories?

Scene 2

In groups of four, begin writing a letter to Sangtin Writers, introducing yourselves to them, and taking this opportunity to revisit the stories about your lives that you have shared earlier in the class. As you do so, reflect on the resonances and dissonances between your own storytelling and that of the Sangtin Writers. What might these reflections teach us about the workings of privilege, vulnerability, politics, and poetics in the work of building situated solidarities?

Scene 3

Reassemble as a large group and summarize the key points from your small group discussion.

Of the stories you revisited and remembered, let us choose one fragment to enact together. As we do so, let us ask: what would it take to deepen that fragment? What might it mean for the person who initially shared the fragment to let go of their story so that we can begin the process of adding more layers to it in order to do justice to the people, context, and struggles from which that fragment emerged? As we enact and improvise, let all of us recall and draw on our own journeys so that we can grapple more fully with the story.

End of Act Ten

Preparation for Act Eleven

Read:

- Premchand, "The Shroud," translated by Frances Pritchett, http://www .columbia.edu/itc/mealac/pritchett/oourdu/kafan/translation_kafan.html.
- From this book: part 3, "Living in Character: 'Kafan' as *Hansa*."
- Alok Rai, "Poetic Justice and Social Justice: Some Reflections on the Premchand-Dalit Controversy."
- Saidiya Hartman, "Venus in Two Acts."

Reflect:

- How does each translation of the story "Kafan" allow for some meanings to evolve while foreclosing other possibilities? Which meanings emerge for you and which meanings are foreclosed?
- What does the concept of hunger do in the readings?
- In what ways did *Hansa* try to grapple ethically with "Kafan"? To what extent do you think it succeeded or failed? Why?
- What are the key arguments made by Hartman and Rai in their essays?
- With "Kafan" and *Hansa* as examples, consider what poetic and social justice to Budhiya, Ghisu, and Madhav might look like for each author.

Act Eleven. Poetic Justice and Social Justice

Synopsis: How are teaching and learning linked with recognizing our responsibility as translators who absorb, feel, process, and act on a story? What kind of labor is involved in making a story do a particular kind of political work? What might it mean to translate ethically when the writer's intention may not be the same as that of the student, teacher, actor, or director?

Scene 1

In groups of three, share your reflections on the questions provided for this week's preparation.

Scene 2

Return to the large group and share key points from the small group reflections. Then, we discuss the following questions:

- Under what conditions does storytelling do the work of justice? Who is able to tell which stories and when? When does a story empower and when does it dispirit? How might we imagine pedagogies of just storytelling across the borders of time, place, community, and struggle?
- How do the readings help us grapple with translation as telling in turn, and also as a refusal to tell? What possibilities of justice are lost, violated, or made possible through such translations? When does translation become ethical mediation?
- Can theater, when conceptualized as continuous improvisation, help us approach ethical mediation through embodied pedagogy? Can such continuously improvised embodied pedagogy enact hungry translations in search of poetic and social justice?

Scene 3

Reassemble in groups of four and revisit the stories you began to work on during Acts 8 and 9. Choose any one story to linger with. Collectively rewrite the story in a way that opens up spaces for ethical mediation through collective improvisation.

End of Act Eleven

Preparation for Acts Twelve, Thirteen, Fourteen, and Fifteen

Throughout these weeks, you will meet for at least ten hours of rehearsals in and outside of the class period to build a polyvocal script that processes the lessons we have learned together thus far. We will meet in small and large groups to revisit the emerging narratives we have rehearsed before, and to finalize a script that interbraids key moments and concerns from those narratives in conversation with stories of others we have listened to, read, or watched for this course. The revised script should explore more than one form of writing, moving, or performing and can be a combination of prose, poem, skit, play, spoken word, letter, video created by you, or any other form of expression. Work creatively and generously with the different kinds of skills, strengths, and passions that exist in our group. Our jointly crafted script can juxtapose or blend genres and languages (e.g., a dance, a play, a graphic image, a song, an equation) to bring to life diverse forms of embodied retellings.

Most of your energies should be devoted to the development of the script, rehearsals, blocking, and improvisation. However, I encourage you to continue reflecting in your journals at the same time. Some themes to consider in your writing are:

- the specific labor you are undertaking to refine the emerging coauthored script and what is generative and challenging about this work;
- your process of researching, absorbing, and embodying stories; your dilemmas or difficulties about relaying and retelling stories with a purpose that is just, and in ways where the collective can thrive through the singular, and vice versa;
- rehearsing connections and contradictions to unlearn and relearn the burdens and possibilities of our locations through each practice;
- building a collective through nurturing connections as well as through discomforts that stimulate, unsettle, fracture, or give pause; and
- becoming intentional about which stories to incorporate in our public performances and how, which stories or fragments to backstage and when, and where and how must the backstaged fragments emerge on the frontstage to produce creative restlessness and to sustain the hunger for justice in our retellings.[11]

Acts Twelve, Thirteen, and Fourteen. Choreographing Fragments with a Purpose

Synopsis: Delving deeper, through rehearsals and continuous revision and improvisation, into embodied writing, scripting, and performance. In what ways are we trying to embody stories responsibly? What does it mean to coauthor a story? What is changing in each one of us as we become one with the script that is emerging?

End of Acts Twelve, Thirteen, and Fourteen

Act Fifteen. Staging Polyvocal Scripts

Synopsis: Final performance, followed by discussion with invited audience determined by the class. Afterwards, we will gather over a meal to reflect together on the following:

- What did you learn from the final performance and from the discussion with the audience about the responsibility of receiving, feeling, telling, and performing stories?
- What could not be staged?
- If you had the authority to revise our collective script, what revisions would you undertake and why?
- How has the class informed your thinking about research, scholarship, and creativity in the context of the global politics of knowledge making?
- What kinds of journeys and struggles must continue for each one of us so that the work of receiving and telling stories for justice can go on?
- What did our journey over the course of the semester teach us about participating in the labor of hungry translations?
- Any other reflections about the course.

Instructor exits. Participants do formal class evaluations. Informal conversations about lessons from this journey shall continue.

END OF FIFTEEN ACTS

Closing Notes

Retelling Dis/Appearing Tales

Siddharth Bharath, Sara Musaifer, and Richa Nagar

All politics are politics of storytelling. Stories shape who we believe we are, our sense of our own inherited privileges and misfortunes, our affinities, identifications, and allegiances. Stories impart humanity and inhumanity; they are implicated in both violence and struggles for justice. Retelling Dis/Appearing Tales *emerges from a collective grappling with how to retell stories ethically and responsibly. The play's polyvocal script— created by all the members of Spring 2017 Global Studies class, 'Stories, Bodies, Movements'—explores questions of belonging, memory, and erasures in relation to the intimate and global politics of feeling, reliving, and retelling stories across borders.*[1]

Pull a thread here and you'll realize the whole world is attached, [says] Nadeem Aslam, in The Wasted Vigil. Fractured Threads *is a patchwork of reflections on the (im)possible work of storytelling. It struggles with the stakes of telling or not telling a story, of embodying stories that may not be ours to tell, and of revisiting our own stories in order to grapple with the t(r)apestry of the i/we/you/they. In attempting to do so, we sing, we break, we crawl, we dream. Using theater as a mode of inquiry, we begin a journey to invent our own transgenre and translingual retelling—one where we refuse to separate the protagonist from the antagonist. This process of creating and co-traveling over the semester has involved fracturing and breaking in every sense of the words. We break to reveal while also keeping in mind that the act of revealing also breaks us.*[2]

These closing notes are yet another collective journey undertaken by three of the twenty-seven people who traveled together at different junctures over the course of two semesters, and who played various roles in the creation of at least one of the two performances—*Retelling Dis/Appearing Tales* and *Fractured Threads*—that evolved in spring and fall 2017, respectively, from the vision laid out in part 4, "Stories, Bodies, Movements: A Syllabus in Fifteen Acts." In addition to the three of us, these people included Alaina Szostkowski, Beaudelaine Pierre, Chip Chang, Colin Wingate, Devan Dupre, Devleena Chatterjee, Esmae Heveron, Esther Ouray, Jada Brown, Janani Eswar, Jason Noer, Julie Santella, Anuradha Marwah, Keavy McFadden, Kriti Budhiraja, Laura Seithers, Lisa Santosa, Maria Schwedhelm, Naimah Petigny, Nithya Rajan, Rebecca Lieser, Tarun Kumar, Valentina Schwedhelm Rios, Veera Vasandani, and Veronica Quillien. For us, writing these closing notes—from different locations but with many shared investments—offered a way to reflect on the processes and power of the collective labor and creativity that taught us some valuable lessons about grappling with hungry translations.

Why bother with this joint reflection now if we do not believe in writing merely for the sake of creating another academic product? The classes are done, the performances are over. We enjoyed and learned much from the experience, and the sixty or so people who came to watch the two plays appreciated them. So, why reflect now when we can be moving on to other important things that require our energies in our many worlds of violence and struggle, of love and hope? In these last pages, we take turns at lingering with this question with our singular *i*'s and eyes, and also at merging our voices into a *we* without following a predictable formula or template. We also consider how Stories, Bodies, Movements and the performances that emerged from it in 2017 represent only a few instances of learning enabled by collectivity and struggle in dynamic spaces such as SKMS and Parakh Theatre. Our stories of what we learned as co-travelers in the classroom are hard to separate from the stories retold in the previous parts of *Hungry Translations*; thus, our reflections on the course commingle with those on the whole book.

Sara opens the next section ("Connecting") with poetic images that both haunt and ground her in a search for situated solidarities through creative divergences. She underscores the need for translating stories that can gain resonance in struggles—stories that are at once deeply intimate *and* penetratingly global—while also refusing the terms that smother certain ways of being, knowing, and telling in and through the academy. In the subsequent section ("Reflecting"), Siddharth asks: what had to change in each of us in order to blur the neat borders of i and you; of theater and politics; of places we know as Mexico,

The making of *Retelling Dis/Appearing Tales* (left to right): Rebecca Lieser improvises as Alaina Szostkowski, Naimah Petigny, Siddharth Bharath, Maria Schwedhelm, and Devleena Chatterjee look on. (Photo by Tarun Kumar)

India, Europe, and the United States; of the classroom, academic writing, and the apparatus known as Development? He meditates on the shared labor of refusing borders that are prone to becoming suffocating spaces of discipline and propriety, of knowledge and knowers, and that kill spirits of collectivities in struggle. Subsequently (in "Unfolding"), Richa reflects on the continuities between *Sangtin Yatra*, *Hansa*, and Stories, Bodies, Movements and on the processes of unlearning and relearning that define these journeys—journeys where hungers for justice meld with multiple and shifting expressions of radical vulnerability that unfold and enfold in an all-encompassing praxis. This praxis refuses such reductive compartments as mind-spirit-body, past-present-future, life-death, real-unreal, inner-outer, or spiritual-theoretical-empirical-political. In threading our sections together, however, we have also become co-editors and coauthors of all the parts that make these "Closing Notes," of the dance of *i/I* and *we* that entangles our singulars and plurals and allows them to coexist and grow. In forging this conversation in these ending pages of *Hungry Translations*, we find affinities between a commitment to unlearn and relearn the world through radical vulnerability and Simona Sawhney's point that all hospitality must arise from first unhousing oneself. It is with these thoughts, then, that we close *and* reopen *Hungry Translations*.

Connecting

Why bother?

because

an aching longing
an insatiable hunger
a situated solidarity
crawls on my soft brown skin
grapevines
steadily
overtaking
a cedar pergola
quietly
colonizing my closet
peeking through keyholes
a craving

                     irreplicable
             incommensurable
     incalculable

swelling
unapologetically
red, white, blue weeds
bullying
the foliage of my backyard
swaying
to the beats of al-khamari drums
the divine summer sun
kissing
surrendering leaves
birthed from dust
bones
broken stones

it is only with my spirit and I
entangled in you and yours
that paths emerge
and merge

burning urge
cradling me to sleep
jerking my body awake
as dawn thunders
through glass windows
this urge
no longer
mine
     alone

I bother

  because

this journey
a riot of fissures
infiltrating
solid brick walls
boiling
underneath the corpse of summer
teeming
sawing
patiently for
this baheemat,
this academy
to explode like hope
stretching
     in agony

—Sara Musaifer

As my year of journeying with Stories, Bodies, Movements concludes, I (Sara) find myself pondering on the manner in which this collective journey complicated my understandings of doing the ethics, aesthetics and politics of storytelling, introducing instead a commitment to translations hungry to "abide by the terms of the struggles we stand with, even as they escape the limits imposed by the disciplined terms of the academy" (page 8). Throughout the months of the course, we "slow[ed] down reasoning," making space for "the composition of that which does not have a political voice . . . [to] put my preconceived ideas at risk."[3] At times, the texts we read, the stories we shared, and the companions we walked with unleashed a grounded intellectual humility and an enthusiasm to unlearn singular ways of knowing justice, truth, and knowledge production—ways that derive their logics from alienated premises. Laboring with, and through, an emerging collectivity opened up possibilities for learning how difficult and how soulful it is to move with situated solidarities, weaving tightly 'us' and 'them' to form a delicate fabric that would cease to exist in the absence of either.[4] This movement does not ask us to entirely unknot the points of disagreement, and it does not demand superficial sameness. Rather, collectivity is made possible by the intricate moments of tension and turbulence that rip and tear: by the "blended but fractured *wes*" that propose "pluriversal politics" through creative divergence.[5] Our entangled embodied existences in Stories, Bodies, Movements and in the plays, *Retelling Dis/Appearing Tales* and *Fractured Threads*, allowed us to share tears of laughter, irony, fury, and frustration, along with our own humanity and inhumanity, making us hungry for an otherwise mode of being in, despite, and beyond the academy.

For the collectives that began to form in the class—at times going through deep confusion, pain, and resistance to becoming vulnerable with one another— embodying pluriversal politics meant confronting our egos and our taken for granted ideas about academic success and self-worth. It meant relearning the epistemological and political labor of "back and front staging" centered around the ethos of "radical difference" that is not a stabilized essence, but an ever-flowing, transforming relation manifesting through expected and unexpected encounters.[6] Grappling with the poetics and politics of radical difference implies a careful engagement with what we deem to be legible or intelligible, and it includes decisions about which stories are told and untold, by whom, how, and under what circumstances. It leaves open the possibilities of disagreements within the collective, and in relation to the stories and storytellers we find ourselves in conversation with. What we achieved collectively—without reducing our labor to a replicable concept or a named process—became most obvious to us when we chose the titles, *Retelling Dis/Appearing Tales* in spring 2017 and *Fractured Threads* in fall 2017, for our polyvocal scripts. In underlining our conviction that every reappearance of a tale carries with it the possibility of violating or erasing other tales, and that ever-emergent threads that bind us together can also be deeply fractured, we became aware of the theoretical and political value of our labor and creative processes. The titles of our performances acknowledged that the work of seeking justice through retelling is fragile, faulted, and risky, and that we are never too far from becoming the perpetrators of the same epistemic violence that we may critique from a distance.

Indeed, Stories, Bodies, Movements brought us closer to understanding what it might mean to labor for what Alexander and Mohanty call a new political culture based on the decolonizing principle of thinking oneself out of the spaces of domination, but always in and through collective or communal processes.[7] In

Transforming the classroom through *Retelling Dis/Appearing Tales*. Clockwise from left: Jada Brown, Sara Musaifer, Siddharth Bharath, Maria Schwedhelm, and Nithya Rajan. (Photo by Tarun Kumar)

Devleena playing Maria's sister, Ana, in *Retelling Dis/Appearing Tales*. (Photo by Tarun Kumar)

thinking and rethinking, acting and reenacting, both classes carved out spaces to critically dissect what *is*, forging in its place paths to serendipitous imaginations of what *can be*, and what it might take to get there.

Yet, continuing such learning produced in relation to particular bodies and embodiments of politics does not suggest an already defined form of resistance. Nor does it prescribe a set of normative conventions commensurate to the inherently incommensurable labor of collective storytelling. Rather, such embodied learning becomes a serious invitation to reflect on the journeys walked, to reshuffle the chess pieces, to carve out new paths that are necessarily embedded in the contexts within which our movements are born and nurtured. Thus, the work of those who are called upon to take on leadership or facilitation roles cannot be understood in the absence of a particular constellation of time, place, and politics. As such, labels of instructor, leader, director, student, and actor do not entail an already delineated subject-position; rather, they become part and parcel of reimagining through the praxis itself. In other words, an understanding of political subject positions cannot emerge prior to the process of living or rescripting those politics.

With all of this in mind, let us return to the provocation we articulated for ourselves at the outset: why bother with this reflection now when we can be moving on to other important things in our many worlds of violence and struggle, of love and hope? Taking time and space to reflect is not a luxury; it is a political necessity. If "decolonization has a fundamentally pedagogical dimension—an imperative to understand, to reflect on, and to transform relations of objectification and dehumanization, and to pass this knowledge along to future generations"—then we must bother to slow down, to seize serendipitous moments of connection and learning through which to interrogate, undermine, undo, and redo the dominant scripts, syllabi, and pedagogies that colonize our imaginations.[8] Only then can we hope to build situated solidarities with authors and actors whose histories, struggles, tunes, and accents have been consistently obliterated or nihilated in the reigning scripts.

Reflecting

Since struggles never end, it is important to pause and to reflect on what we unlearn and earn by sweating, aching, and singing together. So we gather at the end of *Hungry Translations*, this rendition of collectively orchestrated music and imaginations in Sitapur, Mumbai, and Minneapolis. We remember the lessons learned from ever ongoing journeys of so many bodies. We recognize the beginnings of new vital worlds we breathe into our movements, while also accepting the imperfections in those beginnings, for journeys are not meant to arrive at final versions of stories; they can only long for just translations.

Theater as critical and ethical storytelling enabled the performers of *Retelling Dis/Appearing Tales* to transport ourselves to a place from where we could begin to embody the choices, knowledges, and actions of another. In a way, this 'transporting' began with mimicry of the other—of paying full attention to the movements and manners of the characters we were performing, or creating detailed imaginations of the stories we were reading; for example, through physically sculpting key scenes with our own bodies. As we journeyed, we recognized that mimicry was grossly inadequate to learn acting or reading *us* radical vulnerability, which asks for a deep search for the unexpected commonness, a negotiated merging between self and other, over the course of tellings and retellings.

Reflecting on it, I (Siddharth) realize that a journey into radical vulnerability first encounters a barrier of a different side of commonness. Hannah Arendt reminds us of the crucial role of 'common sense' in our knowing the world: "it is a kind of sixth sense needed to keep my five senses together. . . . This same sense . . . fits the sensations of my strictly private five senses . . . into a common world shared by others."[9] This privately held common sense of our relationality in the world can be understood as a root of marginalization. In the common senses of privileged social locations, I can ignore the daily struggles of kisans and mazdoors in SKMS; of Budhiya, Ghisu and Madhav; of Mumtaz, Sajjan, and Alok; of the protestors at Standing Rock; of those who fought for the civil rights in the United States; of those who are compelled to write earthquakes in Haiti, because they are not a part of my (anti-ebony) ivory tower realities. Further, once I have been validated by a few people, this sense of commonality can lead me to think that everyone else experiences the world this way. As the syllabus points out, such prevailing common senses constantly dismiss and erase Othered lives as bodies and sites of knowledge. The pedagogy of *Hungry Translations* seeks to radically disrupt this common sense, or socially imposed embodiment, by melting the labor of telling and receiving stories into the labor of acting.

Responsible embodiment implied that our world change while telling the story of another, even of other-than-humans. We did not just sit and talk about powerful writers and artists like Suheir Hammad, Sterlin Harjo, June Jordan, and Nina Simone; we picked, enacted, and embodied scenes in which, to be responsible to those powerful stories, I had to feel the hurt of an uprooted olive tree, or the conflicted love and violence of a father beating his only daughter so that she could become a soldier in a brutal world that insisted on diminishing them both. All the while, I knew that my understanding, enactment, and embodiment of that story was ever partial, ever situated, and ever a part of more responsible learning. With the same senses and body, I had to shift what I thought was common sense—situating my story in relation to the story I was telling, a translation among related but irreducibly different people, none of whom is denied agency in the process of forming solidarity. How would it be

Team members give feedback as class gets ready for the public performance of *Retelling Dis/Appearing Tales*. Clockwise from left: Alaina, Nithya, and Tarun Kumar (Photo by Richa Nagar)

Maria's daughter, Valentina, joins in as the group rehearses the last scene of *Retelling Dis/Appearing Tales*. (Photo by Tarun Kumar)

if encountering every story was accompanied by this responsibility? Coming from a story of many privileges in life, the class pushed me to begin searching for the intimate connections of my story, Siddharth's story, to the deep violences each of us read and spoke of, violences that i needed to grasp and acknowledge in order to begin a journey of solidarity with those whose stories i had received. This hunger for deepening my understanding of myself in relation to every other in the world is now unstoppable.

The world we breathe in continuously reduces, reroutes, and re-roots the worlds of so many bodies to the stories of so few.[10] Can the spaces of a university—those elite spaces of discipline and propriety, of knowledge and knowers—honor the stories and spirit of collectivity in struggle? Can Development encompass meanings and imaginations radically different from the six-lane highways on concrete pillars that grid and fissure the land of North America, uprooting the lives of Adivasi communities thousands of miles away in South Asia through online sales and transfers of land to extractive corporations?[11] I have felt hungers for these imaginations manifest in many different spaces at the University of Minnesota, as students passionate about questions of social justice in their personal lives negotiate and agitate within professional spaces that were never built to deal with them as full people. The likelihood of hungry translations plants hope of ethical living in and against institutionalized spaces including the academy, a possible port from which to begin endless journeys of building and living in situated solidarities, and invaluable saathis and relations to walk alongside. Stories, Bodies, Movements is not a recipe for social justice pedagogy. It is only one example of a radical beginning inspired by creativity and movements far away from, yet intimately linked to, the academy—an opening that asks us to mobilize, for justice, our own stories, bodies, and movements.

Unfolding

Why bother to reflect on a class in the final pages of this book that, by its very nature, opposes stable conclusions in a journey that must continue to unfold? Maybe because the vision for this journey evolved from other sites of engagement in which i (Richa) had participated with countless others, but where the politics was one without guarantees: there was no assurance that the poetics of that vision would become meaningful for participants who registered for a course in the formal spaces of a university, oceans away from the soils of SKMS and Parakh-Mumbai. As a process of evolving together, this pedagogical exploration could only work if each participant found it worthwhile to become a saathi in a journey whose most critical lessons could only be serendipitous.

The success of the class hinged on each member recognizing organically that what we would gain would more or less be in direct proportion to what each of us was willing to offer. In some ways, the journey reminded me of *Sangtin Yatra*—where nine women opened their pages and pens to all that challenged and moved us—despite the tensions and scars that inevitably accompanied us. As the imaginations of the first group of students who took the Stories, Bodies, Movements class in spring 2017 evolved into the play, *Retelling Dis/Appearing Tales*, the participants needed no further redefinitions of keywords, props, premises, or rules. Radical vulnerability unfolded before us; it enfolded all of us in a profound praxis of spirit and body. Indeed, Siddharth remembers that when we sat down as a class midway through the semester to expand and redefine the keywords and props tentatively proposed in the syllabus, he felt no interest in perfecting those definitions: the words for doing so seemed lifeless in comparison to just doing the work of retelling through acting that we were engaged in. This class's initial idea of embodying collectivity was to juxtapose and merge the writings of all the members of the class into pieces that we could begin to perform and improvise in conversation with one another. However, no matter how much we tried, this mode started slipping into worries about whose memories and words were being centered in the emerging fragments of performances, and whose were not. Similarly, the idea of being generous to the antagonist posed enormous challenges, and sometimes grave suspicion and doubt: when victim and victimizer can be defined so easily in certain contexts, why consider this requirement to listen to the antagonist?

During the weeks that we read Viet Thanh Nguyen's *Nothing Ever Dies*, and as the group continued to struggle through these difficult questions, an exercise in practicing "just remembering" stimulated the sharing of told and untold stories of parents and grandparents. Tarun encouraged the entire class to dive into a richly layered family story of one member of our group—Maria. While journeying with tales of Maria's mother, Gabi, and her grandmother, Olga, an unexpected figure emerged—Carlotita, who worked in their household and raised their children. After having co-created a space for everyone to be antagonists and protagonists, each member of the group could see characters to whom our families and histories had been antagonists, and whose stories never became part of the family archives. Carlotita's appearance in the story created a rupture through which the threads of our stories became entangled with Maria's. In a curious and serendipitous way, the absence of Carlotita in Maria's family story inspired our efforts to do justice to her in ways that were reminiscent of how Mumtaz was moved to do justice to Budhiya. As an actor playing Carlotita, Sara was inspired to travel to apartheid South Africa to explore a particular shape and form of politics governing the world of domestic servitude. More importantly, the role inspired Sara to turn the gaze inward and bring into question her own memories, histories, and genealogies—reliving and collapsing many intimate worlds she had known in and across the United States, Mexico, Bahrain, and the Philippines—sites where she learned the meanings of these very politics. The responsibility of doing justice to Carlotita's story pushed Sara to embrace a different kind of labor that was ethical, political, and what Anzaldúa would call essentially "paralogical"—a site in which unconventional subjectivities and knowledges could be reimagined and rewritten.[17]

Retelling Dis/Appearing Tales allowed the spring 2017 class to relive crucial moments of Maria's mother's and grandmother's journeys with an aim of doing justice to the forgotten story of Carlotita. *Fractured Threads* paved a different, albeit no less challenging, path for the class who traveled with the course during the following semester. Through its fractures seeped the (im)possibilities that emerge from honestly confronting the scars of an other that one may never be able to touch or embody. For Surafel Abebe, a theater scholar who watched the show and wrote about it in a letter to the class that same night, *Fractured Threads* redefined performance as a critical act of co-making patchwork. We share Abebe's letter below because it not only generously engages with the spirit of what the class created through profound turbulences and critical refusals, it also invited us to more responsibly theorize the affect and potential of such labor:

> To the "stories, bodies, movements" team,
>
> It was a great pleasure and honor to watch *Fractured Threads* tonight. Indeed, your performance is a "patchwork of reflections." It brings together incongruous yet related stories of the everyday life. You also redefined performance as a critical act of *making* patchwork together. . . .
>
> Portraying neither a protagonist nor an antagonist, *Fractured Threads* allowed me to refrain from claiming sameness with any of the characters but to understand myself as a fractured being who is always in the process of (precarious) becoming. For instance, looking [at] how *Fractured Threads* showed the institutional racism embedded even in the space that claimed 'radical criticality,' I reflected back on my particular journey . . . as a black international student. Your 'team's' bravery to allow students to think-act with their professors (with a great deal of mutual self-reflexivity) reminded me of a professor who does 'activism' with 'marginalized communities' in the Twin Cities but showed no empathy to me (her student) when I was racially profiled.
>
> Given that your performance as a patchwork complicates the seemingly unrelated but related polka spots of the quilt called life, your drumming, singing, dancing, speaking, reciting, reading, gesture(ing), projection, etc. interrupted the ways in which I desired to dwell on my raced subjectivity. The ways in which you used your "transgenre" storytelling fractured my desire to plot a single uni-

fied linear story. You forced me to face my own historicity as a man who enjoys his own privilege in particular time-spaces. Though it presents specific polka spots to let us see particularities, your work does not reside there but traverses the spaces between the dots revealing the tensions thereof. Your aesthetic allowed me to think what the political is in your performance. I found myself struggling in the manifold, fleeting tensions.

While academic papers/dissertations (ways of knowing and knowledge *productions*) sustain the tyranny of *writing* in most of the academia, *Fractured Threads* shows the ways in which critical reflections can be embodied acts of "revealing." Given that the bodies that I saw on the stage have their own historicities, their embodied acts would "break" them or make them vulnerable. Yet, that vulnerability is, I think, a self-reflexive move that would allow the performers to come out of a 'solitary' act of writing and co-navigate with historically marked and privileged bodies in the interstices of peripheries and centers. This is one possibility that your performance has created. . . . [P]erformance does not radiate innate promise of freedom and one cannot (especially those marked by multiple marginalizations) step in and outside of a performance/character. I saw, for instance, your decisions to switch roles (black bodies embodying white subjectivity and vice versa) as a conscious aesthetic choice that would not leave the audience in a simple identification of characters in a realistic way but as a critical creation that provoked spectators to actively engage with *Fractured Threads*.

Not an end in itself, as freedom is a continuous act of self-recreation, this performance opens avenues for critical engagement and healing. For students who have been trained to do laboratory work and writing, performance is a messy process where lines could not be memorized, lights and sounds may not 'perfectly' fit into the play and 'staying in character' might be difficult. Yet *Fractured Threads*, as a mode of thinking, has already made it possible for students to take performance as an open-ended and shaky yet critical co-recreation: an act of writing, reading, singing, crawling, dreaming, healing and traveling.[13]

The paralogical journeys of both classes enabled new connections—sometimes through disconnections—and inspired new improvisations all the way through to the final performances, which were staged before invited audiences of family members, friends, students, staff, and faculty.[14] Each member of both classes slowly became an embodied co-creator of new modes of knowing, articulating, feeling, and being in the spaces and structures of what we often label flatly as the "academy." In lingering, imagining, singing, patching, refusing, and moving together, the collectives began to learn what it might take to reject conformity to dominant principles of academic propriety that intentionally or unintentionally steal or stifle embodied tongues that do not seek individualized credit or stardom.

Every effort to forge collectivity is undergirded by difficult lessons—including those related to stepping into stories that we may never be able to know or feel. The duration of a semester may be too limited for these lessons to be enunciated and honestly confronted by all the members of a class, and the process is inevitably accompanied by both pleasures and heartaches. At the same time, the collective journey of relearning the world through radical vulnerability can plant a hope that hungry translation as a relation does not always require situated solidarities built among thousands of saathis over a decade and a half. A search for situated solidarities can rupture the borders of the traditional classroom by firing our yearning for deep, ongoing, ethical, and politically committed relationships with people and histories with whom we walk in our everyday lives. Such a search can push us to merge our multiple lives into a mode of living where the singular and the collective strive to support one another in a restless quest for justice—even when the threads that entangle us are inevitably fractured.

Unhousing

"I always wanted to be a writer," wrote the Dalit student activist, Rohith Vemula, in his first and final letter before departing this world, this world that reduces the value of a man "to his immediate identity and nearest possibility. To a vote. To a number. To a thing . . . in studies, in streets, in politics, and in dying and living." Calling his birth a "fatal accident," Vemula stated that he could never recover from "the unappreciated child from my past." He declared, "I loved Science, Stars, Nature, but then I loved people without knowing that people have long since divorced from nature. Our feelings are second handed. Our love is constructed. Our beliefs colored. Our originality valid through artificial art. It has become truly difficult to love without getting hurt." As he prepared to leave for the stars, he wrote:

> There was no urgency. But I always was rushing. Desperate to start a life. All the while, some people, for them, life itself is curse. My birth is my fatal accident . . . I am not hurt at this moment. I am not sad. I am just empty. . . . I don't believe in after-death stories, ghosts, or spirits. If there is anything at all I believe, I believe that I can travel to the stars. And know about the other worlds."[15]

Simona Sawhney reflects on the difficult thoughts and practices that Rohith Vemula's letter has bequeathed to us. Invoking specifically the context of Hindu nationalist, casteist, cow-mother saving, neoliberalized, corporatized India, she writes:

If the nation is the most ambitious attempt to render organic and spiritual a proprietary relation to the land, the rivers, the forests—and to render, in turn, the spiritual itself as a proprietary category—then Vemula was certainly anti-national. His letter prompts us to find a new way of speaking about the earth, the stars, the soul and body—a way that neither the religious nor the secular has thus far been able to alight on and pursue. If the Dalit (in this sense, like the proletariat) is a category whose project is to destroy itself, to annihilate, indeed, the very frame that birthed it, then it perhaps has something particular and singular to teach us about the pain of belonging, the travails of identity-as-home, and the joyful affirmation of transience and unbelonging. It was not Rohith Vemula but instead his opponents who seem to have drawn the line connecting the annihilation of caste with the annihilation of the nation. For us, the task is to draw and read that line in an entirely different way: recasting, first and foremost, all belonging as that which can only arise because of a prior and essential unbelonging; and hence all hospitality as that which can only arise from first unhousing oneself.[16]

Sawhney's reading of Vemula's letter is reminiscent of Stefano Harney's and Fred Moten's argument that the undercommons—that is, black people, indigenous peoples, queers and poor people—"cannot be satisfied with the recognition and acknowledgement generated by the very system that denies a) that anything was ever broken and b) that we deserved to be the broken part." Refusing to ask for recognition, then, this undercommons wants to dismember and dismantle the structure "that limits our ability to find each other, to see beyond it and to access the places that we know lie outside its walls." This is not because we know what structures must replace the current ones; rather it is with the dismantling that we will "inevitably see more and see differently and feel a new sense of wanting and being and becoming. What we want after 'the break' will be different from what we think we want before the break and both are necessarily different from the desire that issues from being in the break."[17]

The journeys shared in *Hungry Translations* travel in and across the interstitial spaces of being and becoming, of refusing and breaking, of rising and flowing from within the breaks, and of hungrily searching for relations and connections. Connections and relations that push us to participate in translations that unsettle, to embrace the refusals that remain hungry for justice, and to look for liberatory knowledges and for modes of living and dying that can never be adequately understood, accessed, or contained within the structures, genres, formats, and languages celebrated by the university, and the narrow worlds it reinforces and reproduces.

We continue, then, on this never-ending path of learning about the ways in which we must unhouse our selves even as we struggle to grapple ethically with new senses of wanting and being and becoming that necessarily accompany the dismantling. As we do so, we are reminded of Tarun Kumar's words at the end of our first public staging of *Retelling Dis/Appearing Tales:* "I was catching disappearing tales . . . finding their threads and trying to connect them with their souls and their roots [so that we could collectively do justice to them]."[18] We also remember the refrain from a song—composed by our colleagues, Julie Santella, Keavy McFadden, and Laura Seithers—to tentatively tie together the pieces that constituted *Fractured Threads:*

> And can we remember
> to do right by these stories
> they weren't made for me
> they were made to be free
> and when we are parted
> plant my body in the ground
> so roots of new mem'ries
> can grow all around.

For us, all of these are powerful invitations to keep reopening the meanings and responsibilities of hungry translations.

Backstage Pages

Hungry Translations marks a culmination of some journeys, and a beginning and continuation of others. It strings together learning moments from various struggles, settings, and stages so that stories can breathe meanings into concepts that might otherwise become pulseless. The seeds of this writing were planted during a period of unprecedented sorrow in my personal and professional life: a time that also witnessed new friendships and creativity that come from touching the unexpected. These backstage pages are an incomplete attempt to acknowledge a handful of the countless people whose journeys converged with the journeys of this book.

This book emerges from the inspiring struggles of the saathis of Sangtin Kisaan Mazdoor Sangathan in Sitapur; from the profound contributions of Parakh-Mumbai team, which created the play, *Hansa, Karo Puratan Baat*; and from the committed labor of students at the University of Minnesota who taught me so much in the fall 2014 Humanistic Commons Freshmen Seminar titled Stories, Bodies, Bordercrossings (co-taught with Diyah Larasati), in the Caste, Race, and Indigeneity seminars in spring 2015 and spring 2016, and in the Stories, Bodies, Movements course (co-facilitated with Tarun Kumar in spring and fall 2017). I thank Provost Karen Hanson, Dean John Coleman, and former Associate Dean for Faculty Ana Paula Ferreira at the University of Minnesota (UMN) for providing critical resources to support this work through a Russell M. and Elizabeth M. Bennett Chair in Excellence and a Beverly and Richard Fink Professorship in Liberal Arts and by giving me the opportunity to teach in the Department of Geography, Environment and Society and the Institute for Global Studies, alongside my home department of Gender, Women, and Sexuality Studies, during my first five years as Professor of the College.

Without Himadeep Muppidi's generous engagements and sharp insights this book would not have taken its current form. Himadeep's intellectual and pedagogical partnership helped to form fresh communities of co-thinkers through the Race, Caste and Indigeneity (RCI) and Writing Political Struggles workshops supported initially by Institute for Global Studies and subsequently by the Interdisciplinary Center for the Study of Global Change (ICGC) at UMN—platforms where the first threads of this writing emerged. I am also indebted to him for his incisive comments on a preliminary draft of the book, and for introducing me to Naeem Inayatullah, Akta Kaushal, and Elizabeth Dauphinee, whose intellectual presence and encouragement have nourished this work in crucial ways. The support from Karen Brown, Evelyn Davidheiser, Raymond (Bud) Duvall, Rachmi Diyah Larasati, Laura Bell, and Shereen Sabet was critical in enabling the RCI workshops, as was the vigorous participation by all the colleagues, students, and visitors who attended these workshops between 2013 and 2017.

The penning of *Hungry Translations* began with an urge to process the collective churnings that created the play, *Hansa,* soon after the passing of my babuji, Sharad Nagar. बाबूजी, आपकी पैनी नज़र और ज़बरदस्त सहारे के बिना ये सारे सफ़र अधूरे रह जाते। For giving so much to the yaadgar safar with *Hansa*, dili shukriya to Meena Jitendra Bariya, Bhagwan Das, Purnima Kharga, Gaurav Gupta, Gabbar Kumar Mukhiya, Neeraj Kushwaha, Satish Kumar, Sujit Kumar, Alok Panday, Aijaz Patel, Mohammad Patel, Mumtaz Sheikh, Sushil Shukla, Kaajal Singh, Munira Surati, Sumit Singh Tomar, Satish Chandra Trivedi, Anil Yadav, Avi Kumar Yadav, and Yasmin ji. My sincere gratitude, also, to Aparna Chaudhari, Wazir Lakra, and the entire staff of Central Institute of Fisheries Education in Mumbai for their generous support. Meenacshi Martins, Devendranath Misra, Sanjay Mishra, Natasha Rana, Abdul Sattar Tatari, and Atul Tiwari provided important feedback during the making of the play. Writing a chapter on hunger, theater, and politics with Dia Da Costa, combined with discussions in various contexts with Dia and with Antonadia Borges, Christopher Chekuri, Bud Duvall, Jim Glassman, Naeem Inayatullah, Vicky Lawson, Nida Sajid, Anuradha Sajjanhar, Suvadip Sinha, Ajay Skaria, and Ashwini Srinivasamohan proved crucial in writing about *Hansa* since 2015, and in drawing connections between *Hansa* and the rest of *Hungry Translations*.

Invitations by Heather McLean to speak at the Arts and Precarity workshop in Glasgow and by Ron Glass, Natalie Baloy, and Sheeva Sabati to participate in the Unsettling Research Ethics workshop in Santa Cruz in 2016 inspired fresh reflections on the distances covered since 1996 with the original group of sangtins as well as with thousands of SKMS saathis and supporters who have taken the journey forward. Three of these saathis—Kamlesh, Radha Pyari, and M. R. Sharma—left this world during the writing of this book. What I have learned from them and from hundreds of other saathis, both named and unnamed on the pages of this book, cannot be summarized here. The saathis of SKMS enabled my writing with Richa Singh of *Ek Aur Neemsaar: Sangtin Atmamanthan aur Andolan*, a book in Hindi that documents the making of the Sangathan between 2004 and 2011, as well as petitions and issues of the community newspaper, *Hamara Safar*. These publications have formed the basis for many of the stories retold in *Hungry Translations*. साथियों, आपके संघर्षों और हिम्मतों ने ही इस किताब के हर लफ़्ज़ को जान दी है। आपको बार-बार सलाम!

The Syllabus in Fifteen Acts began as a dream that woke me up in the middle of the night after a conversation with Imani Vaughn Jones during the spring 2016 semester, when she worked with me as a Dean's Freshman Research and Creative Scholar. Imani's immersion in the politics of race through theater enabled her to offer fresh readings of some of the texts I had been teaching since 2007. The dream continued to become real through conversations with Alissa Case, Ezekiel Joubert, Medha Faust-Nagar, and Sofia Shank in Minnesota, and with Sophie Oldfield, Koni Benson, and Elaine Salo during and after the Radicalizing Collaboration workshop hosted by Sophie and Anna Selmeczi at the University of Cape Town in 2016. Tarun Kumar and Esther Ouray, along with Evelyn Davidheiser, Danielle Dadras, Barbara London, and Amy Selvius made it possible for me to realize the vision of the syllabus in the classroom through IGS.

Engagements with audiences, organizers, and co-presenters in multiple venues have energized this work. I thank David Edmunds, Chesha Wettasinha, and Lini Wollenberg for inviting Richa Singh, Rambeti, and me to the Climate Change, Innovation and Gender workshop in Phnom Penh (2013); Richard Pithouse and Michael Neocosmos for hosting me at the Unit for Humanities at the Rhodes University in Grahamstown (2016); Carly Manion and Payal Shah for inviting me to speak at the presidential sessions at the annual meeting of the Comparative and International Education Society in Atlanta (2017); Tariq Jazeel, Andrew Kent, and the Antipode Editorial Collective for the invitation to deliver the 2017 Antipode Lecture at the Royal Geographical Society in London; and Simona Sawhney for the invitation to speak at the Indian Institute of Technology in New Delhi (2018).

Siddharth Bharath, Hale Konitshek, Sara Musaifer, and Naimah Petigny accompanied me with their inspired intellects at key junctures. Hale's close readings and careful annotations in the summer of 2016 helped to shape this manuscript, and especially part 4, in its early stages. I also appreciate Hale's thorough work in creating the book's final index. Naimah made suggestions on an early draft and also accompanied the Stories, Bodies, Movements class in spring 2017. Siddharth's and Sara's deep involvement in the spring 2017 class resulted in their partnership as coauthors of the "Closing Notes."

Beaudelaine Pierre joined me in the last stages of this book's unfolding and helped me ask what it means to do justice to the poetry of the stories and struggles we end up retelling or refusing to tell. She taught me about cages of propositions and adverbs and about swimming more daringly in the spirit of *Hungry Translations*. Thank you, Beaudelaine, for your bold imagination and intellectual and creative companionship.

I am grateful for the serendipitous merging of my journey with that of AnaLouise Keating and Dawn Durante, the editors of the Transformations series published by the University of Illinois Press. AnaLouise's generous listening to this work, supported by Dawn's consultative approach to editing and publication, has allowed me to flow and grow in this work. I am especially indebted to AnaLouise and to Ajay Skaria for their engaged comments on an early draft of the manuscript, and to Surafel Abebe, María José Méndez, and Frances Vavrus for their thoughtful comments at critical stages of this book's making. I would also like to acknowledge the partnership of my copyeditor, Deborah Oliver, whose queries and suggestions allowed me to undertake revisions that have improved the book. I thank Akshay Nagar for giving his permission to use as the book's cover illustration the image of a painting by his father and my grand-uncle, Madan Lal Nagar.

Tahe dil se shukriya to Mazhar Al-Zo'by, Ayşe Gül Altınay, A. Mangai, Bitoli, Koni Benson, Mukesh Bhargava, Piya Chatterjee, Margalit Chu, Jeanne Faust, Louise Fortmann, Vinay Gidwani, Dwiji Guru, Gillian Hart, Allen Isaacman, Zenzele Isoke, Sangeeta Kamat, Divya Karan, Lori Law, Vibhoo Misra, Nasreen Mohammed, Chandra Talpade Mohanty, Sudha Nagavarapu, Sophie Oldfield, Quỳnh N. Phạm, Prakash, Rambeti, Richard Pithouse, Laura Pulido, Abdi Samatar, Naomi Scheman, Sofia Shank, Sima Shakhsari, Celina Su, Surbala, Richa Singh, Mumtaz Sheikh, Tama, Shruti Tambe, Edén Torres, Shiney Varghese, Narendra Kumar Verma, Ganesh Visputay, Char Voight, Marion Werner, and Shana Ye; to the entire Shukla family—especially Abhishek, Apoorva, Ayush, Neelam, and Shivam Shukla; and to my mother, Vibha Nagar, and my sister, Deeksha Nagar. Each of you has anchored me at some of the toughest moments in the turbulent safars that have accompanied the making of this book.

David Faust, Medha Faust-Nagar, and Tarun Kumar have nourished this work from near and far. In David, I continue to find my key sounding board as well as my most challenging critic and editor. Medha's creative partnership has been vital in the shaping of this book and in the making of *Hansa*. Collaborations with Tarun constitute some of the most challenging journeys I have embraced in life, each time offering rich new worlds to unlearn and relearn. Without these journeys there would be no hungry translations.

. . .

An earlier version of "Aalaap" appeared at http://richanagar.blogspot.com/2016 /05/aalap-no-italics.html.

Sections of part 1 of this book appear in

- *Antipode: A Radical Journal of Geography* 51, no. 1 (2019): 1–22, as "Hungry Translations: The World through Radical Vulnerability." © 2018 Richa Nagar. *Antipode* © 2018 Antipode Foundation Ltd.
- UC Center for Collaborative Research for an Equitable California, *Unsettling Research Ethics: A Collaborative Conference Report*, 43–46, as "Translating Struggles Ethically." https://www.academia.edu/29509417/Unsettling _Research_Ethics_A_Collaborative_Conference_Report.

Sections of part 3 of this book appear in Dia Da Costa and Richa Nagar, "Theater, Hunger, Politics: Beginning a Conversation," in *Relational Poverty Politics*, edited by Victoria Lawson and Sarah Elwood (Athens: University of Georgia Press, 2018).

Glossary of Selected Words and Acronyms

aana	old Indian currency
Awadhi	language of Awadh, predominantly spoken in the rural areas of central and eastern Uttar Pradesh. Often labeled as a dehati zubaan (language of the village), Awadhi is frequently contrasted with khadi boli or 'standard' Hindi taught in schools.
bahu, bahuriya	daughter-in-law
block	community development block, an area earmarked for rural development administration
BDO	block development officer
belan	rolling pin
Bhaiyya	brother
bindi	dot
bitiya	daughter
BJP	Bharatiya Janata Party
chachi	auntie
chakla	circular wooden board for rolling rotis
chilam	clay pipe
chulha	clay stove
Dalit	grounded down; political name embraced by members of scheduled castes in India

dehati	of the dehat, or village, often used synonymously with "grameen"
dhaba	small road-side restaurant
dhankun	midwife
dharna	sit in, protest
dholak	drum
dua	blessing
dupatta	scarf
ghat	cremation ground
gram panchayat	village council
grameen	dehati, rural
kisan	farmer
kulhad	clay cup
lota	container
mazdoor	laborer
MGNREGA	see NREGA
nahar	distributary channel
natak, nautanki	forms of theater
NGO	nongovernmental organization
NREGA	The Government of India's National Rural Employment Guarantee Act of 2005, renamed as the Mahatma Gandhi National Rural Employment Guarantee Act (MGNREGA) in 2009
nyaya panchayats	judicial components of the panchayat system, the lowest rung of the Indian judiciary created for dispute resolution and the administration of justice at the local or rural level
OBC	Other Backward Classes
ojha	healer
padyatra	foot march
pangat	people seated in rows, often on narrow strips of dari, to be fed and served during special feasts
pradhan	elected head of the gram panchayat, also referred to as 'sarpanch' in common parlance
pramukh	elected president
rangmanch	theater
saathi	the one who accompanies. In SKMS, 'saathis' refers to all those companions who share a vision and who travel together to achieve a collective goal.
safar	journey

sangtin	a term of solidarity, reciprocity, and close companionship among women
Sangtin	the organization registered by sangtins in 1998, out of which SKMS emerged
Sangathan	organization, refers here to SKMS
sangtin yatra	the journey of sangtins, which began as a journey of nine women in Sitapur district in 2002 and evolved into SKMS
Sangtin Yatra	the title of a book in Hindi (Anupamlata et al. 2004)
sarpanch	see pradhan
Satyagrah	literally, insistence on truth; a nonviolent political struggle for truth
Savarna	those regarded as upper caste in the caste hierarchy
SKMS	Sangtin Kisaan Mazdoor Sangathan or Sangtin farmers and laborers organization
tehsil	administrative subdivision of district
Vikas Bhawan	the building where the official work pertaining to rural development of a district takes place
yatra	journey

Notes

Part One. Staging Stories

1. Muppidi 2015, 1.
2. Ibid., 5–6.
3. Apter 2006, 6. Also, Nagar 2014, 23; Spivak 2000.
4. For a brief overview of the initial years of the movement, see Sangtin Kisan Mazdoor Sangathan 2010.
5. King 2017, 212; Wynter 1989, 639.
6. See Satyanarayana and Tharu, 2013, 11.
7. Other Backward Classes, or OBCs, is an official classification of the government of India. An OBC, who is regarded as "higher" than Dalit in the caste hierarchy, qualifies as "backward" based on a complex set of social, economic, and educational criteria, as specified by the National Commission for Backward Classes (NCBC). OBCs include small cultivators, agricultural laborers, artisans, and also weavers, fisher-folk, and construction workers—occupations that they share with many of those classified as Scheduled Castes (SCs), who identify as Dalit. See "Guidelines for Consideration of Requests for Inclusion and Complaints of Under Inclusion in the Central List of OBCs"—http://ncbc.nic.in/html/guideline.htm (last accessed 1 September 2017); United Nations Development Program, "Caste, Ethnicity and Exclusion in South Asia: The Role of Affirmative Action Policies in Building Inclusive Societies," http://hdr.undp .org/sites/default/files/hdr2004_dl_sheth.pdf, p. 44 (accessed 30 October 2018).
8. Anupamlata et al. 2004; a later version of *Sangtin Yatra* appeared under the name of Sangtin Lekhak Samooh 2012.
9. Kunwarapur village is located in the Mishrikh Development Block of Sitapur District, Uttar Pradesh.

10. Although gender-based segregation is quite prevalent in rural Uttar Pradesh, the meetings of SKMS are well attended by women and men of all ages.

11. The Government of India's National Rural Employment Guarantee Act (NREGA) of 2005 was renamed the Mahatma Gandhi National Rural Employment Guarantee Act (MGNREGA) in 2009. Throughout this book, I use the acronyms NREGA or MGNREGA, depending on the time when each acronym was in use.

12. Pisawan Development Block is located in the Sitapur District of Uttar Pradesh.

13. Da Costa 2016; Da Costa and Nagar 2018.

14. Da Costa and Nagar 2018.

15. Ibid.

16. Phạm 2018, 16.

17. Morrison 1988, 136–37.

18. Phạm 2018, 45.

19. Ibid., 45.

20. Ibid., 12.

21. Ibid., 12, 42.

22. Ibid., 36, 37.

23. I borrow the term "word-poor" from Muppidi 2015, 1.

24. Duvall and Çıdam 2014, 39.

25. Phạm 2018, p. 47.

26. Research, CGIAR, http://www.cgiar.org/about-us/, accessed 7 February 2018. CGIAR is formerly the Consultative Group for International Agricultural Research.

27. Merrill 2008, 5.

28. Nagar and Singh 2012, Nagar et al. 2017.

29. Sangtin Kisan Mazdoor Sangathan 2018, 9–10.

30. Ismail 2005, xxx, quoted in Jazeel 2018, 12.

31. Méndez 2018, 1.

32. Dayamani Barla, a journalist, leader, and activist from the Munda tribe in Jharkhand, India, discussed this issue in a conversation with Cânté Sütá-Francis Bettelyoun, Oglala Lakȟóta-Očhéthi Šakówiŋ, Educator of Indigenous History, Biological & Ecological Knowledge; Coordinator of Native American Medicine Gardens-University of Minnesota; and Co-Creator of Buffalo Star People Healing Circles for Adult Survivors of Childhood Abuses. The conversation was held at Native American Medicine Gardens, Saint Paul, Minnesota, 6 June 2017. Parts of this conversation appear in a YouTube film made by Tarun Kumar. See Barla and Bettelyoun 2017.

33. "Editor's Interview with Nagar" 2016; see also Connolly 2018.

34. Butler 2004.

35. Hall 1996, 45.

36. Nagar with Aslan et al. 2016.

37. Sangtin Kisan Mazdoor Sangathan 2018.

38. Shank and Nagar 2013.

39. See also R. Brown 2013.

40. Jazeel 2018, 12.

41. Barad 2012; Glissant 1997.

42. Rai 2008, 153.

43. See Chakravarti 1993 for an explanation of the term "brahmanical patriarchy."

44. Pierre, Petigny, and Nagar forthcoming.

45. See also Bhattacharyya and Basu 2018.

46. Prakash in a rally against NGOization of MGNREGA. The speech from which I have translated this excerpt is at https://www.youtube.com/watch?v=ePfHHmg7g70 (at ca. min. 1:00–1:48).

47. For a detailed discussion of this attack and the battle around it, see Nagar 2006a, 2006b.

48. A more literal translation of 'parakh' would be 'examination' or 'assessment.' However, the vision of this theater group is better translated as 'critical eye.'

49. I discuss the concept of radical vulnerability in Nagar with Aslan et al. 2016, "Editor's Interview with Nagar" 2016, and Nagar and Shirzai 2019.

50. See Spivak 1998.

51. Inayatullah 2013a, 2013b.

52. Da Costa 2016, 210.

53. Keating 2013, 7.

54. Latour 2004, 225.

55. The critique of sangtins finds strong resonances in Drishadwati Bargi's writing. Bargi (2014) writes: "The word Dalit . . . refers to dignity of the person concerned without taking away the history of prejudice and discrimination that he or she still faces in forms that cannot be explained through Bhadrolok Marxism. It has gradually incorporated within itself the long history of resistance against caste system as well as our claim to an autonomous identity that cannot be equated with the predicament of being poor, working class or an untouchable but includes something more than that. When I identify myself as a Dalit I am making a claim and seeking recognition for that discrimination, prejudice as well as that resistance. But inadvertently by identifying myself as a Dalit I am also doing something more. I am challenging a practice of 'division of labourers' . . . between emancipators (which includes writers, intellectuals, social activists, doctors, economists, trade union leaders, Naxalite leaders) and the to be emancipated (which includes peasants, workers in factories and homes, taxi drivers, rickshaw pullers etc). . . . The identity Dalit challenges the hierarchy between the caste of emancipator and the caste of emancipated and renders the emancipator redundant and useless."

56. See also Oldfield 2018.

57. A. Mangai 2015, 15–16.

Part Two. Movement as Theater

Walking Together

1. For more details, see Nagar 2006a, 2006b, and chapter 5 of Nagar 2014.

2. 'Poor' is frequently a contested term in SKMS and other similar social movements because those regarded as 'poor' may see themselves as living with values and

relationships that make their lives richer than of who are labeled as 'rich.' A similar sentiment is echoed in Ghisu's critique of his society in part 3 of this book.

3. More details about KBAY (National Food for Work Programme) can be found at https://archive.india.gov.in/sectors/rural/index.php?id=14, last accessed, 16 December 2018.

The Journey Continues

1. The Government of India's National Rural Employment Guarantee Act of 2005 was renamed as the Mahatma Gandhi National Rural Employment Guarantee Act (MGNREGA) in 2009. Throughout this book, I use the acronyms NREGA or MGNREGA, depending on the time when each acronym was in use.

2. Anees Chishti's English translation of this story was published in 2016 by the *Tribune*.

3. This story is based on the notes prepared for a letter in Hindi that SKMS saathis sent to the prime minister of India in October 2016 and on the subsequent article that I drafted on behalf of SKMS in November 2016; see Concerned Citizens and Friends 2016.

4. See Abu-Lughod 1990.

5. The IRB at the University of Minnesota "reviews research projects involving human participants, working with investigators to ensure adequate protection and informed, uncoerced consent." See https://research.umn.edu/units/irb.

6. Sheila Kelleher to author, e-mail ("Study 0302S41442 Crossing Borders / okay to close"), 12 December 2016.

Part Three. Living in Character

Mumtaz and Budhiya

1. The Urdu version of the story was published in *Jamia* (December 1935), and the Hindi version of the story was published in *Chaand* (April 1936), a few months before Premchand's death on 8 October 1936. The story has been republished many times, including in the *Premchand Rachna-Sanchayan*, edited by Nirmal Verma and Kamal Kishore Goenka (2004). It was translated into English by Frances W. Pritchett as "The Shroud" (Premchand, n.d.).

2. Chamars are classified as a scheduled caste and regard themselves as Dalit. *Chamar* can also be considered a derogatory label imposed by the Savarna.

3. Emily Durham (2018, 17) points out that Premchand sought to challenge colonial, nationalist, and casteist notions of what 'the Indian subject' can and should be; however, his Dalit critics argue that even as they describe the dynamics of the oppressive sociopolitical system in which they live, Premchand's characters fail in their own dynamism. Indeed "it becomes difficult to conceive of a Dalit character that is able to exceed the constraints of her condition." Durham engages with this critique of Premchand's work by considering Ajay Navaria's contemporary short story "Uttarkatha," translated into English as "Hello Premchand" by Laura Brueck

(see Navaria 2013). In this story, Navaria "uses some of Premchand's most recognizable characters who then work together to challenge the restricted fortunes of low and high-cast[e] figures alike. Instead of emphasizing the gaps between characters that consist of the symbolic particularities in an oppressive system, Navaria's story highlights the connections between characters that are able to reveal the cracks in that system" (Durham 2018, 17).

4. Bal auditorium of Central Institute of Fisheries Education in Versova was available free of charge, and it allowed us to reach a large audience who could enjoy a play in Awadhi.

5. In part 3, I have used aliases to retain the anonymity of some people due to the sensitive nature of the information they shared.

Hansa, Karo Puratan Baat!

1. Sharma 2010.

Entangled Scripts and Bodies

1. This builds on Merrill 2008; see part 4 of *Hungry Translations*.

2. Gaurav Gupta (workshop participant), journal entry and workshop discussion, 8 Aug. 2014.

3. There were twenty-six participants, counting all those who provided different kinds of support during the six months of the theater workshop.

4. Only three participants—Mumtaz Sheikh, Meena Bariya, and Yasmin—were women, and all three are domestic workers. This acquired significance in the relationships that developed during the workshop as well as the aesthetics pertaining to the adaptation of "Kafan" into *Hansa*.

5. The "Challenge Called 'Kafan'" section is based on verbal and e-mail communication between Tarun Kumar and me (July 2014–September 2015), and on sections of journals shared by Alok Panday and Gaurav Gupta . It also draws on my participation in the workshop during June, July, August, and December 2014.

6. The "Swimming with *Hansa*" section is based mainly on written reflections shared by Alok Panday from his journals. I complement it with conversations with, and journals written by, other participants as well as with my own observations as a co-facilitator of the workshop during June, July, August, and December 2014.

Hungry for *Hansa*

The discussion in this chapter builds on Da Costa and Nagar 2018.

1. Tarun Kumar and author, Skype discussion, 27 July 2015.

2. Rai 2008, 153.

3. Mumtaz Sheikh, reflections dictated to co-participants and shared in discussions, 21, 24, and 25 Dec. 2014.

4. Rai 2008, 151.

5. Skaria, 'Response to Courtney Gildersleeve, Naeem Inayatullah, Molly McGlennen, Richa Nagar,' IGCC Research Circle Workshop on Trans-border Conversations on 'Caste, Race, and Indigeneities,' University of Minnesota, Twin Cities, March 2015.

6. Vineet Kumar, theater and film actor, Mumbai, 21 Dec. 2014.

7. Saurabh Shukla, theater and film actor, in discussion after the first show on 27 Dec. 2014.

8. Da Costa in Da Costa and Nagar 2018, 204.

9. Alok Panday, diary, Hansa: Karo Puratan Baat Theater Workshop, Mumbai, India, 2014.

10. See Guru 2001.

11. Sajid 2016, 114; Satyanarayana and Tharu 2013, 18. See also Valmiki's preface in Valmiki 1997, Guru 2003, Guru and Sarukkai 2012.

12. Rege 2006.

13. Sajid 2016; Naimishraya 1995; Naimishraya 2008.

14. Bhagwan Das (workshop participant), journal entries and workshop discussions, 19 and 21 Dec. 2014.

15. Mumtaz Sheikh, in journal entries (dictated to co-participants) and workshop discussions, 21, 24, and 25 Dec. 2014.

16. Alok Panday (workshop participant), entries from journal 3, pp. 5–6; and unnumbered entry from 12 Aug. 2014.

17. This situation presented new contradictions. One glimpse can be found in the journal that my daughter Medha Faust-Nagar wrote for her eleventh-grade theater class at Great River Montessori in Saint Paul: "One thing that I've really been grappling with [since last August] is how people can ideologically believe something is ethical or not ethical, but still not see the contradictions of their ethical standpoint in their own lives. An example that I saw specifically was the way [Sajjan] (a young man in the "Kafan" cast, who is also a domestic worker for one of the director's friends' homes) was treated like an equal and important member of the group during rehearsals, but one day after rehearsal there was a party at Sajjan's bosses' house. The director, my mom, me, and one other member of the cast who was the bosses' nephew were the only ones involved in "Kafan" there (excluding [Sajjan]). I felt so awkward when [Sajjan] (who is my age) was being told to serve food to all the guests and to manage the pets' behavior all evening. My mother and the director said they felt it too, especially the way the nephew and all the other guests were just treating him like a servant. At 6 pm the nephew was treating [Sajjan] like a Bollywood hero and at 10 pm [Sajjan] was just the live-in dog nanny. I wanted to talk to him and apologize, but what could I have said? It wouldn't change anything, so I smiled at him, served myself, and played with the dogs so he could have a break to eat."

18. This point builds on Da Costa and Nagar 2018.

19. See Sajid 2016.

20. Da Costa and Nagar 2018.

21. See Nagar and Shirazi 2019.

22. Inayatullah 2013a, 336.

23. Ibid., 341.

24. Premchand, n.d.

25. Ibid.

Part Four. Stories, Bodies, Movements

One More Time

1. To quote Édouard Glissant: "Agree not merely to the right to difference but, carrying this further, agree also to the right to opacity that is not enclosure within an impenetrable autarchy but subsistence within an irreducible singularity. Opacities can coexist and converge, weaving fabrics. To understand these truly one must focus on the texture of the weave and not on the nature of its components" (1997, 190).

Synopsis and Backdrop

1. For example, caste, race, gender, class, sexuality, and other categories to which we connect our origins, identities, and/or ideas about belonging.

2. See Pratt and Rosner 2012.

3. Spivak 2004, 81.

Initial Keywords, Props, Premises

1. This definition comes from Skaria 2016.

2. See also Nagar and Shirazi 2019.

The Fifteen Acts

1. I thank Dominique Johnson from my spring 2016 Gender and Global Politics class for introducing me to the two video clips mentioned in Act 1.

2. See Merrill 2008 for a rich discussion of this idea.

3. I discuss this point as the 'first truth' of storytelling in chapter 6 of *Muddying the Waters* (Nagar 2014).

4. Pratt and Rosner 2012 and Abu-Lughod 2013.

5. On radical vulnerability, see Nagar 2014; Nagar with Aslan et al. 2016, Chowdhury et al. 2016, Nagar and Shirazi 2019.

6. See Wolfe 2006.

7. A. Simpson 2014, 22.

8. Tuck and Yang 2014, 817.

9. Satyanarayana and Tharu 2013, 17.

10. Ibid., 19. Guru 2003, 70–71. See also Guru and Sarukkai 2012.

11. On frontstaging and backstaging, see Shank and Nagar 2013.

Closing Notes

1. Blurb created by the spring 2017 Stories, Bodies, Movements class to describe their performance, *Retelling Dis/Appearing Tales*.

2. Blurb created by the fall 2017 Stories, Bodies, Movements class to describe their performance, *Fractured Threads*.

3. De La Cadena 2010, 358. See also Stengers 2005, 994.

4. See Nagar 2014.

5. Nagar 2006a; De La Cadena 2015, 286.

6. Shank and Nagar 2013; De La Cadena 2015, 275.

7. Alexander and Mohanty 1997, xxviii–xxix.

8. Ibid.

9. Arendt 1981, 50. Arendt writes: "Our certainty that what we perceive has an existence independent of the act of perceiving, depends entirely on the object's also appearing as such to others and being acknowledged by them. Without this tacit acknowledgement by others we would not even be able to put faith in the way we appear to ourselves" (46).

10. Palmer 2014, 268.

11. Dayamani Barla, a journalist, leader, and activist from the Munda tribe in Jharkhand, India, discussed this issue in a conversation with Cânté Sütá-Francis Bettelyoun, Oglala Lak óta-Očhéthi Šakówi , educator of Indigenous History, Biological & Ecological Knowledge; coordinator of Native American Medicine Gardens–University of Minnesota; and co-creator of Buffalo Star People Healing Circles for Adult Survivors of Childhood Abuses. The conversation was held at University of Minnesota Native American Medicine Gardens, Saint Paul, 6 June 2017. Parts of this conversation appear in a YouTube film made by Tarun Kumar. See Barla and Bettelyoun 2017.

12. See Anzaldúa 1996.

13. Abebe 2017.

14. On "paralogical," see Anzaldúa 1996.

15. Vemula 2016.

16. Sawhney 2016, 118–19.

17. Halberstam 2013, 6.

18. Tarun Kumar, in discussion with the *Retelling Dis/Appearing Tales* audience at Heller Hall, University of Minnesota, Minneapolis, 8 May 2017.

Works Cited

Abebe, Surafel. 2017. Letter to "Stories, Bodies, Movements" Team. Personal communication. 18 December 2017.

Abu-Lughod, Lila. 1990. "The Romance of Resistance: Tracing Transformation of Power through Bedouin Women." *American Ethnologist* 17, no. 1: 41–55.

———. 2013. *Do Muslim Women Need Saving?* Cambridge: Harvard University Press.

Alexander, M. Jacqui. 2005. *Pedagogies of Crossing*. Durham, NC: Duke University Press.

Alexander, M. Jacqui, and Chandra Talpade Mohanty. 1997. *Feminist Genealogies, Colonial Legacies, Democratic Futures*. New York: Routledge.

Anupamlata, Ramsheela, Reshma Ansari, Vibha Bajpayee, Shashibala, Shashi Vaish, Surbala, Richa Singh, and Richa Nagar. 2004. *Sangtin Yatra: Saat Zindgiyon Mein Lipta Nari Vimarsh*. Sitapur: Sangtin.

Anzaldúa, Gloria E. 1996. "Spiritual Mestisaje, an Other Way." Box 64, folder 28, Gloria Evangelina Anzaldúa Papers, Nettie Lee Benson Library, University of Texas, Austin.

———. 2015. "Preface: Gestures of the Body—Escribiendo para idear." In *Light in the Dark / Luz en lo Oscuro: Rewriting Identity, Spirituality, Reality*, edited by AnaLouise Keating, 1–8. Durham, NC: Duke University Press.

Apter, Emily. 2006. *The Translation Zone: A New Comparative Literature*. Princeton, NJ: Princeton University Press.

Arendt, Hannah. 1981. *The Life of the Mind*. Boston: Houghton Mifflin Harcourt.

Barad, Karen. 2012. "On Touching—The Inhuman that Therefore I Am." *Differences: A Journal of Feminist Cultural Studies* 23, no. 3: 206–23.

Bargi, Drishadwati. 2014. "The Dilemma of an Upwardly Mobile, English Speaking, Bengali Dalit Woman." *Round Table India*, 20 January 2014. http://roundtableindia

.co.in/index.php?option=com_content&view=article&id=7175%3A, last accessed 2 December 2018.

Barla, Dayamani, and Cânté Sütá-Francis Bettelyoun. 2017. In *Indigeneity Colonialisms, and Justice: A Conversation between Dayamani Barla and Cante Suta-Francis Bettelyoun*. A film by Tarun Kumar. Parakh Theatre. Posted 27 September 2017. https://youtu.be /ZcLdYDfMMWk.

Bhattacharyya, Asmita, and Sudeep Basu, eds. 2018. *Marginalities in India: Themes and Perspectives*. Singapore: Springer.

Brown, Brené. No date. "Brené Brown on Empathy." RSA Shorts. Video, 2:53. [Posted December 2013.] www.youtube.com/watch?v=1Evwgu369Jw.

Brown, Ruth Nicole. 2013. *Hear Our Truths: The Creative Potential of Black Girlhood*. Urbana: University of Illinois Press.

Butler, Judith. 2004. *Precarious Life: The Powers of Mourning and Violence*. New York: Verso.

Cerat, Marie Lily. 2011. "Maloulou." In *Haiti Noir*, edited by Edwidge Danticat, 179–91. New York: Akashic Books.

Chakravarti, Uma. 1993. "Conceptualising Brahmanical Patriarchy in Early India: Gender, Caste, Class and State." *Economic and Political Weekly* 28, no. 14 (3 April 1993). www .epw.in/journal/1993/14/special-articles/conceptualising-brahmanical-patriarchy -early-india-gender-caste, last accessed 2 December 2018.

Chowdhury, E. H., L. Pulido, N. Heynen, L. Rini, J. Wainwright, N. Inayatullah, and R. Nagar. 2016. "Muddying the Waters: Coauthoring Feminisms across Scholarship and Activism." *Gender, Place and Culture* 23, no. 12: 1800–1812. doi: 10.1080 /0966369X.2016.1221880.

Concerned Citizens and Friends of Sangtin Kisan Mazdoor Sangathan, Sitapur, Uttar Pradesh. 2016. "MGNREGA Workers Demand Their Wages Now: How Does GoI's Failure to Pay Affect the Everyday Lives of Those Whom It Is Cheating?" *Wire*, 21 November 2016. https://thewire.in/politics/mgnrega-workers-demand- their-wages-now.

Connolly, Patricia. 2018. *Transnational Testimonios: The Politics of Collective Knowledge Production*. Seattle: University of Washington Press.

Da Costa, Dia. 2016. *Politicizing Creative Economy: Activism and a Hunger Called Theater*. Urbana: University of Illinois Press.

Da Costa, Dia, and Richa Nagar. 2018. "Theater, Hunger, Politics: Beginning a Conversation." In *Relational Poverty Politics: Forms, Struggles, and Possibilities*, edited by Victoria Lawson and Sarah Elwood, 201–18. Athens: University of Georgia Press.

De la Cadena, M. 2010. "Indigenous Cosmopolitics in the Andes: Conceptual Reflections beyond Politics." *Cultural Anthropology* 25, no. 2: 334–70.

———. 2015. *Earth Beings: Ecologies of Practice across Andean Worlds*. Durham, NC: Duke University Press.

Du Bois, W. E. B. 1868. *The Souls of Black Folk*. New York: Vintage Books / Library of America.

Durham, Emily A. 2018. "Magic, Madness and Mud: The Progressive Realism of Premchand, Manto and Chughtai." PhD diss., University of Minnesota.

Duvall, Raymond, and Çiğdem Çıdam. 2014. "Power in the Analysis of World Orders." In *Civilizations and World Order: Geopolitics and Cultural Difference*, edited by Fred Dallmayr, M. Akif Kayapınar, and İsmail Yalacı, 35–50. Lanham, MD: Lexington Books.

"Editor's Interview with Richa Nagar, Interview Forum: On Feminist and Postcolonial Thought." 2016. *Journal of Narrative Politics* 2, no. 2: 73–81. http://journalofnarrativepolitics.com/wp-content/uploads/2016/03/JNP-Vol-22-Nagar.pdf.

Garbus, Liz, dir. 2015. *What Happened, Miss Simone?* Netflix documentary.

Gidla, Sujatha. 2017. *Ants among Elephants: An Untouchable Family and the Making of Modern India*. New York: Farrar, Straus and Giroux.

Glissant, Édouard. 1997. *Poetics of Relation*. Translated by Betsy Wing. Ann Arbor: University of Michigan Press.

Guru, Gopal. 2001. "Politics of Representation." *Seminar* 508 (December). www.india-seminar.com/2001/508/508%20gupal%20guru.htm.

———. 2003. "Review of *Joothan: A Dalit's Life* by Omprakash Valmiki." *Seminar* 530 (October). www.india-seminar.com/semframe.html.

Guru, Gopal, and Sundar Sarukkai. 2012. *The Cracked Mirror: An Indian Debate on Experience and Theory*, New Delhi: Oxford University Press.

Halberstam, Jack. 2013. "The Wild Beyond: With and for the Undercommons," In Stefano Harney and Fred Moten, *The Undercommons: Fugitive Planning and Black Study*, 5–12. New York: Minor Compositions.

Hall, Stuart. 1996. "The Problem of Ideology: Marxism without Guarantees." In *Stuart Hall: Critical Dialogues in Cultural Studies*, edited by David Morley and Kuan-Hsing Chen, 25–46. New York: Routledge.

Hammad, Suheir. 2010. *Born Palestinian, Born Black: And The Gaza Suite*. Brooklyn, NY: UpSet Press.

———. 2008. *Breaking Poems*. New York: Cypher Books.

Harjo, Sterlin. 2010. *Barking Waters*. Film. Directed by Sterlin Harjo. New York: Lorber Films.

Harney, Stefano, and Fred Moten. 2013. *The Undercommons: Fugitive Planning and Black Study*. New York: Minor Compositions.

Hartman, Saidiya. 2007. *Lose Your Mother: A Journey along the Atlantic Slave Route*. New York: Farrar, Straus and Giroux.

———. 2008. "Venus in Two Acts." *Small Axe* 12, no. 2: 1–14.

Husain, Zakir. No date. "Abbu Khan ki Bakri." Translated by Anees Chishti, in "Abbu Khan's Goat and Lessons It Teaches." *Tribune*, 3 May 2016. www.tribuneindia.com/news/comment/abbu-khan-s-goat-lessons-it-teaches/230995.html, last accessed 16 December 2018.

Inayatullah, Naeem. 2013a. "Pulling Threads: Intimate Systematicity in the Politics of Exile." *Security Dialogue* 44, no. 4: 331–45.

———. 2013b. "Distance and Intimacy: Forms of Writing and Worlding." In *Claiming the International*, edited by Arlene B. Tickner and David L. Blaney, 194–213. New York: Routledge.

Ismail, Qadri. 2005. *Abiding by Sri Lanka: On Peace, Place, and Postcoloniality*. Minneapolis: University of Minnesota Press.

Jazeel, Tariq. 2018. "Singularity. A Manifesto for Incomparable Geographies." *Singapore Journal of Tropical Geography*, 10 October 2018, 1–17. https://onlinelibrary-wiley-com .ezp1.lib.umn.edu/doi/epdf/10.1111/sjtg.12265.

Jordan, June. 2000. *Soldier: A Poet's Childhood*. New York: Basic Civitas Books.

———. 2007. "Poem about My Rights." In *Directed by Desire: the Collected Poems of June Jordan*, edited by Jan Heller Levi and Sara Miles. Seattle: Copper Canyon Press.

Kapadia, Karin. 2017. "Introduction: We Ask You to Rethink: Different Dalit Women and Their Subaltern Politics." In *Dalit Women: Vanguard of an Alternative Politics in India*, edited by S. Anandhi and Karin Kapadia, 1–50. New York: Routledge.

Kauanui, J. Kēhaulani. 2016. "'A Structure, Not an Event': Settler Colonialism and Enduring Indigeneity." *Lateral Journal of Cultural Studies Association* 5, no. 1 (spring). http:// csalateral.org/issue/5-1/forum-alt-humanities-settler-colonialism-enduring -indigeneity-kauanui/, last accessed 13 December 2018.

Keating, AnaLouise. 2013. *Transformation Now! Toward a Post-Oppositional Politics of Change*. Urbana: University of Illinois Press.

King, Joyce E. 2017. "2015 AERA Presidential Address: Morally Engaged Research/ers Dismantling Epistemological Nihilation in the Age of Impunity." *Educational Researcher* 46, no. 5: 211–22. Also, www.aera.net/EventsMeetings/AnnualMeeting /PreviousAnnualMeetings/2015AnnualMeeting/2015AnnualMeetingWebcasts /AERAPresidentialAddressJoyceEKing.

Latour, Bruno. 2004. "Why Has Critique Run Out of Steam? From Matters of Fact to Matters of Concern." *Critical Inquiry* 30 , no. 2 (winter): 225–48.

Lorde, Audre. No date. Poems. At: https://frankroberts.files.wordpress.com/2012/10 /audrelordepoems.pdf.

Loudermilk, A. 2013. "Nina Simone and the Civil Rights Movement: Protest at Her Piano, Audience at Her Feet." *Journal of International Women's Studies* 14, no. 3: 121–36.

Mangai, A. 2015. *Acting Up: Gender and Theatre in India, 1979 Onwards*. New Delhi: Left-Word.

Méndez, María José. 2018. "'The River Told Me': Rethinking Intersectionality from the World of Berta Cáceres." *Capitalism Nature Socialism* 29, no. 1: 7–24. doi: 10.1080 /10455752.2017.1421981.

Merrill, Christi A. 2008. *Riddles of Belonging: India in Translation and Other Tales of Possession*. New York: Fordham University Press.

Middle East Research and Information Project. 2014. "Primer on Palestine, Israel and the Arab-Israeli Conflict." www.merip.org/primer-palestine-israel-arab-israeli -conflict-new.

Mohamed, Saredo Qassim. No date. "The Process of De-Colonization." www.facebook .com/WesternUSC/videos/1375581585825465/, last accessed 18 December 2018.

Morrison, Toni. 1988. "Unspeakable Things Unspoken: The Afro-American Presence in American Literature." Tanner Lectures on Human Values, delivered at the

University of Michigan, 7 October 1988, pp. 123–63. https://tannerlectures.utah
.edu/_documents/a-to-z/m/morrison90.pdf, last accessed 17 December 2018.

Muppidi, Himadeep. 2015. *Politics in Emotion: The Song of Telangana*. New York: Routledge.

Nagar, Richa. 2006a. "Introduction: Playing with Fire: A Collective Journey Across Borders." In Sangtin Writers and Richa Nagar, *Playing with Fire: Feminist Thought and Activism through Seven Lives in India*, xxi–xlvii. New Delhi: Zubaan Books; Minneapolis: University of Minnesota Press.

———. 2006b. "Postscript: NGOs, Global Feminisms, and Collaborative Bordercrossings." In Sangtin Writers and Richa Nagar, *Playing with Fire: Feminist Thought and Activism through Seven Lives in India*,132–55. New Delhi: Zubaan Books; Minneapolis: University of Minnesota Press.

———. 2014. *Muddying the Waters: Coauthoring Feminisms across Scholarship and Activism*. Urbana: University of Illinois Press.

Nagar, Richa, Kathy Davis, Judith Butler, AnaLouise Keating, Claudia De Lima Costa, Sonia E. Alvarez, and Ayşe Gül Altınay. 2017. "A Cross-Disciplinary Roundtable on the Feminist Politics of Translation." In *Feminist Translation Studies: Local and Transnational Perspectives*, edited by Emek Erun and Olga Castro, 111–36. New York: Routledge.

Nagar, Richa, with Özlem Aslan, Nadia Z. Hasan, Omme-Salma Rahemtullah, Nishant Upadhyay, and Begüm Uzun. 2016. "Feminisms, Collaborations, Friendships: A Conversation." *Feminist Studies* 42, no. 2: 502–19.

Nagar, Richa, and Richa Singh. 2012. *Ek Aur Neemsaar: Sangtin Atmamanthan aur Andolan*. New Delhi: Rajkamal Prakashan.

Nagar, Richa, and Roozbeh Shirazi. 2019. "Radical Vulnerability." In *Keywords in Radical Geography: Antipode at 50*, edited by The *Antipode* Editorial Collective: Tariq Jazeel, Andy Kent, Katherine McKittrick, Nik Theodore, Sharad Chari, Paul Chatterton, Vinay Gidwani, Nik Heynen, Wendy Larner, Jamie Peck, Jenny Pickerill, Marion Werner, and Melissa W. Wright, 236–42. Hoboken, NJ: Wiley-Blackwell.

Naimishraya, Mohandas. 2008. *Dalit Patrakarita: Sahityik evam Sanskritik Chintan*. Vol. 2. New Delhi: Nataraj Prakashan.

———. 1995 (2009). *Apne-Apne Pinjre, Parts 1 and 2*. New Delhi: Vani Prakashan.

Navaria, Ajay. 2013. *Unclaimed Terrain*. Translated from Hindi by Laura Brueck. New Delhi: Navayana Publishing.

Nguyen, Viet Thanh. 2016. *Nothing Ever Dies: Vietnam and the Memory of War*. Cambridge: Harvard University Press.

NYC Stands with Standing Rock Collective. 2016. "Timeline of US Settler Colonialism." In #StandingRockSyllabus. https://nycstandswithstandingrock.wordpress
.com/standingrocksyllabus/.

Oldfield, Sophie. 2018. "In Everyday City Struggles: Collaborative Research and Its Inspirations." In *Across Theory and Practice: Thinking through Urban Research*, edited by Monika Grubbauer and Kate Shaw, 223–30. Berlin: JOVIS Verlag.

Palmer, Vera. 2014. "The Devil in the Details: Controverting an American Indian Conversion Narrative." In *Theorizing Native Studies*, edited by A. Simpson and A. Smith, 266–96. Durham, NC: Duke University Press.

Phạm, Quỳnh N. 2018. *Politics Beyond Dominance: Subaltern Power and World Making*, PhD diss., University of Minnesota, Twin Cities.

Pierre, Beaudelaine, Naimah Petigny, and Richa Nagar. Forthcoming. "Embodied Translations: Decolonizing Methodologies of Knowing and Being." In *The Routledge International Handbook of Gender and Feminist Geographies*, edited by Anindita Datta, Peter Hopkins, Lynda Johnston, Elizabeth Olson, and Joseli Maria Silva.

Pierre, Beaudelaine, and Nataša Ďurovičová, eds. 2011. *How to Write an Earthquake: Comment écrire et quoi écrire. Mo pou 12 Janvye*. Iowa City: Autumn Hill Books.

Pratt, Geraldine, and Victoria Rosner. 2012. *The Global and the Intimate: Feminism in Our Time*. New York: Columbia University Press.

Premchand. 2004. "Kafan." In *Premchand Rachna-Sanchayan*, edited by Nirmal Verma and Kamal Kishore Goenka, 218–25. New Delhi: Sahitya Akademi.

———. No date. "The Shroud." Translated by Frances Pritchett. www.columbia.edu/ itc/mealac/pritchett/00urdu/kafan/translation_kafan.html.

Rai, Alok. 2008. "Poetic and Social Justice: Some Reflections on the Premchand-Dalit Controversy." In *Justice: Political, Social, Juridical*, edited by Rajeev Bhargava and Michael Dusche, 151–69. New Delhi: Sage.

Rege, Sharmila. 2006. *Writing Caste / Writing Gender: Narrating Dalit Women's Testimonios*. New Delhi: Zubaan.

Sajid, Nida. 2016. "Resisting Together Separately: Representations of the Dalit-Muslim Question in Literature." In *Dalit Literatures in India*, edited by Joshil K. Abraham and Judith Misrahi-Barak, 108–27. New Delhi: Routledge.

Sangtin Kisan Mazdoor Sangathan. 2010. *Sangtin Yatra: A Short Introduction (2002–2010)*. www.youtube.com/watch?v=Ml4vEeGL6OY&t=24s.

———. 2018. "Ek aur Manthan: Jati, Dharm, aur Pahchan ki Rajneeti." *Hamara Safar* 13, no. 1: 7–10.

Sangtin Lekhak Samooh (Anupamlata, Ramsheela, Reshma Ansari, Richa Nagar, Richa Singh, Shashibala, Shashi Vaish, Surbala, and Vibha Bajpayee). 2012. *Sangtin Yatra: Saat Zindgiyon Mein Lipta Nari Vimarsh*. Rev. ed. New Delhi: Rajkamal Prakashan.

Sangtin Writers and Richa Nagar. 2006. *Playing with Fire: Feminist Thought and Activism through Seven Lives in India*. New Delhi: Zubaan Books; Minneapolis: University of Minnesota Press.

Satyanarayana K., and Susie Tharu, eds. 2013. *The Exercise of Freedom: An Introduction to Dalit Writing*, New Delhi: Navayana.

Sawhney, Simona. 2016. "End Notes." *Cultural Critique* 94 (fall): 113–23.

Shank, Sofia, and Richa Nagar. 2013. "Retelling Stories, Resisting Dichotomies: Staging Identity, Marginalization and Activism in Minneapolis and Sitapur." In *Rethinking Feminist Interventions into the Urban*, edited by Linda Peake and Martina Rieker, 90–107. Oxford: Routledge.

Sharma, Ram Kishore, ed. 2010. *Kabir Granthavali (Sateek)*. 8th ed. Allahabad: Lokbharti Prakashan.

Simpson, Audra. 2014. *Mohawk Interruptus*. Durham, NC: Duke University Press.

Simpson, Darius, and Scout Bostley. 2015. "Lost Voices." Button Poetry / College Union Poetry Slam Invitational (CUPSI). Video, 2:59. Posted 17 June 2015. www.youtube .com/watch?v=lpPASWlnZIA&sns=em.

Simpson, Leanne Betasamosake. 2017. *As We Have Always Done: Indigenous Freedom through Radical Resistance*. Minneapolis: University of Minnesota Press.

Skaria, Ajay. 2015. "Response to Courtney Gildersleeve, Naeem Inayatullah, Molly McGlennen, Richa Nagar." Interdisciplinary Center for the Study of Global Change (ICGC) Research Circle Workshop on Trans-border Conversations on 'Caste, Race, and Indigeneities,' University of Minnesota, Twin Cities, March.

———. 2016. "The Death and Rebirth of Gandhi," *Outlook*, 7 November 2016. www .outlookindia.com/magazine/story/the-death-and-rebirth-of-gandhi/298047.

Spivak, Gayatri Chakravorty. 1998. *In Other Worlds: Essay in Cultural Politics*. New York: Routledge.

———. 2000. "The Politics of Translation." In *The Translation Studies Reader*. 2nd ed. Edited by Lawrence Venuti, 369–88. New York: Routledge.

———. 2004. "Terror: A Speech after 9–11." *boundary* 2, 31, no. 2: 81–111.

Stengers, I. 2005. "The Cosmopolitical Proposal." In *Making Things Public: Atmospheres of Democracy*, edited by B. Latour and P. Weibel, 994–1004. Cambridge, MA : MIT Press.

Tinsley, Omise'eke Natasha, Ananya Chatterjea, Hui Niu Wilcox, and Shannon Gibney. 2010. "So Much to Remind Us We Are Dancing on Other People's Blood: Moving Toward Artistic Excellence, Moving from Silence to Speech, Moving in Water, with Ananya Dance Theatre." In *Critical Transnational Feminist Praxis*, edited by Amanda Lock Swarr and Richa Nagar, 147–65. Albany, NY: SUNY Press.

Tuck, Eve, and K. Wayne Yang. 2012. "Decolonization Is Not a Metaphor." *Decolonization: Indigeneity, Education and Society* 1, no. 1: 1–40.

Tuck, Eve, and K. Wayne Yang. 2014. "Unbecoming Claims: Pedagogies of Refusal in Qualitative Research." *Qualitative Inquiry* 20, no. 6: 811–18.

Valmiki, Omprakash. 1997 (2014). *Joothan* (Hindi). New Delhi: Radhakrishna Prakashan.

Vemula, Rohith. 2016. "My Birth Is My Fatal Accident: Full Text of Dalit Student Rohith's Suicide Letter." *Indian Express*, 19 January 2016. http://indianexpress.com/article/india /india-news-india/dalit-student-suicide-full-text-of-suicide-letter-hyderabad/.

Wolfe, Patrick. 2006. "Settler Colonialism and the Elimination of the Native." *Journal of Genocide Research* 8, no. 4: 387–409.

Wynter, Sylvia. 1989. "Beyond the Word of Man: Glissant and the New Discourse of the Antilles." *World Literature Today* 63, no. 4 (autumn): 637–48.

Xaxa, Abhay. 2011. "I Am Not Your Data." *Roundtable India*, 19 September 2011. http:// roundtableindia.co.in/lit-blogs/?tag=abhay-xaxa.

Index

Aag Lagi Hai Jangal Ma (play), 16
"Aalaap" (poem), 1–3
Abbu Khan ki Bakri (story by Zakir Husain), 93
Abebe, Surafel, 253–54
academy, xi; going beyond the mainstream, 7–8, 101, 199, 206, 242–57; negotiating ethics within, 10, 32
acting, 11, 108, 112; gender, class, and, 115–19, 154–55, 167; industry of, 160, 182; labor of, 158, 162, 182, 189, 249; learning through, 161, 166–69, 175, 248; living and, 189, 193; power of, 177, 181; radical vulnerability and, 179, 188, 249; reading through, 179; responsibility of, 159; retelling through, 162, 252
activism, 32, 43–45, 199, 206; contradictions of, 253; Dalit-Savarna politics in, 72, 87–88; political, 43; scholarship and, 32; spiritual, 43, 178; of women, 9
Adivasi people, 87, 91–92, 101, 147, 251
aesthetics, 34, 43, 254; creativity and, 110; definition of, 211; ethics and, 43, 110, 147, 179, 188; of *Hansa*, 179, 273n4; just, 157–59; politics and, 43, 110, 147–48, 159; of protest, 38, 45; of receiving and

telling stories, 218, 233. *See also* ethics; performance; politics
Afrazul [Khan], murder of, 99–100
agitation, 8–9, 20, 53; political, 32, 36, 58–59
Aijaz [Patel] (*Hansa* backstage worker), 115–16, 123, 165–66, 172
Akbarabadi, Nazeer, 116
Alexander, M. Jacqui, 35, 41–42, 246
allegiances, 205, 241
alliances: embodied, 224 (*see also* embodiment); samanvaya, 181–82, 187
Ansari, Reshma, 51
antagonist: generosity toward, 189, 212, 229, 232, 252; non-separation between protagonist and, 37–39, 43–46, 189–91, 199, 231, 241, 252–53. *See also* protagonist
anti-Muslim attitudes, 54
Anzaldúa, Gloria, 35, 41–42, 253
Apter, Emily, 9, 269n3
Arendt, Hannah, 249, 276n9
Arthapur village, 96
Aslam, Nadeem, 241
atmakatha (story of the self), 180
audit, social, 74

authority, 7, 71–72, 168, 234, 239; sharing, 31, 42, 213

authorship, 10. *See also* coauthorship

autobiography, 224; Dalit, 233

Awadhi (language): coauthoring *Hansa* in, 34, 112–13, 123; glossary description for, 265; journeys in, 9, 169; politics of, 117–18, 157–58; translating *Hansa* to English from, 146. See also *Hansa, Karo Puratan Baat*

babuji, author's (Sharad Nagar), v, 114, 260

backstaging, 238, 246, 275n11

Bahrain, 253

Bargadiya village, 94

Bariya, Meena Jitendra: on the acting industry, 155; acting with, 155–58, 167–68; Alok reflecting on, 168–71, 181; co-dreaming with, 120–22; featured in "Kafan," 123, 273n4; journey of, 156, 185; meeting, 117–18

Barla, Dayamani, 270n32, 276n11

belly: Ghisu's full, 135; hunger of, 18–19, 28, 92, 124, 184–88; taking care of one's, 151–56, 178–79. *See also* hunger

Bhaiyya (brother): becoming a, 26–27, 154, 158; Sunita and, 12–14, 18, 27, 114; as term of endearment, 124, 128, 140–42. *See also* Kumar, Tarun

Bhakti poetry, 112, 114, 178, 185

Bharath, Siddharth, xi, 34, 45, 241–57

Bharatiya Janata Party, 97

Bhargava, Mukesh, 14, 49–50

Bhole Dada, 115–18, 162, 173. *See also* Shukla, Sushil

bhookh, 3, 15; defined, 28. *See also* hunger

Bitoli, 75, 88, 96

Block Development Officer (BDO), 66, 68

bodies, v, 52–53, 248–51; entangled scripts and, 146–76; healthy, 98; hungry, 19, 21, 27–32, 100; of knowledge, 35; moving, 7–8, 36, 207; Othered, 37–40, 45, 209; overlaying memories with, 229–30; privileged, 254; and radical vulnerability, 179; rallying, 10, 70, 75; reproducing our, 187; spirit or being and, 110, 131, 207, 212 (*see also* mind, body, and soul/spirit); on stage, 44; stories, borders, and, 219, 222–23; unequal, 213

Bollywood, 39, 146, 160, 182–85, 274n17

borders: authorship across and within, 10; bodies and, 223; of the classroom, 255; between i and you, 208, 242; politics and possibilities of crossing, 23–24, 30, 46, 117–18, 147, 191; refusing, 243; stories and, 31, 205, 207, 219–20, 237, 241

Bostley, Scout, 214

Brahma Prasad, 86–89

brahmanical patriarchy, 33–34, 59, 65, 152–53, 271n43

Brown, Brené, 214

Brown, Jada, 242, 247

Budhiraja, Kriti, 242

Budhiya: doing justice to, 108, 112–22, 150–64, 169–95, 252; of *Hansa,* 124–39, 145; Madhav and, 118 (*see also* Madhav); Mumtaz as, 108–9, 114–22, 158, 168, 187 (*see also* Sheikh, Mumtaz); students reflecting on, 192–95, 236, 249. See also *Hansa, Karo Puratan Baat*

Butler, Judith, 30

Carlotita, doing justice to, 252–53

caste: annihilation of, 256; Dalit identity and, 180–81; engaging caste in the context of *Hansa,* 157; everydayness of, 118; gendered practices of labor and, 155; hierarchies and politics of, 39, 54, 87–89, 94, 119, 175–90, 269n7, 272n2 (2); nuances of, 146; privilege, 79; rethinking and rewriting scripts of, 11, 176, 190; unlearning, 60, 86–88, 156; untouchable, 9; upper, 94, 147, 156, 233, 267; woman as, 137, 139. *See also* brahmanical patriarchy; Dalit(s); Dalit-Savarna politics; Savarna; Savarna privilege

casteism: anti-Dalit, 159; capitalist patriarchy and, 37; deconstructing and opposing, 87–90, 113, 150–56; Hindu nationalism and, 255–56; psychological price of, 188; stereotypes of, 192–94

Cerat, Marie Lily, 222

CGIAR, 22–27; CCAFS program of, 23–27; Climate Change, Innovation and Gender Workshop of, 22–27, 191, 270n26

chamar (caste), 174–75, 272n2; combating stereotypes of, 189; *Hansa* and the significance of, 113, 134, 156; politics, 146.

See also Ghisu; *Hansa, Karo Puratan Baat*; Madhav

character, living in, 110, 171, 176, 192. *See also* acting; *Hansa, Karo Puratan Baat*; *and names of specific characters*

Chatterjee, Devleena, 242–43, 247

childhood, 231–32

Chowdhury, Ritwik (backstage participant), 123

Chughtai, Ismat, 112, 149

citizenship, 9, 231

classism, 153

classroom: co-traveling in, 242–43; ethical storytelling in, 40, 209; poetic and social justice in, 190–91; reimagining pedagogy through theater in, 34, 40, 247; rupturing borders of, 40–43, 193, 206–8, 210, 219, 255; translating through, 199

Climate Change, Agriculture, and Food Security (CCAFS), 23–27

Climate Change, Innovation and Gender Workshop, 22–27, 191, 270n26

co-acting, praxis of, 166

coauthorship, 213; in the classroom, 223, 238, 243; radical vulnerability and, 30–31, 39, 42; of *Sangtin Yatra*, 35

co-learning, 26, 146–47, 191, 207–8; serendipitous and playful, 38; as uncoercive arrangement of desires, 210

collaboration, 22, 40, 187, 215

collective: doing justice to, 213; individual or singular in relation to, 34, 188, 219, 233, 238, 254–55; organized, 58

collectivity: becoming and learning through, 224–46; challenges of forging, 186, 209, 213, 235, 246, 255; embodying and honoring the spirit of, 218, 251–55; forging, 94; killing the spirit of, 30, 243; labor and processes of, 27–38, 110, 113, 157, 214–17, 241–48; praxis of solidarity and, 40–42, 85–86, 187–89, 199; radical vulnerability through, 210, 221, 223–24; resistance to, 43; sustaining, 184

colonialism, settler. *See* settler colonialism

color line, 227

common sense, 39, 42, 56, 178, 189, 249

communalism, 34, 90, 100, 155

community, 207; engagement, 43, 206; as "out there," 45, 206; of struggle, 33, 64, 160, 214; theater and, 119, 185, 186 (*see also* theater: community)

consciousness, 32, 35, 219; oppositional, 41; planetary, 45; raising, 57

Cornelius, Chandra, 191

corruption, 14, 16, 29, 36; fighting, 77, 96; in government, 59–71

cosmopolitanism, 20, 156

Da Costa, Dia, 40, 179

Dalit(s): autobiographies by, 233; casteism against, 159; communities, 57, 180; critique of Premchand by, 272n3 (*see also* Premchand: Dalit controversy); cultural upsurge, 177; literature, 180; Muslims who are, 9, 111, 147, 182; representation of, 180; status and meaning of, 9, 87–89, 147, 256, 265, 271n55; stereotypes about, 189; struggles for dignity, recognition, and rights, 23, 34, 73–75, 99; women who are, 23–25, 63–67, 93–95, 164, 232. *See also* caste; casteism

Dalit kisans and mazdoors: casteism and, 90, 156; exploitation and marginalization of, 9, 118; gender and, 23–25, 80; resistance and transgression of, 68–69, 72–77; status as, 175; struggles of, 94–98. *See also* kisans and mazdoors; mazdoors and kisans; Sangtin Kisan Mazdoor Sangthan (SKMS)

Dalit-Savarna politics: in activism, 72, 87–88; of land and resources, 62, 94–97; living, 146, 159; in the workplace, 54. *See also* brahmanical patriarchy; caste; casteism; Savarna; Savarna privilege

Das, Bhagwan (BD), 115–23, 154, 160–67, 172–73, 181–87, 195

decolonization, 20, 228–29, 246–48; pedagogy of, 248

dehumanization, 248

development, 23–24, 34, 55, 94, 98, 251; apparatus of, 29, 33, 36–37, 103, 243; corporate, 91; critiques of, 77, 101; global machinery of, 20; rural, 56–103

Dhankun (character), 134–35, 147, 169, 266

diary, 54, 223–24; *Hansa*, 148; SKMS, 66–85, 91. *See also* journals

difference, 26, 37, 86, 187, 205, 225; radical, 246

discussion, animated, 212, 215
district magistrate, 62, 68, 80
distrust, 43. *See also* trust
doing justice to: Budhiya, Ghisu, and Madhav, 112–95; the characters of "Kafan" and *Hansa*, 116, 120, 146–76; the hungry belly and soul, 188; a story, 113, 147, 152, 156–57, 189, 252–53 (*see also* stories). *See also* ethics; justice
domestic labor. *See* labor
Du Bois, W. E. B., 34, 226–27
Dupre, Devan, 242
Durban, South Africa, conference in, 180
Ďurovičová, Nataša, 222

education, 54, 57–58, 98–100, 176, 206, 233
ego: complicating, 223; confronting or recognizing, 223–24, 246; creative, 184; dissolving or surrendering, 29–30, 42, 64, 168, 212; individualized, 212
elitism, critiques of, 150, 165
embodiment, 148, 208–9, 249; definition of, 211; engaged, 227; knowledge and, 43, 116, 203, 205, 235; pedagogy of, 188–90, 206, 237; praxis of, 110; writing, 215, 228
employment. *See* Mahatma Gandhi National Rural Employment Guarantee Act; National Rural Employment Guarantee Act
episteme, 39, 43–45, 213. *See also* hunger: as episteme
epistemology, 43; critical, 213; labor of, 246
equality/equity (samata), 181, 187; expectation of, 186; in-, 26, 42, 213; and sociopolitical change, 60. *See also* caste
erasure, 7, 22, 39, 241. *See also* nihilation
ethics: alternative vision of, 21, 153; definition of, 211; desires, dreams, and, 184; institutionalized, 101; justice and, 43, 45, 207, 233 (*see also* justice); performance and, 147; poetics, aesthetics, and, 38, 101, 179–80, 188, 245; responsibility of telling and receiving stories, 40, 218, 220, 223, 235, 249 (*see also* storytelling); shared, 157; shifting, 29; uneven, 213. *See also* aesthetics; politics
Europe, 23, 243

expertise, critique of, 26, 31, 42, 208. *See also* elitism

Faust-Nagar, Medha, 49, 111, 115–17, 123; reflecting on visit to Sajjan's house, 274n17
feminism, 54, 65, 116, 150
Fifteen Acts, 218–39
Film Actors' Association, 154
food: insecurity, 25, 27; security, 22–23, 27
forgetting, just, 179, 230–31
Fractured Threads (play), 241–42, 246, 253–54, 257
fractured *we*, 41–42, 235, 246
fragments: of journeys, 38, 46, 214, 252; pedagogy of, 223, 228–29, 238; of *we*, 42
freedom, 61, 93, 103, 119, 178; promise of, 254; spiritual, 184
frontstaging, 246, 275n11

Garbus, Liz, 227
gaze, 225, 253–55
gender: acting and, 115–19, 154–55, 167; Dalit kisans and mazdoors and, 23–25, 80; labor and, 155; NGOs and, 60; performance and, 64, 116; Savarna privilege and, 72, 87–88, 164; SKMS and, 92–95, 270n10. *See also* Climate Change, Innovation and Gender Workshop
Ghisu (character), 113–18, 154–56, 169, 173–75, 181–85; doing justice to, 157; of *Hansa*, 124–46, 172–73; immersion in, 146–53, 162–69, 174–78, 187–95; students reflecting on, 172, 191–95, 236, 249. See also *Hansa, Karo Puratan Baat*
Gidla, Sujatha, 232
Girdhari (character), 132–33
Glissant, Édouard, 9, 275n1
global, the, 207, 220–21; the intimate and, 241–42. *See also* imperialism, global; politics: global
global peasant, 20–21
Gomez Cerna, Marvin, 24
Gopalpur village, 94
gram panchayat, 72–74, 78, 80. *See also* panchayat system
Gujarat, Oona District, 99
Gupta, Gaurav: acting with, 115, 119,

167–68, 173, 187–88; diary of, 148, 182; experience in film industry of, 154, 185; gratitude to, 195; *Hansa* featuring, 123; on the other play of *Hansa*, 157

Guru, Gopal, 233

Haiti, 249

Hamara Safar (newspaper), 28

Hammad, Suheir, 34, 225, 228, 249

Hansa, Karo Puratan Baat (play): actors of, 123, 182 (*see also names of individuals*); Alok's journey with, 160–76; backstage participants and supporters, 123 (*see also names of individuals*); collective labor of, 157; doing justice to, 120, 152; embodied pedagogies of, 186; journals from, 148; journey of, 38–40; learning to let go of, 190; Parakh Theatre's production of, 110, 193, 195; rehearsals of, 119–22; script of, 123–45; stipends, 153; transforming "Kafan" into, 34, 39, 113–91, 236, 273nn3–6; translating, 146–48. *See also* acting; Awadhi; Parakh Theatre; translation

"Hansa, Karo Puratan Baat" (song of Kabir), 112, 119, 145. *See also* Kabir

Hardoi (district of Uttar Pradesh), 119, 146, 158

Hariya (character), 132–33

Harjo, Sterlin, 226, 249

Harney, Stefano, 228, 256

Hartman, Saidiya, 35, 227, 236

Hasnain, 58

Heveron, Esmae, 242

hierarchy, 26, 116, 210, 271n55; epistemic, 30. *See also under* caste; movement(s); religion

Hill Collins, Patricia, 35

Hindi (language): journeys in, 9, 35, 49–50; literature in, 112–14; politics of, 54, 158, 182, 185. *See also* Awadhi; language; translation

'Hindi belt' (linguistic region), 160

Hindu-Muslim divide, 88

Hindu nationalism, 255. *See also* Hindutva

Hindustan Times (newspaper), 80, 82

Hindutva, 57, 100

hope, 119; building and nourishing, 28, 58, 88; gaining and losing, 92; hunger and, 21, 45; for the journey, 43, 98; love and, 242, 248–49; politics and pedagogies of, 9; refusal and, 22

hopelessness, 88, 119, 192

Hoshangabad, 87

humanity and inhumanity, 43, 136, 153, 241, 246

human rights, 29, 57, 224

humiliation, 23, 74, 88, 90, 179; poverty and, 176, 188. *See also* casteism

humility, 7, 24, 69, 187, 191; intellectual, xii, 245

hunger, xi, 33, 53, 65, 189; Alok reflecting on, 163, 173–74; collective, 184–85, 187; concept of, 236; continuous, 28, 205; creative, 19, 110, 184, 187; discourses of, 45; divergent, 28; entangled, 150, 181, 184; as episteme, 22, 39–46, 179–85, 208–13, 223, 244–46; Ghisu and Madhav's, 192, 194; insatiable, 244; for justice, 19–20, 28–29, 209–10, 238, 243, 256; kinds of, 27–28, 110, 150, 177; for learning, 8, 251; multiply intertwined, 184; newly found, 188; pedagogies of, 9; political, 18, 186–87; of the soul, 177, 184, 188, 194; Tarun reflecting on, 151; for theater, 15, 18–19, 21, 177–79, 186. *See also* bhookh; translation

hunger strike, 79

hungry translations: argument for, 8–9; definition of, 213–14, 220; as ethical translation, 43, 191–95; labor and responsibilities of, 237–57; participation in, 21–46; seeking justice through, 176–78. *See also* hunger; translation

Hungry Translations (this book), 33–34, 39–45, 101, 110, 242–43, 256; pedagogy of, 248–49

Husain, Zakir, 93

i. *See* i and you; i/I, I/i; i/we/you/they

i and you, 65, 224, 242

Ibn-e-Insha, 112

identification, 41, 66–67, 147, 184–89, 205, 254

i/I, I/i, 34, 42, 209–12, 224, 233, 243

imaginary, social, 19, 36–39

imperialism, global, 54

improvisation: continuous, 117–18, 237–38; creating *Hansa* through, 146; as mode of cocreation, sharing, and social reflection, 39, 113, 146, 155, 182; revision and, 208–9

Inayatullah, Naeem, 34, 189, 212, 229

incommensurability, xii, 24–26, 30–33, 38–40, 213, 244–48

India: corporatized and neoliberalized, 255; government of, 33–34, 96, 98; Hindi belt of, 160; migration throughout, 39; national politics of, 34; schools of, 113; societies of, 181

Indira Housing Scheme, 94

individual, 35, 46, 147, 184, 209, 233; ego, 30, 223–24. *See also* collective

individualism, 192

inequality, 26, 42, 213

inhumanity and humanity, 43, 136, 153, 241, 246

injustice, 42, 55, 57, 93, 96, 117; epistemic, 213. *See also* justice

Institutional Review Board (IRB), 102–3, 272n5

International Relations (IR), 20

irrigation, 58–63, 91

Irrigation Department, 59, 61–63, 73

Islamnagar distributary, 58, 64

Ismail, Qadri, 29

italics, refused, 3

i/we/you/they, 241

jatiwaad. *See* casteism

Jayasi, Malik Mohammad, 116

Jazeel, Tariq, 29; on singularity, 32

job cards, 66–72. *See also* unemployment allowance

Jordan, June, 34, 227, 231–35, 249

journals, xiii; from Parakh Theatre Workshop, 148–49, 160, 170, 182; from Stories, Bodies, Movements, 215–16, 223, 225, 238. *See also* diary

journey, 8–10, 42–46, 53–60, 146–49, 187; collective, 9, 38, 148, 177–79; doing justice to, 213; embodied, 34, 38, 208; of *Hansa* cast, 146–76, 181–91; map for, 214; paralogical, 254; poetic, 113; of sangtins, 35–39, 52–103; of students,

191–95, 200, 204–57; translational, 190; unfolding or ongoing, 27–31, 248. *See also* safar; yatra

justice: alternative vision of, 7, 21; beyond familiar frameworks of, 189; collective stake in, 205; contextual meanings of, 45; doing, 9–10, 26–29, 110, 146 (*see also* doing justice to); epistemic, 7–46, 52; hunger for, 19–20, 28–29, 209–10, 238, 243, 256; local conceptions, imaginaries, and negotiations of, 27, 40, 95, 210; poetic, 33, 45, 177–91, 214, 236–37; possibilities of, 39, 42–43, 237; rescripting stories for, 213–14, 228–30; rethinking, 223; and serendipity, 22; singular, 245; situated solidarities for, 224; social, 33, 45, 57, 177–81, 189–91, 251–57; storytelling, retelling, and, 113, 206–9, 221, 233–39, 246; struggles and quests for, 53–55, 90–91, 220, 224, 241, 255. *See also* injustice

Kaam ke Badle Anaaj Yojana (KBAY, National Food for Work Programme), 61–62, 93, 272n3 (1)

Kabir, 112, 116, 119, 178–79, 182; Granthavali, 123

kafan, 113, 117, 140, 142–44

"Kafan" (story), 110–18, 123, 146–67, 174–85, 189–95, 236; controversies surrounding, 113, 272n3; feeling vs. reading, 156, 158; improvising, 117–18; as "The Shroud," 191; transforming into *Hansa*, 34, 39, 113–91, 236, 273nn3–6

Kamlesh, 10, 12; death of, 28

Kamleshwar, 112, 149

Kannada, 118

Kapadia, Karin, 232

Karnataka, 110, 147, 154, 156

Kauanui, J. Kēhaulani, 224

KBAY (National Food for Work Programme), 61–62, 93, 272n3 (1)

Keating, AnaLouise, xi–xii; on post-oppositional politics and oppositional consciousness, 41

Khan, Afrazul, murder of, 99–100

Khan, Junaid, murder of, 99

Khan, Pahlu, murder of, 99

Kharga, Purnima, 123, 170, 172

Khilawan (character), 132–33, 136, 147
Khusro, Ameer, 116
King, Joyce, 9
kisans and mazdoors (farmers and laborers): climate change impacts on, 15; disrupting boundaries between activist, artist, educator, writer, and, 31, 33; political strategies of, 94–99; recognizing the power of, 59, 102; representing, 130–31, 152, 174; stereotypes of, 189, 193; struggles of, 36–37, 61–81, 249; victories of, 95. *See also* Dalit kisans and mazdoors; Sangtin Kisan Mazdoor Sangathan (SKMS)
knowledge: authority to make claims, 7; collective and co-owned, 8, 45, 102, 243–46; colonial, 226; contingencies of, 207; community, 225; dominant and totalizing, 19, 44, 213; embodied, 43, 116, 203, 205, 219, 235; erased, 7; escape from, 20; fragmented, 35; global politics of, 35, 100, 192, 221, 239; Indigenous/ Native, 225; just, 32–33, 213; making, 30–36, 180, 213; mobilizing, 9; self-, 9; shared, 33; yearning for, 9, 28. *See also* epistemology
Kumar, Sujit (backstage participant), 123
Kumar, Tarun: on casteism and work, 188–89; co-building theater with, 37–38, 111–18; contributions to performances, 242, 257; gratitude to, 195; *Hansa* workshop facilitated by, 123, 147; photos by, 250–52; reflections on "Kafan" and *Hansa*, 148–51, 153–57, 159–62, 165–67, 174, 178; Sunita and, 10–14, 18, 21–22, 26–27. *See also* Bhaiyya (brother)
Kunwarapur village, 10, 18, 26, 59–62, 269n9
Kushwaha, Neeraj, 116, 119, 123, 182–83, 195
Kusuma, 16, 39
Kutubnagar, 67, 100

labor: creative, 45, 147, 150, 184–85, 217; epistemic, 246; migrant, 34, 110–11, 155, 160, 182, 185; politics of domestic, 34–40, 111–12, 147, 185, 252, 273n4; stigmas of domestic, 155, 274n17. *See also* kisans and mazdoors

language: body, 172; borders of, 44, 157; contextual, 175; dominant, 9; embodied practices of, 188, 219; incoherent, 225; limitations of, 10; politics of, 113, 117–19, 146, 168, 179; spoken, 159–61; translating, 8, 235 (*see also* translation). *See also* Awadhi; Hindi
Larasati, Rachmi Diyah, 191, 193
Latour, Bruno, 41
learning: borderless sites of, 37; creative journeys of collective, 38–40, 70–72, 86–103, 146–59, 242–45; embodied, 188, 248; hunger for, 8, 251; by living in character, 176, 192; modes of, 101; neverending, 256; playful and serendipitous, 39; radical vulnerability and, 189; through unlearning and relearning, 116–17. *See also* classroom; co-learning; pedagogy; relearning; unlearning
Lieser, Rebecca, 242, 243
likkhaad, 49–50, 52
listening, 30, 212, 222–23
living in character, 110, 171, 176, 192. *See also* acting; *Hansa, Karo Puratan Baat*
local, the, 19, 26–27, 35
Lorde, Audre, 227
Loudermilk, A., 227
love: death and, 119; hope and, 242, 248–49; politics and, 227; radical, 42; reflections on, 192; respect and, 166; translation as an act of, 9; Vemula on, 255; violence and, 199, 231; work of, 182
Lucknow: collaborations in, 38; memories of, 191; migration to and from, 94; SKMS battles in, 69, 82; theater in, 112, 114, 186

Madhav (character), 113–18, 154–55, 185; Budhiya and, 118; from *Hansa*, 124–46; doing justice to, 147, 157, 163–76; reflections about, 149–53, 160–62, 168, 178, 181–84, 187–95; teaching through, 236, 249. See also *Hansa, Karo Puratan Baat*; Panday, Alok
Madhurani, 63
Mahadeva, Devanoora, 232
Maharashtra, 91, 112
Mahatma Gandhi National Rural Employment Guarantee Act (MGNREGA), 14–16, 36, 90–93, 266, 270n11, 272n1;

killing of, 96–97. *See also* National Rural Employment Guarantee Act

Mangai, A., 44

marginality: multiple, 254; radical rethinking of, 187; roots of, 249

margins, 9, 31, 99, 187, 194, 209; inhabiting, 41

Marxism, 179, 271n55

Mazdoor characters from *Hansa*, 124–25, 128, 130–33, 136, 140; connecting with, 152–56, 169, 174. See also *Hansa, Karo Puratan Baat*

mazdoors and kisans (laborers and farmers). *See* Dalit kisans and mazdoors; kisans and mazdoors

McFadden, Keavy, 242, 257

melodies, resistance through, 7–8, 10, 17, 38

memoir, 224

memory, 229–31, 241; justice and, 179, 252

Méndez, María José, 30

Merrill, Christi, 26

metanarrative of knowledge production, 225

metaphor, 146, 203, 213, 228–29

Mevani, Jignesh, 99

Mexico, 242, 253

MGNREGA. *See* Mahatma Gandhi National Rural Employment Guarantee Act

Middle East Research and Information Project, 225

migration, 34, 160, 182. *See also* labor: migrant

migratory translations, 223. *See also* translation

mind, body, and soul/spirit, 19, 209, 212, 219, 243. *See also* bodies

Minneapolis, 38, 112, 186, 192, 248. *See also* Twin Cities

Minnesota, 8, 116. *See also* University of Minnesota

Minnesota Chapter of the Association for India's Development (AID-MN), 54

Mishrikh Development Block, 56–57, 59

Mohamed, Saredo, 222

Mohanty, Chandra Talpade, 234, 246

monsoons, 107, 114

Morrison, Toni, 20

Moten, Fred, 228, 256

movement(s): building, 33, 57; collective, 52–53, 102, 199, 212–15; embodied, 188; hierarchies within, 10; ongoing, 186–88; pedagogy and politics of, 27–29, 206–7; representation of, 23; retelling and, 31; SKMS, 9, 36–46 59, 82, 92; social, 23, 199, 207, 271n2; questioning, 91; theater as, 47–103. *See also* Stories, Bodies, Movements

Muddying the Waters (Nagar), 42

Mukhiya, Gabbar Kumar, 120, 123

Mumbai: caste and gender in, 155; leaving, 117, 120; looking for better futures in, 39, 111, 147, 154; migrant domestic workers in, 34, 110–11, 185; monsoons of, 107, 114; Mumtaz's journey to, 110–11; rehearsals in, 116; theater workshops in, 13, 114, 153, 170, 192–93. *See also* Bollywood; *Hansa, Karo Puratan Baat*; rehearsal; Yari Road

Mumtaz. *See* Sheikh, Mumtaz

Munshi (character), 140, 169

Muppidi, Himadeep, 7, 8, 21

Musaifer, Sara, xi, 34, 45, 241–57

Muslim(s), 112, 121; Dalit, 9, 111, 147, 182. *See also* anti-Muslim attitudes

Nagar, Richa, as backstage participant, 123

Nagar, Sharad (babuji), v, 114, 260

Naimishraya, Mohandas, 181

narration, 31–32, 40, 209, 212; collectively owned, 38, 234; ethics and politics of, 180

"narratives of suffering," Satyanarayana and Tharu on, 233

natak. *See* theater

National Food for Work Programme (KBAY), 61, 93, 272n3 (1)

National Rural Employment Guarantee Act (NREGA), 63, 73–74, 77–78, 80–81, 86; corruption within, 11; guidelines of, 67. *See also* Mahatma Gandhi National Rural Employment Guarantee Act (MGN-REGA)

nautanki, 14–19, 21, 36, 64. *See also* acting; living in character; Parakh Theatre; theater

Naxalites, 91, 271n55

NGOization, 35, 184, 187; critique of, 56,

59; of grassroots politics, 42. *See also* nongovernmental organizations

Nguyen, Viet Thanh, 34, 179, 229–30, 252

nihilation: concept of, 9, 19–20, 26–27; epistemic, 213, 248. *See also* erasure; obliteration

Noer, Jason, 242

nongovernmental organizations (NGOs), 23–24, 35–36, 56, 186; attacks, 54; critiques of, 53; dominant imaginations of, 52; gender and, 60; violations by, 49. *See also* NGOization

North America, 23, 225, 251

"Nourishment" (poem), 107–9

NREGA. *See* National Rural Employment Guarantee Act

nyaya panchayat, 66–67, 70. *See also* panchayat system

OBCs (Other Backward Classes), 9, 88, 147, 269n7

objectification, 248

obliteration, 19, 27–28, 213, 248. *See also* erasure; nihilation

"One More Time" (poem), 201–4

openness, radical, 9, 43. *See also* radical vulnerability; vulnerability

oppositional consciousness, 41

Other Backward Classes (OBC), 9, 88, 147, 269n7

Others, 40, 42, 46, 87, 88, 249

Ouray, Esther, 242

paasi, 87, 159

panchayat system. *See* gram panchayat; nyaya panchayat

Panday, Alok, 115–23, 154, 160–77, 182–88, 195, 249; on hunger, 163–64; journal of, 148, 160–76, 182

Parakh Theatre (also Parakh-Mumbai): collaborations with SKMS, 207, 242, 251; journeys of, 34–35, 38–39; journey with "Kafan" and *Hansa* in Mumbai, 107–91

paralogical, the, 253–54

Patel, Aijaz (*Hansa* backstage worker), 115–16, 123, 165–66, 172

Patel, Mohammad (Patel Saheb), 123, 159, 165–66, 170

pathshala (site of learning), 37–38, 79

patriarchy, 33–34, 37, 59–65, 153–55, 194. *See also* brahmanical patriarchy

peasants: emancipation and, 271n55; global vs. provincial, 20; as political subjectivity, 20–21

pedagogy, 9, 34–40, 191, 208–10, 224–25, 249; collective, 38, 116; creative, 36; critical, 213, 224; embodied, 36, 190, 206, 237; epistemology, theory, and, 43; of movements, 27–29, 206–7; social and poetic justice and, 190–91, 251; strategic retelling and, 45. *See also* classroom; epistemology; learning; unlearning

performance: dramatic, 157; embodied, 206; final, 238–39; fragments of, 252; gender and, 64, 116; honest, 151; labor of, 182; learning through, 206, 208, 216–19, 231; Mumtaz on, 120; politics and, 147, 254; rebellion through, 12; redefining through, 253; Sajjan's, 185. *See also* acting; ethics; *Hansa, Karo Puratan Baat*; movement(s); Stories, Bodies, Movements

Petigny, Naimah, 242–43

Phạm, Quỳnh, 20–21

Philippines, 253

Phnom Penh, 22–24, 26

Pierre, Beaudelaine, 34, 222, 242

Pisawan Block, 13–15, 67–68, 79–83, 86, 93–95, 100

Pita, 10, 12, 64, 114

planetary consciousness, 45

Playing with Fire (Sangtin Writers and Nagar), 35, 42, 55, 59, 102; interpretations of, 23; teaching with, 234–35

poetic justice, 33, 45, 177–91, 214, 236–37. *See also* justice; social justice

poetics: collective search for, 189; of collective vision, 251; of justice, 178–81; politics and, 119, 206, 230, 235, 246; of protest 38, 43; responsibility of, 32; of teaching, 45. *See also* aesthetics; ethics

poetry, Bhakti, 112, 114, 178, 185

political theater, 33–37, 110, 177–78, 184–88, 207, 242. See also *Hansa, Karo Puratan Baat*; Parakh Theatre; theater

politics: aesthetics and, 43, 110, 147–48, 159; of authenticity, 224; of caste, 146,

175–76, 179–80, 233; Dalit, 233; of domestic labor, 34–40, 111–12, 147, 185,
252, 273n4; embodied, 241–42, 248,
252–53; feeling, 227; global, 199, 205,
208, 220, 239, 241; without guarantees,
30, 32, 45–46, 251; of hate, 99–100;
hungry, 213; of knowledge, 35, 100, 192,
221, 239; of language, 113, 117–19, 146,
168, 179; of MGNREGA, 96; of movements, 27–29, 206–7; performance and,
147; pluriversal, 246; radical, 94; shared,
233–35; of situated solidarities, 101;
story as, 118–19; of storytelling, 205–9,
220, 234–35, 241, 245; transformative,
187–92; of writing, 230. *See also* activism; ethics; justice
polyvocality, 118, 235
polyvocal script(s), 213, 216–17, 237–38,
241, 246; staging, 238
post-oppositional politics, 41
poverty, 34, 41, 153, 175–76, 189, 191; discourses of, 19–22, 187–91, 271, 272n2;
figure of, 100
power: axes of, 35; collusion and, 78, 91;
creative, 38, 64, 70, 182, 242; dominant,
21, 73, 152–53, 179, 194; embodying, 116;
negotiating, 234; privilege and, 224–26;
of SKMS saathis, 59, 72, 84; structures
of, 205, 220; unjust, 86, 91
Prakash, 14–19, 21–22, 37–38, 88, 95,
271n46; speech by, 35–36
Prasad, Brahma, 86–89
praxis: all-encompassing, 243; of co-
acting, 166; creative, 21; critical, 40;
definition of, 211; embodied, 44, 110, 184,
199, 206–8, 252; ethical, of stories, 40,
52–53; ethical engagement through, 10,
205, 220; of ethical responsibility, 9–10,
18, 39, 147–50, 191, 235; interbraided,
30–31; pedagogy and, 44, 184, 206–7;
reimaging through, 248; of retelling, 45,
52, 205, 241; of solidarity and collectivity, 40–42, 85–86, 187–89, 199; of
spirit, 252; translational, 31, 224. *See also*
activism; politics; radical vulnerability;
refusal; telling in turn
Premchand: Dalit controversy, 178, 181,
236; death of, 272–73n1; Emily Durham on, 272n3; interpretations of, 34,

146–50, 156, 167, 178–79; "Kafan" by, 39,
110–17, 123; Mumtaz and Kabir as *Hansa*
coauthors with, 182; rereading and rescripting, 188
Pritchett, Frances, 191, 236
privilege: caste, 79; inequalities of, 42;
inherited, 205, 241; learning to deconstruct, 235; within movements,
92; power and, 224, 249–54; of the researcher, 50–52; Savarna, 180
props, 212, 214–15, 252
protagonist: Dalit, 180; non-separation
between antagonist and, 37–39, 43–46,
189–91, 199, 231, 241, 252–53. *See also*
antagonist
protest: as pathshala, 79; playful, 37–38;
rethinking, 8, 45; shifting labors of, 31–
33; SKMS and, 63–64, 71–90, 96
provincializing, 33, 45. *See also* peasants:
global vs. provincial, 20
pseudonyms, 233, 235
Pundit (character), 126–27, 161

Quillien, Veronica, 242

radical, definition of, 211
radical openness, 9, 43
radical vulnerability: acting, reading, and,
179, 188, 249; collectively owned praxis
of, 29–31, 199, 204–13, 243, 252–55;
contradictions of, 43; definition of, 212,
271n49, 275n5; *Hansa* and, 188; hungry translation and, 46; mode of, 189,
210–12; politics through, 38–39; situated solidarities through, 199 (*see also*
situated solidarities); skeptics of, 45;
SKMS and, 42–46; unlearning and relearning through, 148–51, 221–25, 235
(*see also* relearning; unlearning). *See also*
vulnerability
Rai, Alok, 178, 181, 236
Raibahadur, 58
Rajan, Nithya, 242, 247, 250
Rajaram Bhai, 98
Rajpati, 58, 62
Rambeti, 14–17, 22–24, 67, 80, 93–95, 191;
on CCAFS conference, 22, 25; refusing
money from CCAFS, 26, 37; as source of
profound knowledge, 38–39, 88

Ramdevi, 95

Ramsheela, 51

Reena, 10–11, 56, 59, 61–62, 86–88

recognition: feeling of, 168; politics of, 178, 185, 205, 256, 271n55; refusal of/and, 225

reflection: collective, 45, 84; critical, 45, 86; empathetic, 212, 215; *Hansa* as, 150; honest, 215; necessity of, 40, 242, 248; online, 225; pedagogy of, 216; small-group, 237; sociopolitical, 147, 182; theorizing through, 209; vulnerability and, 92

reflexivity, 253; self-, 182, 253–54

refusal: as analytic practice, 226; to be nihilated, 9, 226; collective, creative, and critical, 21, 101, 192–93, 253; to cross borders, 220; difficult, 30; hungry, 256; kinds of, 22; moments of, 27; pedagogy, politics, and praxis of, 21, 40, 215, 225–26; radical, 225; Rambeti's, 25–26; reciprocal, 21; SKMS's, 9, 37; Sunita's, 27; stories and, 29, 226, 237; to translate perfectly, 29; translating, 22–27

rehearsal, 112–22, 158–93, 237–38

Rekha, 28, 96

relearning: across borders, 24; collective, 41, 243, 255; continuous, 117; critical epistemic, 213; against ego, 167–68; politics through, 190–93, 199; through radical vulnerability, 148; in Sitapur, 68–70; staging and, 246; struggles of, 87; unlearning and, 31–33, 44–45, 101, 158, 179, 206–9. *See also* learning; pedagogy; unlearning

religion: hierarchies of, 33; liberation from, 185; rituals of, 88; rules of, 111. *See also* brahmanical patriarchy; Hindutva; Muslim(s)

remembering, just, 179, 252

representation, 39, 151, 177, 180, 191, 232

rescripted stories, 40, 188, 229–31; 248; performance and, 231. *See also* stories

resistance, 191, 194, 206; to becoming vulnerable 43, 246; collective, 87; from employers, 40; epistemological, 37–38; Ghisu's and Madhav's, 189; living, 45; romance of, 101

resonances, 101, 218, 223–27, 235; analytical, 187; imperfect, 44

responsibility: acting and, 159, 176–77;

aesthetics, ethics, and, 218; collective pedagogy and, 99, 116, 187; embodied, 249; praxis of ethical, 9–10, 18, 39, 147–50, 191, 235; receiving and retelling stories with, 26–32, 52, 206–26, 232–39, 248–53; of the Sangathan (SKMS), 28–29, 83–84, 89, 98–99; of the State, 57–58, 63, 98. *See also* ethics

retelling: through acting, 162, 252; authoritative, 30–32; across borders, 207; collective, 21, 34, 49, 53–55, 59, 98; embodied, 238; ethical, 178–79, 207–12, 224, 230, 238; hungry, 31; just, 188–89; modes of, 43, 223; performing, 45–46; praxis of, 40, 52, 205, 241; receiving and, 24, 35; seeking justice through, 246; translation as, 224; uneven, 101

Retelling Dis/Appearing Tales (play), 242–43, 246–53, 257

revision, 238; collective, 31, 223, 230, 235, 239; continuous, 208, 220, 235

revolution, 93–95

Richa S. *See* Singh, Richa

Roshan (alias), 116, 148, 165

rurality, 21. *See also* development, rural

saathis (of SKMS), 9–38, 52–53, 60–103, 207, 251, 255; defined, 266; harassment of, 81; as interlocutors, 20; pakke, 58–59

safar, 95, 98, 206, 212, 266. *See also* journey

sahaanubhuti, 187

Sahu (character), 141, 143

Saint Paul, MN, 14, 23, 38. *See also* Twin Cities

Sajid, Nida, 180–81, 232

Sajjan (alias), 115, 181, 249; on the acting industry, 155–58; class position of, 185–88, 274n17; experiences shared by, 165–72; gratitude to, 195; journals of, 148

samaanubhuti, 181–82, 186–87

Samajwadi Party, 97

samanvaya (alliance), 181–82, 187. *See also* situated solidarity

samata (equality/equity), 181, 187

Sangathan. *See* Sangtin Kisan Mazdoor Sangathan (SKMS)

Sangtin (organization), 50, 58–59, 267

sangtin (term): definition of, 50, 57–59, 267; work of, 22–23

Sangtin Kisan Mazdoor Sangathan (SKMS): background and members, 9–18, 59–60, 269n4; battle for rights, 33, 66–84; CCAFS engagement with, 22–26; collective statement to mazdoors, 98; confrontation with CDO, 74, 78; epistemic labor of, 34; funding of, 84; gender and, 92–95, 270n10; IRB on research with, 102; on job cards and unemployment allowances, 66–85; journeys with, 27–28, 34, 36–38, 146, 261; methodologies, principles, and visions of, 29, 42, 271n3; Parakh Theatre and, 207, 242, 251; stories of, 49–53; sustaining, 186; women's leadership in, 60–64, 92. *See also* Dalit kisans and mazdoors; kisans and mazdoors; mazdoors and kisans; political theater; saathis (of SKMS)

'Sangtin Samooh,' 53

Sangtin Writers, 23, 42, 56, 102, 234–35; letter to, 235

sangtin yatra, 35–37, 243, 252, 267; beginning of, 42

Sangtin Yatra (Anupamlata et al.), 9, 35–37, 51; battles after, 53–59, 102, 243, 252, 267, 269n8. *See also Playing with Fire*

Santella, Julie, 242, 257

Santosa, Lisa, 242

Santosh, 58

Santoshi, 64

Santram Dada, 88–89

Saraswati Amma, 10, 58, 64

Sarvesh, 12, 68–70, 88

Satyanarayana, K., 232

Savarna: caste(ism), 9, 159, 272; heteropatriarchy, 72, 164, 174; kisans, 94; Premchand's status as, 113; reflexivity on being, 33, 101. *See also* caste; casteism; Dalit-Savarna politics; upper caste

Savarna privilege, 147, 156; controversies around, 54; gender and, 72, 87–88, 164; mode of narration, 180; violence of, 187

Sawhney, Simona, 243, 255–56

Schwedhelm, Maria, 242–43, 247, 250, 252–53

scripts: of caste, 11, 176, 190; collective, 7, 239; dominant, 147, 248; embodied, 146–76; formal, 37; fragmented, 110; language that bears, 44; polyvocal, 213,

216–17, 237–38, 241, 246; stories and, 45; undoing, 127, 39, 190. *See also* justice: rescripting stories for; rescripted stories; *and names of specific plays*

SDM (subdistrict magistrate), 68, 71, 80–81

Seithers, Laura, 242, 257

Sen, Binayak, 91

serendipity: creative, 33, 179–81; embodied learning and, 210, 248, 251–52; epistemic hunger and, 213; journeys sustained by, 46, 181; movements and, 207; remaining open to, 22; research and, 102; translation and, 152

settler colonialism, 224–28; territorialization and, 225

Shahjahanpur, 119, 161, 169, 174, 176

Shamsuddin (Shammu), 10, 58, 59, 61

Shashibala, 51

Sheikh, Mumtaz, 1, 249; as Budhiya, 107–23, 195, 252, 272; diary of, 148–62, 182; life of, 273n4; reflections on, 167–88. *See also* Budhiya

Shivram, 58

"Shroud, The" 191–95, 236. *See also* "Kafan"

Shukla, Sushil, 123. *See also* Bhole Dada

Simone, Nina, 34, 227, 249

Simpson, Audra, 225

Simpson, Darius, 214

Simpson, Leanne Betasamosake, 35, 225

Singh, Kaajal, 123, 170

Singh, Richa (Richa S.): CGIAR conversations with Rambeti and, 22–25; home of, 49–50; on IRB rejection, 103; leadership of, 80, 98; NGO controversy and, 54, 59; resistance by, 77, 86; SKMS and, 10, 14–15

Sitapur: climate change impacts on, 15; community theater in, 43, 112; development and political corruption in, 58–63, 90; *Hungry Translations* and, 248; organizing resistance in, 67–82, 95–97; rural, 35; SKMS and, 23; villages of, 9, 36

situated solidarity: definition of, 34, 42, 187; possibilities and contradictions of, 46; relationalities inspired by, 30; search for, 44, 244; across uneven terrains, 101. *See also* samanvaya; solidarity

Skaria, Ajay, 178, 274n5, 275n1

SKMS. *See* Sangtin Kisan Mazdoor Sangthan

Sobran Dada, 58, 61

social, the, 33, 40, 45, 207–8, 227, 233; meanings of, 150–51, 213, 223

social justice: goal of, 33; grand discourse of, 57; pedagogical labor of, 190–91; poetic justice and, 45, 177–81, 214, 236–37; translations that seek, 26. *See also* justice; poetic justice

social structure, 38, 93, 153, 155–56, 159, 164, 194, 256. *See also* transformation, social

solidarity, 13, 194, 210, 249, 267; embodied, 38, 39, 148; ethical, 24; evolving, 31, 37; among *Hansa* cast, 33–34; labor of, 39; power of, 84–85; romance of, 18; stories and, 7. *See also* situated solidarity

soul: feeding, 28; hunger of, 177, 184, 188, 194; journey of, 119, 162; mind, body, and, 19, 131, 136, 209, 212, 219, 243; mysterious, 133, 189; sharing and, 190

South Africa, 252

South Asia, 251

sovereignty, 212, 225

spirituality and spiritualism: activism and, 43, 178; all-encompassing praxis and, 243; art and, 19, 208; as context, 207; embodied process of, 193; freedom of, 184; as proprietary, 256; questioning and, 114; radical, 185. *See also* soul

stage(s): Budhiya on, 170–71; character growth on, 114–15; classroom as, 40–46; of life, 168, 194; local, 19; as negotiated pedagogy, 45–46; notion of, 44, 206; page as, 7, 31, 46; sharing *Hansa* on, 181–82, 190; site of, 206; stories and, 252; soul-, 1; unbound, 52

staging, 206, 238–39, 246, 254. *See also* backstaging; frontstaging

Standing Rock, 224, 249

stories: aesthetics, ethics, and responsibility of receiving and telling, 7–10, 22–24, 39–46, 178–92, 222–29; crossing and refusing to cross borders with, 199, 220, 241; doing justice to, 110, 257; embodied retelling of, 238–41; ethical praxis of, 40, 52–53; experience of, 219; layers of, 149; letting go of, 40, 222, 236; owning, 222;

partial, 249; restaging, 40; situated, 40, 249, 251; telling someone else's, 79, 222, 232; traveling of, 40. *See also* rescripted stories; retelling; storytelling; translation

Stories, Bodies, and Bordercrossings (freshman seminar), 191–95

Stories, Bodies, Movements (class), 34–38, 199, 206–10, 214, 241–46, 251–53; expectations, grades, and assignments of, 215–16; remaking the classroom through, 40; syllabus for, 40, 197–239, 242; vision of, 218. *See also* classroom; epistemology; pedagogy

storytelling: aesthetics of, 233–34, 244, 246; collective, 248; as embodied praxis, 199, 206–8; ethical responsibility of, 208, 220–22, 232, 245; as global politics, 220; intimate realm of, 220–21; justice and, 231, 233–34, 237, 241; modes of, 43, 223; pedagogies of, 237; politics of, 201–8, 234, 241, 245; transgenre, 253

strategic retelling, 45. *See also* pedagogy; retelling

structure(s), 8, 26, 37–43, 88, 179, 208, 220–24, 256; of the academy, 254; global, 20; and infra-, 35, 56, 96, 186; institutional, 210; locating story in, 212; of power, 220; prevailing, 21, 43, 88, 185; social, 38, 93, 153, 155–56, 159, 164, 194, 256. *See also* transformation, social

struggle, 180–82, 199, 213–14, 239–43, 251, 256; against authority, 168–69; being in, 205–9; collective, 27; communities of, 33, 64, 160, 214; as evolving, 45; for just representation, 150, 176, 221, 228, 237; scenes from, 68–85; of SKMS, 86–101; stories of, 8, 52; as unending, 248

subaltern, the, 20–21, 26; representations of, 39

subalternization, 20

subdistrict magistrate (SDM), 68, 71, 80–81

Sufism: poetry of, 178; traditions of, 112

Sunita, 10–13, 88, 191; Prakash, Tama, and, 19, 22, 39; refusal by, 27, 37; Tarun and, 12–13, 18, 21, 26

Surati, Munira, 123, 170

Surbala, 51, 56, 59–62, 86–89

swaanubhuti, 180, 182, 186, 187
syllabus: as fluid text, 218, 252; moving
away from, 210; rethinking, 40, 199–200,
208; for Stories, Bodies, Movements
class, 197–239
Szostkowski, Alaina, 242–43, 250

Taka (character), 129–33, 147, 154–56, 169;
reflection on, 152
Tama, 10–14, 16, 64, 87; Prakash, Sunita,
and, 19, 22, 39; Tarun and, 18
Tefla's Studio, 116, 160, 166, 169–70
telling in turn, praxis of, 26–27, 220, 237
Thakur (character), 124, 129, 131–32, 134,
140–41; analysis of, 147, 152–56, 169,
190. See also *Hansa, Karo Puratan Baat*
Tharu, Susie, 232–33
theater, 1, 10, 37, 179, 187, 206; in the classroom, 34, 199; community, 43; as embodied creative pedagogy, 36; hunger for,
15–18; intellectual labor of, 37; as mode
of inquiry, 241; as movement, 45; political, 33–37, 110, 177–78, 184–88, 207,
242; of real life, 29; as storytelling, 249
theory, embodied, 43, 45, 206, 227
Tinsley, Omise'eke Natasha, 222
Tomar, Sumit Singh, 115, 123, 157
transformation, social, xii, 32, 44, 56–59,
92–93, 185–87
transgenre, 241, 253
translation, 1–3, 56, 146–57, 185–88,
206–9; through the classroom, 190, 199;
collective, 223; ethics and responsibility
of, 26–29, 150–53, 164–70, 204, 236–37;
fragmented, 110; impossibility of perfect and complete, xii, 101, 150; justice
through, 26, 43, 248; labor of, 24; literal,
13; migratory, 223; notes on, xiii; as ongoing, 22, 27; questions of, 45; refused,
27, 44; responsible, 150, 236; Sajjan and,
185–86; singular, 224; storytelling as,
206, 209, 219–20; as telling in turn,
26–27, 220, 237; undisciplined, 9; across
uneven terrains, 26, 213. See also hungry
translations; retelling; storytelling
translational praxis, 24–28, 31–32, 191,
205, 223–24. See also radical vulnerability

transliteration, xiii, 3
Trivedi, Satish Chandra, 123, 182
trust: distrust and, 43; politics of, 98; praxis
of, 18, 23–24, 33, 40, 221; radical vulnerability inspired by, 38; retelling and,
212–13; violating, 49
truth(s): ancient, 145; basic, 73, 205; being blind to, 22, 25; contingency of, 207;
embodied, 153; feeling, 58; fundamental,
26, 189; hunger for, 181; intimate, 53–54;
living, 162, 176; marginalized and subordinated, 8, 191; momentary, 151; mundane, 32; painful, 190; politics of, 192,
227, 245; radical vulnerability as, 46;
struggle for, 28, 267; translation and, 22
Tuck, Eve, 34, 225, 228
Twin Cities, 253. *See also* Minneapolis;
Saint Paul, MN; University of Minnesota

undercommons, 229, 256
underdevelopment, figure of, 19–20
unemployment allowance, 35, 66, 74,
78–85, 90, 95
United States: knowledge of, 243, 253; settler colonialism and, 224, 249; SKMS
support from, 86; universities in, 33–34,
199
University of Minnesota, 154; honing pedagogical praxis at, 34, 38, 43, 191–93, 251;
IRB at, 272n5154
unlearning, 31, 33, 41, 44, 101; of caste, 86–
88, 156; embodied, 199; labor of, 24, 37;
pedagogy of, 33, 206–9; as praxis, 193;
theater as, 208. *See also* epistemology;
learning; pedagogy; relearning
untouchability: burden of maintaining, 87;
caste and, 9, 192; in *Hansa*, 161; identity
and, 271n55; oppression and violence
of, 118, 174, 185. *See also* caste; casteism;
Dalit(s)
upper caste, 94, 147, 156, 233, 267. *See also*
Savarna
Urdu (language), xiii, 112, 114, 272n1
Uttar Pradesh, 49, 68; gender segregation
in, 270n10; kisans and mazdoors of, 15;
labor department of, 95; NGOs in, 53;
state government of, 97; villages of, 149,
174

Vaish, Shashi, 51
Vasandani, Veera, 242
Vemula, Rohith, 255–56
vernaculars, 26; globalized, 30
Vikas Bhawan (building), 73–78, 80; shutting down, 77
violence: caste-based, 113, 118; communal, 187–92; epistemic, 19–20, 26, 37, 42, 101, 246; of erasure, 7; global context of, 26, 100, 199, grappling with, 251; journeys through, 117, 241–42; love and, 231, 242, 248–49; remembering past, 219; settler colonial, 226; structural, 214
voice(s): collective, 35, 118, 213; dying Budhiya's, 115; merging, 8, 110, 242; political, 245; power, authority, and, 234; as representation, 20, 98–99; stolen, 7; Tama's, 13–14, 87. See also coauthorship; radical vulnerability; we
vulnerability: in the classroom, 222–23, 232–35, 254; frustrations of embracing, 246; radical (see radical vulnerability). See also radical openness

we: blended, 246; fractured, 42, 235, 246; making of, 243
Wingate, Colin, 242

Wolfe, Patrick, 225
workers. See kisans and mazdoors; labor
World Conference Against Racism (2001, Durban), 180
writing, 212, 217; embodied, 215, 222, 228; politics of, 230; relational, 223; tyranny of, 254; as yatra, 212

Xaxa, Abhay, 101

Yadav, Anil: on acting industry, 155; featured in Hansa, 123; journal of, 148; rehearsing for Hansa, 115, 158, 187; relearning Hansa, 167–69; observing, 160–61, 181; Yasmin ji and, 165
Yadav, Avi Kumar, 117, 123
Yang, K. Wayne, 34, 225, 228
Yari Road, 111–12, 114, 147, 160, 170, 185
Yasmin ji: class status of, 165–66, 273n4; featured in Hansa, 123; journey with Hansa, 159, 170–73, 185; rehearsing Hansa, 115. See also Patel Saheb
yatra (journey), 46, 60, 267; of Hungry Translations (book), 33–37; of sangtins, 10, 42; translating through, 27; writing as, 212. See also journey

Richa Nagar is Professor of the College in the College of Liberal Arts and a core faculty member in the Department of Gender, Women, and Sexuality Studies at the University of Minnesota. She writes in English and Hindi. Her books in English include *Muddying the Waters: Coauthoring Feminisms across Scholarship and Activism*, *Playing with Fire: Feminist Thought and Activism through Seven Lives in India*, and *A World of Difference: Encountering and Contesting Development*, 2nd edition.

TRANSFORMATIONS: WOMANIST, FEMINIST,
AND INDIGENOUS STUDIES

Teaching with Tenderness: Toward an Embodied Practice   *Becky Thompson*
Building Womanist Coalitions: Writing and Teaching in the Spirit of Love
    Edited by Gary L. Lemons
Hungry Translations: Relearning the World through Radical Vulnerability
    Richa Nagar, in journeys with Sangtin Kisan Mazdoor Sangathan and Parakh Theatre

The University of Illinois Press
is a founding member of the
Association of University Presses.

———————————————————

University of Illinois Press
1325 South Oak Street
Champaign, IL 61820-6903
www.press.uillinois.edu

Made in the USA
Monee, IL
05 May 2021